Creating Cross Platform C# Applications with Uno Platform

Build apps with C# and XAML that run on Windows, macOS, iOS, Android, and WebAssembly

Matt Lacey

Marcel Alexander Wagner

Packt>

BIRMINGHAM—MUMBAI

Creating Cross-Platform C# Applications with Uno Platform

Copyright © 2021 Packt Publishing

Associate Group Product Manager: Pavan Ramchandani

Publishing Product Manager: Rohit Rajkumar

Senior Editor: Sofi Rogers

Content Development Editor: Feza Shaikh

Technical Editor: Saurabh Kadave

Copy Editor: Safis Editing

Project Coordinator: Manthan Patel

Proofreader: Safis Editing

Indexer: Subalakshmi Govindhan

Production Designer: Vijay Kamble

First published: September 2021
Production reference: 1250821

Published by Packt Publishing Ltd.
Livery Place
35 Livery Street
Birmingham
B3 2PB, UK.

978-1-80107-849-8

www.packt.com

Contributors

About the authors

Matt Lacey has been building desktop and mobile software since the '90s. He currently works as an independent development consultant and focuses on helping developers to create better software. Having worked in companies of all sizes and in a wide variety of industries, he brings this breadth of experience to present a viewpoint that considers technology, business, and design.

Matt is a Microsoft MVP in Windows Development, regularly speaks at user groups and conferences in multiple countries, and is a prolific contributor to a plethora of open source projects. He lives in the UK with his wife and two children.

Marcel Alexander Wagner is a full-stack software developer and open source contributor. He is a Microsoft MVP in Windows Development and a top contributor to the WinUI library and the XAML Controls Gallery, while also contributing to other projects and libraries, including the Windows Community Toolkit and Uno Platform.

Marcel graduated with a Bachelor of Science in computer science and has since been developing applications and services with a wide variety of technologies, including React, Java, C#, C++, UWP, and Uno Platform. He currently resides in Germany.

About the reviewers

David Oliver is an open source framework developer with a .NET background. He is a recovering physicist and lapsed Australian. He is currently a senior developer on the Uno Platform core team.

Martin Zikmund is a freelance software developer and Microsoft Developer Technologies MVP. He specializes in building cross-platform mobile and cloud solutions on the Microsoft technology stack. His passion is contributing to open source, especially to Uno Platform. You can also encounter him on Stack Overflow, where he frequently helps other developers. To document his developer journey, Martin regularly writes articles on his blog and tweets about interesting things he comes across. In his spare time, he likes to play squash, game on Xbox, read, and search for geocaches.

Nick Randolph currently runs Built to Roam, which focuses on building rich mobile applications. He has been identified as a Microsoft MVP in recognition of his work and expertise with Microsoft application platforms.

Nick is an active contributor in the device application development space via his blog. He has been invited to present at a variety of events, including TechEd and Ignite Australia and NZ, DDD, NDC, and local user groups. He has also authored multiple books on Visual Studio and Windows development.

Shimmy Weitzhandler is a skilled full-stack developer and consultant working independently.

He has been coding for nearly two decades, and has used technologies ranging from ASP. NET, HTML, and JavaScript with VB.NET to WPF, Silverlight, WinUI, and, for the past few years, Uno Platform.

Among his projects are an emergency response system, a club card management and points accumulation portal, video conversion software, a school and college system, e-commerce websites, and QuickBooks components.

Shimmy is an active member and contributor on key tech hubs such as GitHub and Stack Overflow.

He is well known for his distinct programming style, his architectural thinking, and his dedication to creativity and transparency, utilizing the latest technologies.

Table of Contents

Section 2:
Writing and Developing Uno Platform Apps

3
Working with Forms and Data

4
Mobilizing Your App

5

Making Your App Ready for the Real World

6

Displaying Data in Charts and with Custom 2D Graphics

Section 3:
Test, Deploy, and Contribute

7
Testing Your Apps

8
Deploying Your Apps and Going Further

Other Books You May Enjoy

Index

Preface

Developers are increasingly being asked to build native applications that run on multiple operating systems and in the browser. In the past, this would have meant learning new technologies and making multiple copies of an application. But Uno Platform allows you to use tools, languages, and APIs you already know from building Windows apps to develop apps that can also run on other platforms. This book will help you to create customer-facing as well as line-of-business apps that can be used on the device, browser, or operating system of your choice.

This practical guide enables developers to put their C# and XAML knowledge to work by writing cross-platform apps using Uno Platform. Packed with tips and practical examples, this book will help you to build applications for common scenarios. You'll begin by learning about Uno Platform through step-by-step explanations of essential concepts, before moving on to creating cross-platform apps for different lines of business. Throughout this book, you'll work with examples that will teach you how to combine your existing knowledge to manage common development environments and implement frequently needed functionality.

By the end of this Uno Platform development book, you will have learned how to write your own cross-platform apps with Uno Platform and use additional tools and libraries to speed up your app development process.

Who this book is for

This book is for developers who are familiar with app development for Windows and want to use their existing skills to build cross-platform apps. Basic knowledge of C# and XAML is required to get started with this book. Anyone with basic experience of app development using WPF, UWP, or WinUI will be able to learn how to create cross-platform applications with Uno Platform.

What this book covers

Chapter 1, Introducing Uno Platform, introduces the Uno Platform, explaining what it is designed for and when to use it. After this, the chapter will cover how to set up the development machine and install the necessary tools.

Chapter 2, Writing Your First Uno Platform App, walks through creating your first Uno Platform app and covers the app's structure. By the end of this chapter, you will have written a small Uno Platform app that can be run on different platforms and display content based on the OS the app is running on.

Chapter 3, Working with Forms and Data, walks you through developing a data-focused line-of-business app for the fictional company UnoBookRail. The chapter covers displaying data, providing input validation on forms, and exporting data to PDF.

Chapter 4, Mobilizing Your App, introduces you to developing mobile apps using Uno Platform. In addition to that, the chapter covers working with remote data on devices with unstable internet connections, styling the app based on the platform it is running on, and using device capabilities such as the camera.

Chapter 5, Making Your App Ready for the Real World, covers writing a mobile app that is aimed at external customers. As part of this, it covers persisting data locally on the device, localizing your app, and writing an accessible app with Uno Platform.

Chapter 6, Displaying Data in Charts and with Custom 2D Graphics, explores displaying graphs and charts in an Uno Platform app. The chapter covers using libraries such as SyncFusion and creating custom graphics using SkiaSharp. Lastly, the chapter covers writing a UI that responds to changes in screen size.

Chapter 7, Testing Your Apps, introduces you to UI testing with Uno.UITest. In addition, this chapter covers writing automated UI tests with WinAppDriver, writing unit tests for the Windows 10 version of the app, and testing the app for accessibility.

Chapter 8, Deploying Your Apps and Going Further, walks you through bringing your Xamarin.Forms app to the web with Uno Platform and deploying WASM Uno Platform apps to Azure. After this, the chapter covers deploying an Uno Platform app and joining the Uno Platform community.

To get the most out of this book

In this book, we will be using Visual Studio 2019 on Windows 10 and the .NET CLI to develop Uno Platform apps. We will cover installing the necessary extensions and CLI tools; however, installing Visual Studio and the .NET CLI will not be covered. To install the required software, you will need a functional internet connection.

Software/hardware covered in the book	Operating system requirements
Uno Platform 3.9	Windows 10 or macOS 11 (Big Sur)

If you are using the digital version of this book, we advise you to type the code yourself or access the code from the book's GitHub repository (a link is available in the next section). Doing so will help you avoid any potential errors related to the copying and pasting of code.

Download the example code files

You can download the example code files for this book from GitHub at `https://github.com/PacktPublishing/Creating-Cross-Platform-C-Sharp-Applications-with-Uno-Platform`. If there's an update to the code, it will be updated in the GitHub repository.

We also have other code bundles from our rich catalog of books and videos available at `https://github.com/PacktPublishing/`. Check them out!

Code in Action

The Code in Action videos for this book can be viewed at `https://bit.ly/3yHTfYL`

Download the color images

We also provide a PDF file that has color images of the screenshots and diagrams used in this book. You can download it here: `https://static.packt-cdn.com/downloads/9781801078498_ColorImages.pdf`.

Conventions used

There are a number of text conventions used throughout this book.

`Code in text`: Indicates code words in text, database table names, folder names, filenames, file extensions, pathnames, dummy URLs, user input, and Twitter handles. Here is an example: "Inside the `UnoAutomatedTestsApp` folder, create a folder named `UnoAutomatedTestsApp.UITests`."

A block of code is set as follows:

```
private void ChangeTextButton_Click(object sender,
                                    RoutedEventArgs e)
{
    helloTextBlock.Text = "Hello from code behind!";
}
```

When we wish to draw your attention to a particular part of a code block, the relevant lines or items are set in bold:

```
<skia:SKXamlCanvas
xmlns:skia="using:SkiaSharp.Views.UWP"
PaintSurface="OnPaintSurface" />
```

Any command-line input or output is written as follows:

```
dotnet new unoapp -o MyApp
```

Bold: Indicates a new term, an important word, or words that you see onscreen. For instance, words in menus or dialog boxes appear in **bold**. Here is an example: "Open the **Test Explorer** by clicking **View** in the menu bar and clicking on **Test Explorer**."

> Tips or important notes
> Appear like this.

Get in touch

Feedback from our readers is always welcome.

General feedback: If you have questions about any aspect of this book, email us at customercare@packtpub.com and mention the book title in the subject of your message.

Errata: Although we have taken every care to ensure the accuracy of our content, mistakes do happen. If you have found a mistake in this book, we would be grateful if you would report this to us. Please visit www.packtpub.com/support/errata and fill in the form.

Piracy: If you come across any illegal copies of our works in any form on the internet, we would be grateful if you would provide us with the location address or website name. Please contact us at copyright@packt.com with a link to the material.

If you are interested in becoming an author: If there is a topic that you have expertise in and you are interested in either writing or contributing to a book, please visit authors.packtpub.com.

Share Your Thoughts

Once you've read *Creating Cross-Platform C# Applications with Uno Platform*, we'd love to hear your thoughts! Scan the QR code below to go straight to the Amazon review page for this book and share your feedback.

https://packt.link/r/1801078491

Your review is important to us and the tech community and will help us make sure we're delivering excellent quality content.

Section 1: Getting to Know Uno Platform

This part of the book will provide you with all the information you need to know about Uno Platform and how to determine which of your projects it is appropriate for. It will then detail how to set up your development environment(s) for building apps with Uno Platform and walk you through creating your first app. It will then explore the basics of working with an app built with Uno Platform and show how you can use the tools and skills you're already familiar with. Additionally, it will show you how to do some of the most common tasks that developers need to do in most apps.

In this section, we include the following chapters:

- *Chapter 1, Introducing Uno Platform*
- *Chapter 2, Writing Your First Uno Platform App*

1

Introducing Uno Platform

Uno Platform is a cross-platform, single-codebase solution for developing applications that run on various devices and operating systems. It does this while building on the rich heritage of Windows development APIs and tooling. This allows you to take the Windows app development skills you already have and use them to build apps for Android, iOS, macOS, WebAssembly, Linux, and others.

This book will be your guide to Uno Platform. It will show you how to use Uno Platform's functionality to build a variety of different applications that address real-world scenarios.

In this chapter, we'll cover the following topics:

- Understanding what Uno Platform is
- Using Uno Platform
- Setting up your development environment

By the end of this chapter, you'll understand why you'll want to use Uno Platform to develop apps, and the types of applications it's best suited to help you build. You'll also be able to set up your environment so that you're ready to start building apps when reading subsequent chapters in this book.

Technical requirements

In this chapter, you will be guided through the process of setting up your development machine. To work through all the examples in the book, you will need a machine running any of the following:

- **Windows 10** (1809) or higher

- **macOS 10.15** (Catalina) or higher

If you only have access to one, you'll still be able to follow along with most of the book. The book will primarily assume you are working with a Windows machine. We will only show examples that use Mac when absolutely necessary.

There is no source code for this chapter. However, the code for the other chapters can be found at the following URL: `https://github.com/PacktPublishing/Creating-Cross-Platform-C-Sharp-Applications-with-Uno-Platform`.

Understanding what Uno Platform is

According to the website (`https://platform.uno/`), Uno Platform is *"the first and only UI Platform for single-codebase applications for Windows, WebAssembly, iOS, macOS, Android and Linux."*

That's a complex sentence so let's break down the key elements:

- As a UI platform, it's a way of building applications with a **User Interface** (**UI**). This is in contrast to those platforms that are text-based and run from the command line (or equivalent), are embedded in hardware, or are interacted with in other ways, such as by voice.

- Using a *single code base* means you only need to write code once to have it run on multiple devices and operating systems. Specifically, this means the same code can be compiled for each platform the app will run on. This is in contrast with tools that convert or transpile code into a different programming language before being compiled for another platform. It's also the only code base that's singular, not the output. Some comparable tools create a unique package that runs inside a host application on each OS, or create everything in HTML and JavaScript, and run inside an embedded browser. Uno Platform does neither of these. Instead, it produces native application packages for each platform.

- Windows apps are based on the **Universal Windows Platform** (**UWP**) for Windows 10. Work is currently being done at Microsoft to make **WinUI 3** the successor to UWP. Uno Platform has partnered with Microsoft to ensure that Uno Platform can easily transition from UWP once WinUI 3 is at a comparable operative level.

- Windows support also includes the **Windows Presentation Foundation** (**WPF**), powered by SkiaSharp, for apps that need to run on older versions of Windows (7.1 or 8.1).

- Applications that run in WebAssembly have all their code compiled to run inside a web browser. This means they can be accessed from any device with a compatible browser, without running code on the server.

- By supporting iOS, the apps that are created can run on iPhones and iPads.

- With support for macOS, the apps can run on a MacBook, iMac, or Mac Mini.

- Support for Android applies to phones and tablets running the Android operating system.

- Linux support applies to specific Linux PC equivalent distributions and is powered by SkiaSharp.

Uno Platform does all of the preceding by reusing the tooling, APIs, and XAML that Microsoft created for building UWP apps.

Another way to answer the "what is Uno Platform?" question is that it's a way to *write code once and have it run everywhere*. The exact definition of "everywhere" is imprecise, as it doesn't include every embedded system or microcontroller capable of running code. Still, many developers and businesses have long had the desire to write code once and run it easily on multiple platforms. Uno Platform makes this possible.

One of the early criticisms of Microsoft's UWP was that it was only *universal* on Windows. With Uno Platform, developers can now make their UWP apps genuinely universal.

A brief history of Uno Platform

With the varied number of cross-platform tools available today, it's easy to forget how limited the options were back in 2013. At that time, there were no general-purpose tools for easily building native apps that ran on multiple operating systems.

It was at that time that **nventive** (`https://nventive.com/`), a Canadian software design and development company, faced a challenge. They had lots of knowledge and experience in building applications for Windows and Microsoft tools, but their customers were also asking them to create applications for Android and iOS devices. Rather than retrain staff or duplicate effort by building multiple versions of the same software for the different platforms, they invented a way to compile the code they wrote for Windows Phone (and later UWP) apps and transfer it to other platforms.

By 2018, it was obvious this approach had been successful for them. They then did the two following things:

1. They turned the tool they had created into an open source project, calling it Uno Platform.

2. They added support for WebAssembly.

As an open source project, this allowed other developers tackling the same problem to work together. Uno Platform has since seen thousands of contributions from over 200 external contributors, and involvement has been expanded to support more platforms and add additional functionality for the initially supported platforms.

As an open source project, it is free to use. Additionally, it is supported by a company with a business model that was made popular by Red Hat, and has been adopted widely. Usage is free and there is some free public support. However, professional support, training, and custom development are available only through payment.

How Uno Platform works

Uno Platform works in different ways and uses multiple underlying technologies, depending on the platform you're building for. These are summarized in *Figure 1.1*:

- If you're building an app for Windows 10, Uno Platform does nothing and lets all the UWP tooling compile and execute your app.

- If you're building an app for iOS, macOS, or Android, Uno Platform maps your UI to the native platform equivalents and uses native `Xamarin` libraries to call into the OS it is running on. It produces the appropriate native packages for each OS.

- If you're building a WebAssembly app, Uno Platform compiles your code against the `mono.wasm` runtime and maps the UI to HTML and CSS. This is then packaged into a `.NET` library that is launched with the Uno Platform web bootstrapper as static web content.

- To create Linux apps, Uno Platform converts your code to the `.NET` equivalent and uses **Skia** to create a version of the UI. It then outputs a `.NET5` app that uses **GTK3** to present the UI.

- Apps for Windows 7 and 8 are created by Uno Platform by wrapping the compiled code in a simple **WPF** (**NETCore 3.1**) app that uses **SkiaSharp** to render the UI.

Refer to the following diagram:

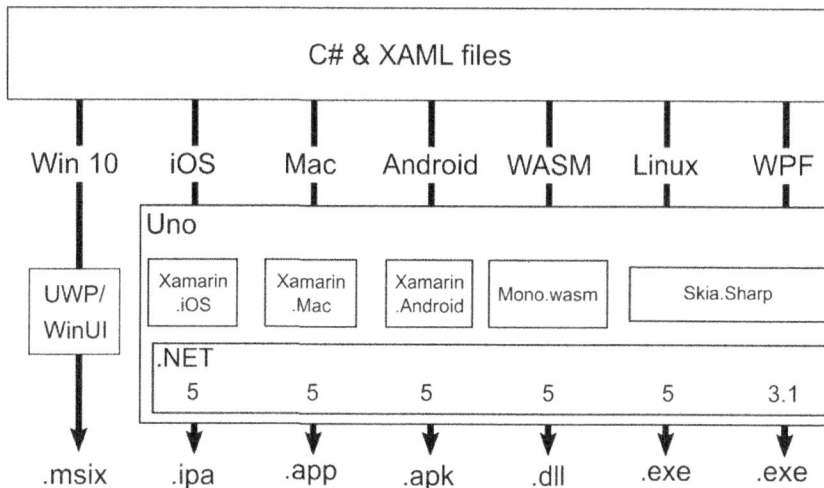

Figure 1.1 – The high-level architecture of Uno Platform

Whichever operating system or platform you're building for, Uno Platform uses the native controls for the platform. This enables your apps to achieve the experience and performance of a fully native app. The exception to this is where it uses SkiaSharp. By using SkiaSharp, Uno Platform draws all UI content on a canvas rather than using platform-native controls. Uno Platform does not add an extra layer of abstraction to the running app (as you might find with cross-platform solutions that use a container, such as an embedded WebView within a shell app).

Uno Platform enables you to do a lot with a single code base. But can it do everything?

Is it a panacea?

The principle of writing code once and running that code everywhere is both powerful and appealing. However, it's necessary to be aware of the following two key points:

- Not all applications should be created for all platforms.

- It's not an excuse for not knowing the platforms the apps will run on.

Additionally, not everything warrants an app. Suppose you just want to share some information that won't be frequently updated. In such a scenario, a website with static web pages would likely be more appropriate.

The lesson *just because you can do something doesn't mean you should* applies to applications too. When you see how easy it is to create applications that run on multiple platforms, you may be tempted to deploy your applications everywhere you can. Before you do this, there are some important questions you need to ask:

- *Is the app wanted or needed on all the platforms?* Do people want and need to use it on all the platforms you make it available? If not, you may be wasting effort by putting it there.

- *Does the application make sense on all the platforms?* Suppose the application has key functionality that involves capturing images while outside. Does it make sense to make it available on a PC or Mac? In contrast, if the application requires the entry of lots of information, is this something people will want to do on the small screen of a mobile phone? Your decision about where to make an application available should be determined by its functionality and the people who will use it. Don't let your decision be based solely on what's possible.

- *Can you support it on all platforms?* Does the value you gain by making an application available on a platform justify the time and effort in releasing, maintaining, and supporting the application on that platform? If you only have a small number of people use the app on a particular type of device, but they generate many support requests, it's OK to reevaluate your support for such devices.

No technology will render a perfect solution for all scenarios, but hopefully, you can already see the opportunity that Uno Platform provides. Let's now look a bit closer at why and when you might want to use it.

Using Uno Platform

Now you know what Uno Platform is, we'll look at what you need to consider when choosing whether to use it. There are four factors to consider:

- What you already know.
- What platforms do you wish to target?
- The functionality required in the app.
- How it compares to alternatives.

Let's explore each of these factors in relation to Uno Platform.

Uno Platform allows you to use what you already know

Uno Platform was initially created for developers using C# and XAML within **Visual Studio**. If this is familiar to you, this will make it easy to start using Uno Platform, as you'll be working with the software you already know.

If you're already familiar with UWP development, the differences will be minimal. If you're familiar with WPF development, there are minor differences in XAML syntax and available functionality. As we go through the book, you'll learn everything you need to build with Uno Platform. As long as you don't expect everything to work as it does in WPF, you'll be fine. Also, as the WinUI and Uno Platform teams are working to remove the minor differences that exist, you may never notice a difference.

If you don't know C# or XAML, Uno Platform may still be suitable for you, but as this book assumes familiarity with these languages, you may find it helpful to first read *C# 9 and .NET 5 – Modern Cross-Platform Development – Fifth Edition, Mark J. Price, Packt Publishing*, and *Learn WinUI 3.0, Alvin Ashcraft, Packt Publishing*.

Uno Platform supports many platforms

One of the great things about Uno Platform is the number of platforms it allows you to build for. Uno Platform has support for the most common platforms, but if you need to build applications that run on a niche platform or specialist device, then it may not be suitable for you. Additionally, if you need to support an old version of a platform or operating system, you may have to find workarounds or alternative solutions. The following table shows the versions of the supported platforms you can build for with Uno Platform:

Platform	Min. Version	Notes.
Windows 10 (UWP)	1607	Although the oldest version supported by Microsoft is 1809.
Android	5.0 (API 21)	
iOS	8	
Mac	10.9	Although the oldest version supported by Apple is 10.14.
WebAssembly Chrome Edge Firefox Safari	 57 16 52 11	All major browsers since 2017, although some features are not available everywhere. See `https://webassembly.org/roadmap/` for more details. Limited/no support on older mobile browsers.
WPF Windows 7 Windows 8	3.1 (Core) SP1 8.1	With extended security updates installed.
Linux Ubuntu ArchLinux Manjaro	 18.04 5.8.14	With GTK3.

Figure 1.2 – The lowest supported platform versions supported by Uno Platform

Support for multiple platforms can also be advantageous, even when you want very different application behaviors or functionalities across different platforms. It's possible to support multiple platforms by creating multiple solutions, rather than by combining everything into a single solution.

Uno Platform boasts up to 99% reuse of code and UI. This is great when you need the same thing on all devices. However, if you require different behavior or a UI that's highly customized for different platforms (something that we'll look into in future chapters), it can be easier to build the different applications in different solutions, as opposed to putting lots of conditional logic in the code. There is no hard and fast rule for how much conditional code is too much, and it varies based on project and personal preference. Just remember it remains an option if you ever find your code is becoming full of conditional comments that make it hard to manage.

Accordingly, it's also possible to use Uno Platform to build for a single platform. You may not want to create an app that runs everywhere. You may only be interested in a single platform. If that's the case, you can use Uno Platform for that too. It also makes it easy to add additional platforms in the future if your needs change.

Can Uno Platform do everything that your app requires?

Core to Uno Platform's ability to reuse the UWP APIs to build for other platforms is that it has code to map the UWP API to its equivalent on the other platforms. Due to time, practicality, and priority limitations, not all APIs are available on all platforms. By way of general guidance, the most common APIs are available on the broadest number of platforms. Suppose you need to use more specialist functionality or are targeting something other than Android, iOS, Mac, or WebAssembly? In that case, it's advisable to check that the features you need are available.

> Tip
> We recommended confirming that the functionality you need for your app is available before you start writing code. This will allow you to avoid any nasty surprises late in the development process.

Due to the permanence of printed books and the frequency with which new functionality is added and more APIs are supported, it's not appropriate to list what is supported here. Instead, you can see a high-level list of supported features at the following URL: `https://platform.uno/docs/articles/supported-features.html`. There's also a list of supported UI elements at the following URL: `https://platform.uno/docs/articles/implemented-views.html`. Of course, the definitive way to confirm what is and isn't available is to check the source code at the following URL: `https://github.com/unoplatform/uno`.

If you try and use an API that is not supported, you'll see a hint inside Visual Studio, as is shown in *Figure 1.3*. If you try and use this at runtime, you'll either get nothing (a `NOOP`) or a `NotSupported` exception:

```
tion = Package.Current.Description;
```

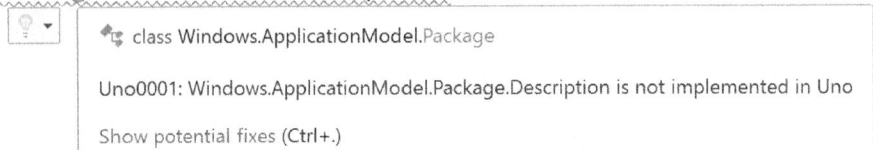

class Windows.ApplicationModel.Package

Uno0001: Windows.ApplicationModel.Package.Description is not implemented in Uno

Show potential fixes (Ctrl+.)

Figure 1.3 – An example of an unsupported API being indicated in Visual Studio

If necessary, you can check for supported features at runtime by using the `Windows.Foundation.Metadata.ApiInformation` class.

As an open source project, there is also the option to add any currently unsupported features yourself. Contributing such an addition back into the project is always greatly appreciated and new contributors are always welcomed by the team.

How does Uno Platform compare to the alternatives?

As mentioned earlier, many tools are available for developing applications that run on more than one platform. It is not our intention to discuss all the options available, as they can be evaluated and compared with the previous three points. However, as this book is intended for developers already familiar with C#, XAML, and Microsoft technologies, it is appropriate to mention `Xamarin.Forms`.

`Xamarin.Forms` was created at around the same time as Uno Platform and has several similarities. The two key ones are using C# and XAML to create apps that run on multiple operating systems. Both do this by providing an abstraction over the `Xamarin.iOS` and `Xamarin.Android` libraries that contain the C# bindings to the underlying operating systems.

The two biggest differences between Uno Platform and `Xamarin.Forms` are as follows:

- Uno Platform supports building for a greater number of platforms.
- Uno Platform reuses the UWP APIs and XAML syntax, rather than building a custom one.

The second point is important for developers already familiar with UWP development. The names of many `Xamarin.Forms` elements and properties are similar-sounding, so remembering the variations can be challenging.

Version 5 of `Xamarin.Forms` was released toward the end of 2020 and is intended to be the last version of `Xamarin.Forms`. It will be replaced with **.NET Multi-platform App UI (MAUI)** as part of .NET 6. .NET MAUI will support building apps for iOS, Android, Windows, and Mac from a single code base. However, it will not include the ability to also build for WebAssembly. Microsoft already has Blazor for building for WebAssembly, and so is not looking to add this capability to .NET MAUI.

.NET 6 will bring with it many new capabilities. Some of these capabilities are being added specifically for .NET MAUI. Once part of .NET 6, these capabilities will not be limited only to .NET MAUI. They will be available to Uno Platform apps too. The most obvious of these new capabilities is in having a single project that can produce different outputs for different platforms. This will enable a significant simplification of the required solution structure.

> **Important note**
>
> As we write this book, Microsoft is preparing to release **WinUI 3** as the next-generation Windows development platform. This will build upon UWP and is part of the **Project Reunion** effort to make all Windows functionality and APIs available to developers, regardless of the UI framework or application packaging technology they use.
>
> As WinUI 3 is the successor of UWP development, the Uno Platform team has publicly stated that plans and preparations are underway for Uno Platform to transition to using WinUI 3 as the base upon which it builds. This is being done in partnership with Microsoft, allowing the Uno Platform team to take the WinUI code and modify it to work elsewhere. You can be confident that anything you make now will have a path to transition to and take advantage of the benefits and functionality that WinUI will bring.

Another similar cross-platform solution that uses XAML to define the UI of an app is Avalonia (`https://avaloniaui.net/`). This, however, is different in that it focuses only on applications for desktop environments.

As you now have a solid understanding of what Uno Platform is and why you'll want to use it, you'll need to set up your machine so you can write code and create apps.

Setting up your development environment

Now that you are familiar with Uno Platform, you're undoubtedly eager to begin writing code. We'll start that in the next chapter, but you'll need to set up your development environment before we can begin.

Visual Studio is the most popular **Integrated Development Environment** (**IDE**) for developing Uno Platform apps. A large part of this is because it has the broadest set of capabilities and the best support for building UWP apps.

Developing with Visual Studio

To build apps with Uno Platform using Visual Studio, you will need to do the following three things:

- Ensure you have **Visual Studio 2019** version **16.3** or higher, although using the latest version is recommended.
- Install the necessary workloads.
- Install the project and item templates.

Installing the required workloads

The many tools, libraries, templates, SDK, and other utilities that can be installed as part of Visual Studio are collectively called **components**. With over 100 components available, related components are grouped into workloads to make it easier to choose what you need. You select workloads in the **Visual Studio Installer**, and these are shown in *Figure 1.4*:

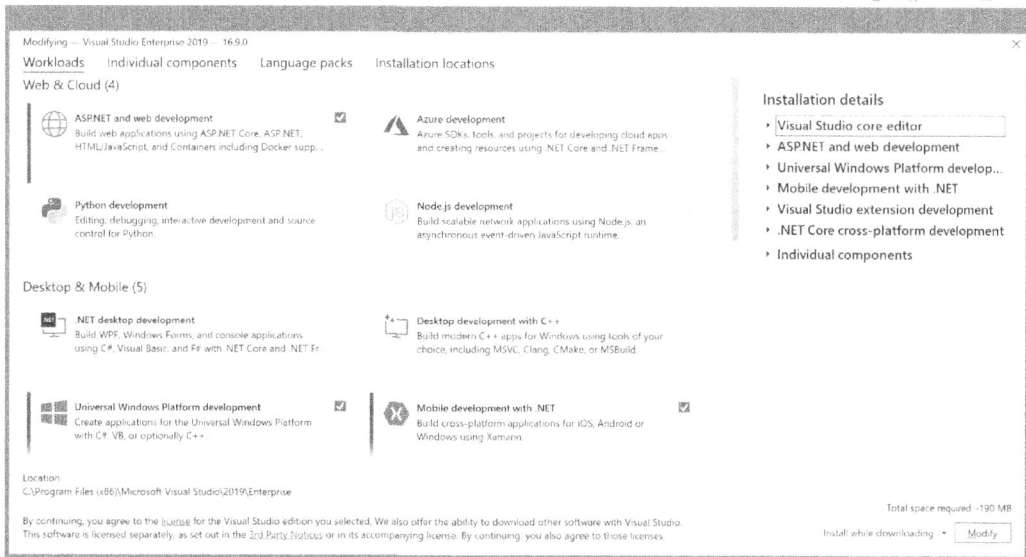

Figure 1.4 – The Visual Studio Installer showing various workload options

To build apps with Uno Platform, you'll need the following workloads installed:

- **Universal Windows Platform Development**

- **Mobile development with .NET**

- **ASP.NET and web development**

- **.NET Core cross-platform development**

Installing the required templates from the marketplace

To make it easier to build your Uno Platform applications, multiple project and item templates are available. These are installed as part of the **Uno Platform Solution Templates** extension. You can install this from within Visual Studio, or directly from the marketplace.

Installing templates from within Visual Studio

To install the extension containing the templates, perform the following actions within Visual Studio:

1. Go to **Extensions>Manage Extensions**.

2. Search for Uno. It should be the first result.

3. Click the **Download** button.

4. Click **Close**, let the extension installer complete, and then restart **Visual Studio**:

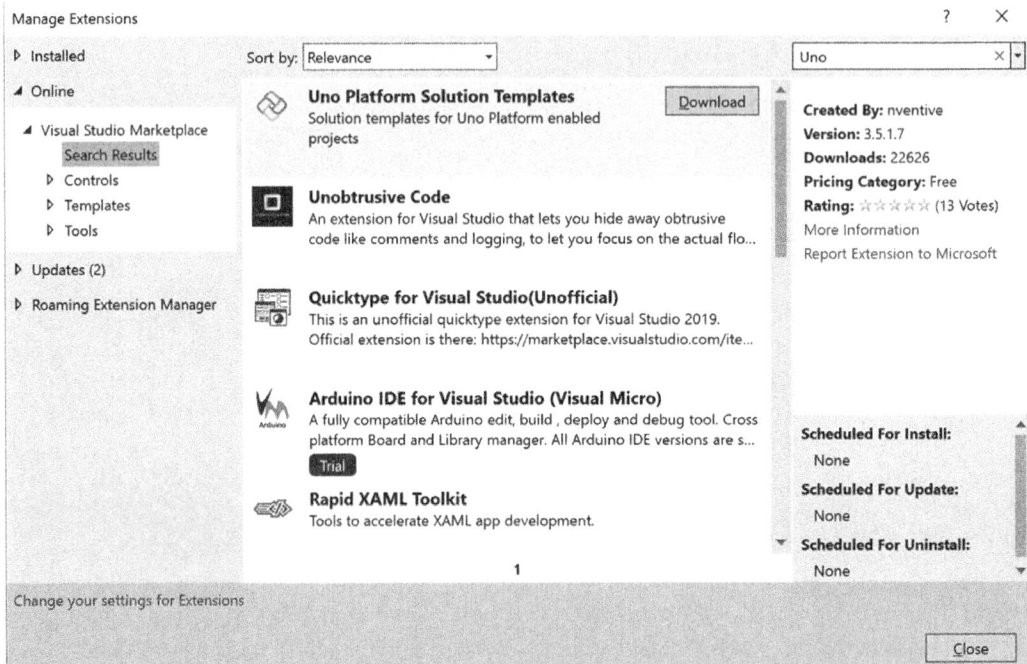

Figure 1.5 – Uno Platform Solution Templates shown in the Manage Extensions dialog

Installing templates from the marketplace

Follow these steps to install the extension from the marketplace:

1. Go to `https://marketplace.visualstudio.com` and search for Uno. It should be the first result returned.

    Alternatively, go directly to the following URL: `https://marketplace.visualstudio.com/items?itemName=nventivecorp.uno-platform-addin`.

2. Click on the **Download** button.

3. Double-click on the downloaded `.vsix` file to start the install wizard.

4. Follow the steps in the wizard.

With the workloads and templates installed, you're now ready to start building apps. However, if you want to develop for iOS or Mac, you'll also need a Mac device set up so that you can connect to it from Visual Studio on Windows.

Using other editors and IDEs

It's not compulsory to use Visual Studio 2019 on a Windows PC, and the Uno Platform team has worked hard to make building Uno Platform apps as flexible as possible. Therefore, you can use it within your existing working patterns and preferences.

Installing the required templates with the command line

In addition to working with the templates inside Visual Studio, it's also possible to install them for use from the command line. To install them this way, run the following at the command line or terminal:

```
dotnet new -i Uno.ProjectTemplates.Dotnet
```

After this command has finished, it will list all the available templates. You should see multiple entries with a short name, beginning with *uno*.

Building Uno Platform apps with Visual Studio for Mac

To build Uno Platform apps using Visual Studio for Mac, you will require the following:

- **Visual Studio** for Mac version 8.8 or higher (using the latest version is recommended).

- **Xcode 12.0** or higher (using the latest version is recommended).

- An Apple ID.

- **.NET Core 3.1** and **5.0 SDKs**.

- **GTK+3** (for running the **Skia/GTK** projects).

- The templates installed (see previous section).

- Enable the templates to be visible in Visual Studio for Mac by opening the **Preferences** menu option and then selecting **Other>Preview Features** and checking **Show all .NET Core templates in the New Project Dialog**.

Links to all these are available at the following URL: `https://platform.uno/docs/articles/get-started-vsmac.html`.

Building Uno Platform apps with Visual Studio Code

You can use Visual Studio Code to build WebAssembly apps on Windows, Linux, or Mac. Using it to build apps for other platforms is not yet supported.

To build Uno Platform apps using Visual Studio Code, you will need the following:

- **Visual Studio Code** (using the latest version is recommended)
- Mono
- **.NET Core 3.1** and **5.0 SDKs**
- The templates installed (see previous section)
- **C#** extension for **Visual Studio Code**
- **JavaScript Debugger** (Nightly) extension for **Visual Studio Code**

Links to all these are available at the following URL: `https://platform.uno/docs/articles/get-started-vscode.html`.

Building Uno Platform apps with JetBrains Rider

It is possible to use **JetBrains Rider** on Windows, Mac, and Linux, but not all platforms can be built for with all versions.

To build Uno Platform apps with JetBrains Rider, you will need the following:

- **Rider version 2020.2** or higher, although using the latest version is recommended
- **Rider Xamarin Android Support Plugin**
- **.NET Core 3.1** and **5.0 SDKs**
- The templates installed (see previous section)

There are some additional points to be aware of when using JetBrains Rider, as follows:

- WebAssembly apps cannot yet be debugged from within the IDE. As a workaround, it's possible to use the Chromium in-browser debugger instead.
- If building the **Skia/GTK** projects on a Mac, you'll also need to install **GTK+3**.
- If you wish to build iOS or Mac apps using a Windows PC, you will need an attached Mac (as you would if using Visual Studio).

Links to all these and more details are available at the following URL: `https://platform.uno/docs/articles/get-started-rider.html`.

> **Important note**
>
> It is also possible to use Blend for Visual Studio (on Windows) to work with code as you can for regular UWP apps. However, Blend does not support all the project types that an Uno Platform solution contains. You may find it beneficial to have a separate version of the solution that doesn't include those projects, and access that version in Blend.

Checking your setup

Uno Platform has a **dotnet global tool** to check if your machine is set up correctly and walk you through addressing any issues it finds. It's called **uno-check** and it's very simple to use, as follows:

1. Open a developer Command Prompt, Terminal, or PowerShell window.

2. Install the tool by entering the following:

   ```
   dotnet tool install --global Uno.Check
   ```

3. Run the tool by entering the following:

   ```
   uno-check
   ```

4. Follow any prompts it gives you and enjoy looking at the following message:
   Congratulations, everything looks great!

Debugging your setup

Whichever IDE or code editor you use, there will be many parts, and the use of multiple tools, SDKs, and even machines can make it hard to know where to begin when things aren't working. The following are general tips to help work out what isn't working. Some of these may seem obvious, but I'd rather look a fool for reminding you to check something obvious than have you waste time on an unchecked assumption:

- Try restarting your machine. Yes, I know, it would be funny if it didn't work so often.

- Read and then re-read any error messages carefully. They can sometimes be helpful.

- Check you have installed *everything* correctly.

- Has anything changed? Even if you didn't do it directly, something might have been changed automatically or without your knowledge (including, but not limited to, OS updates, security patches, IDE updates, other apps being installed or uninstalled, and network security permission changes).

- If one thing has been updated, have all dependencies and referenced components been updated too? It's common that when things are connected, share references, or communicate, they must be updated together.

- Have any keys or licenses expired?

- If there is a problem with a previously created app, can you create a new app and compile and run that?

- Can you create a new app and confirm that it compiles and runs on each platform?

- If on Windows, can you create a new blank UWP app and then compile and debug it?

Trying equivalent actions or creating equivalent apps with other tools can often produce different error messages. In addition, you may also find paths to solutions that fix problems in your Uno Platform project setup:

- If using a WebAssembly app, can you create a new, blank **ASP.NET** web app or **Blazor** project and compile and debug that?

- If a WebAssembly app doesn't work in one browser, are error messages shown in the browser log or debug window? Does it work in another browser?

- For **Android**, **iOS**, or **macOS** issues, can you create, compile, and debug `Xamarin.Forms` apps?

- If there is an Android-specific issue, can you create and debug an app with Android Studio?

- If using a Mac, can you create and debug a blank app with Xcode?

Additional tips for resolving common setup and configuration issues can be found at the following two URLs:

- `https://platform.uno/docs/articles/get-started-wizard.html#common-issues`

- `https://platform.uno/docs/articles/uno-builds-troubleshooting.html`

If the issue comes from connecting to a Mac from a PC, the Xamarin documentation may be helpful. It is available at the following URL: `https://docs.microsoft.com/ en-us/xamarin/ios/get-started/installation/windows/connecting-to-mac/`. This can also help identify and address the issue in Uno Platform projects as well.

Details on where to go for answers to specific Uno Platform-related questions can be found in *Chapter 8, Deploying Your Apps and Going Further*.

Summary

In this chapter, we learned what Uno Platform is, the problem it was designed to solve, and the types of projects we can use it for. We then looked at how to set up your development environment, making it ready in order to build your first application with Uno Platform.

In the next chapter, we will build our first Uno Platform app. We will explore the structure of the generated solution, look at how to debug on different environments, and customize the app when it runs on those different environments. We will look at how you can create reusable libraries for use within your future Uno Platform projects. Finally, we will look at some of the other options available for creating Uno Platform apps.

Further reading

The following titles were mentioned earlier in this chapter and may provide useful background on working with C# and XAML if you are unfamiliar with them:

- *C# 9 and .NET 5 – Modern Cross-Platform Development – Fifth Edition, Price, Packt Publishing (2020)*
- *Learn WinUI 3.0, Ashcraft, Packt Publishing (2021)*

2
Writing Your First Uno Platform App

In this chapter, you will learn how to create a new Uno Platform app and see how a typical Uno Platform app is structured. First, we will go over the default Uno Platform app template, including the different projects included, and get you running on Windows 10 with your first Uno Platform app. After that, we will dive deeper into running and debugging your app on different platforms by showing how to use emulators and debugging the WebAssembly (Wasm) version of the app.

Since Uno Platform supports a plethora of platforms and more and more platforms are being added to the list of supported platforms, in this book, we will only develop for a subset of supported platforms. The following platforms are the most prominent and widely used platforms, and as such, we will target them: Windows 10, Android, Web/ Wasm, macOS, and iOS.

While we mention the other platforms in this chapter for completeness, the other chapters will only include the platforms mentioned earlier. This means that we will not show you how to run or test your app on **Linux**, **Tizen**, or **Windows 7/8**.

In this chapter, we will cover the following topics:

- Creating an Uno Platform app and understanding its structure
- Running and debugging your app, including using **XAML Hot Reload** and **C# Edit and Continue**
- Platform-specific code using C# compiler symbols and **XAML** prefixes
- Other project types besides the Uno Platform app

By the end of this chapter, you will have written your first Uno Platform app and created customizations based on the running platform. In addition to that, you will be able to make use of the different Uno Platform project types.

Technical requirements

This chapter assumes that you already have your development environment set up, including installing the project templates, as was covered in *Chapter 1, Introducing Uno Platform*. You can find the source code for this chapter here: `https://github.com/PacktPublishing/Creating-Cross-Platform-C-Sharp-Applications-with-Uno-Platform/tree/main/Chapter02`.

Check out the following video to see the code in action: `https://bit.ly/37Dt0Hg`

> **Note**
> If you are using the digital version of this book, we advise you to type the code yourself or access the code from the book's GitHub repository Doing so will help you avoid any potential errors related to the copying and pasting of code.

Creating your first app

There are different ways of creating your project, so we will start with the most common one, using Visual Studio.

Creating your project with the Uno Platform solution templates

The process of creating an Uno Platform app project is the same as for other project types in Visual Studio. Depending on the extensions and project templates installed, you will be greeted by the list of options in *Figure 2.1* when filtering for **Uno Platform**. Note that for *Figure 2.1*, only the **Uno Platform Solution Templates** extension was installed:

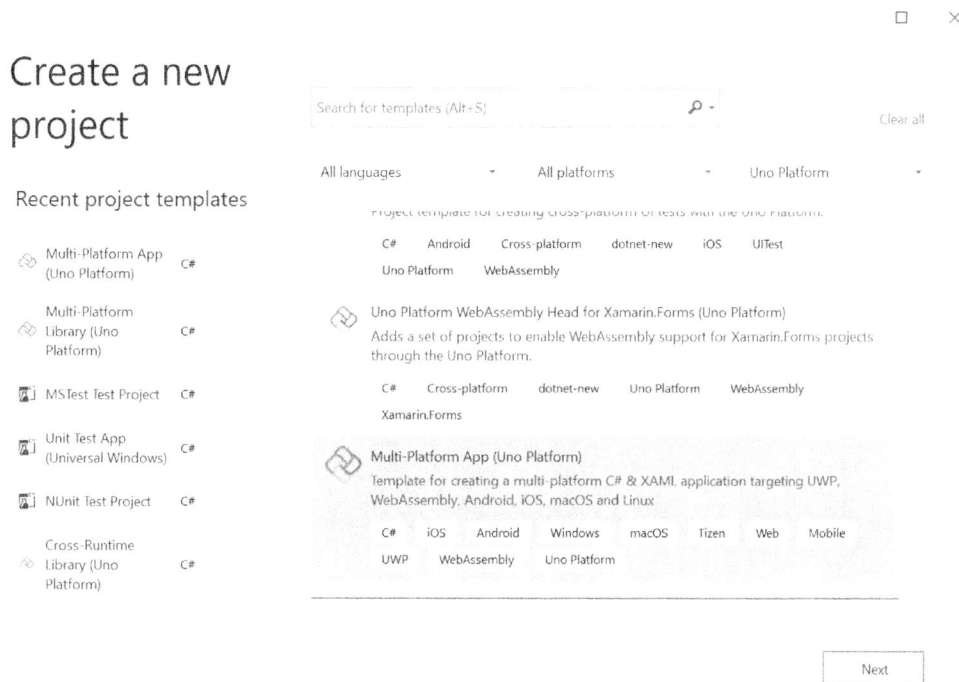

Figure 2.1 – List of Uno Platform project templates in the new project dialog

The easiest way to get started with Uno Platform is using the **Multi-Platform App (Uno Platform)** project template as this contains all the necessary projects to build and run Uno Platform apps for every platform.

Let's start creating your app by selecting the **Multi-Platform App (Uno Platform)** project type and click **Next**. Be careful that you are not selecting the **Multi-Platform Library (Uno Platform)** option as that will create a different project type, which we cover in the *Going beyond the default cross-platform app structure section*. Now you need to choose the name of your project, the location, and the solution name as seen in *Figure 2.2*:

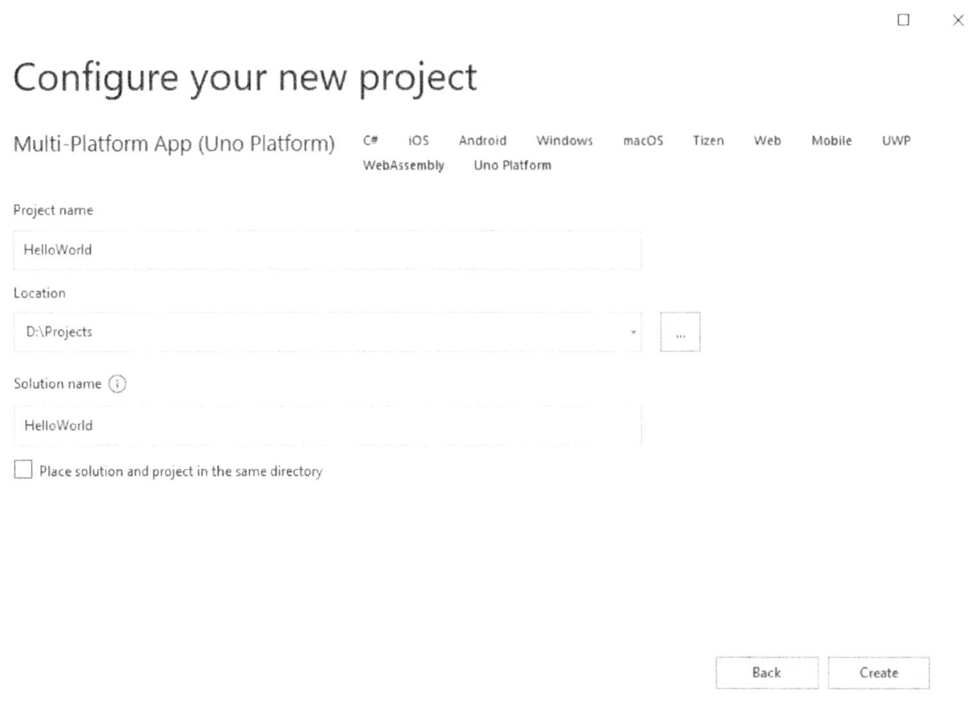

□   ×

Configure your new project

Multi-Platform App (Uno Platform)   C#   iOS   Android   Windows   macOS   Tizen   Web   Mobile   UWP
WebAssembly   Uno Platform

Project name

> HelloWorld

Location

> D:\Projects   ▾   ...

Solution name ⓘ

> HelloWorld

☐ Place solution and project in the same directory

Back   Create

Figure 2.2 – Configuring Multi-Platform App (Uno Platform)

In our case, we will call our project `HelloWorld` and save it under `D:\Projects` meaning that the project will be stored in `D:\Projects\HelloWorld` with the `HelloWorld.sln` solution being the top-level element. Of course, you can create the project in any folder you want; `D:\Projects` is just an example here. Note though that you should create your project as close as possible to the root of your drive to avoid issues with paths that are too long. After clicking **Create**, Visual Studio will create your project and open the solution for you. You will see all the generated projects in **Solution Explorer**.

If you are creating your project in Visual Studio for Mac, the generated solution will include project heads for **Windows Presentation Foundation** (**WPF**) and **Universal Windows Platform** (**UWP**) apps. A project or platform head is the corresponding project that will be compiled when you compile your app for a specific platform. So, in the case of Windows 10, the UWP head will be compiled. You will need to use a Windows PC to build these apps. If you don't want to build for these platforms, you can remove the projects from the solution. If you will build these on a Windows machine separately, unload them from the solution when working on a Mac.

Since your app might not target every platform supported by Uno Platform, you might want to remove those heads for your app. To do that, remove those projects from the solution by right-clicking the project in the project view and clicking **Remove** as shown in *Figure 2.3*:

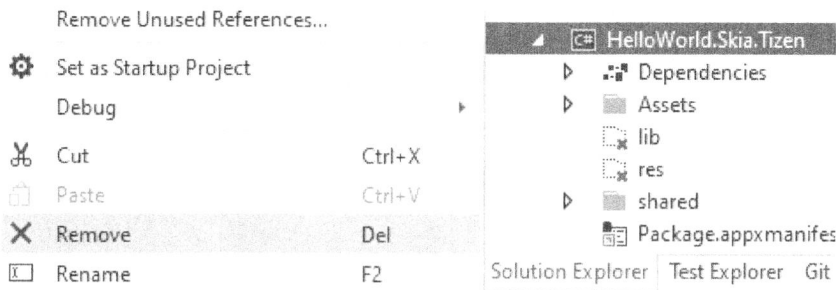

Figure 2.3 – Removing the Skia.Tizen head from the solution

After removing the project from the solution, the project is still on disk. To remove it entirely, you will have to delete the project by opening the project folder and deleting the corresponding folders. Since we will only target Windows 10, Android, Web, macOS, and iOS, you can remove the `Skia.GTK`, the `Skia.Tizen`, `Skia.Wpf`, and `Skia.WpfHost` projects from your solution.

Creating your project with the .NET CLI

Of course, you don't have to use Visual Studio to create your Uno Platform app. You can also use the `dotnet new` templates for Uno Platform. You can create a new project by opening a terminal and typing the following:

```
dotnet new unoapp -o MyApp
```

This will create a new project called **MyApp**. You can find an overview of all the dotnet new templates in Uno Platform's template documentation (`https://platform.uno/docs/articles/get-started-dotnet-new.html`).

Of course, not everyone wants to target every platform with their app nor is it appropriate for every app to run on every platform. You can opt out of creating the target projects for specific platforms (more on those in the next section) by including specific flags in your commands. For example, with the following command, you will create a new project that will not run on Linux and other Skia-based platforms as we exclude the Skia heads:

```
dotnet new unoapp -o MyApp -skia-wpf=false -skia-gtk=false
-st=false
```

To get a list of all the available options for the `unoapp` template, you can run `dotnet new unoapp -h`.

Project structure and the heads

When creating the project in Visual Studio on Windows, with the Uno Platform Solution templates, there are two different top-level elements in **Solution Explorer**: the `Platforms` folder and the `HelloWorld.Shared` shared C# project. Note that in the solution view, those are the two top-level elements, however, the `Platforms` folder does not exist on disk. Instead, all projects including the shared project have their own folder as shown in *Figure 2.4*:

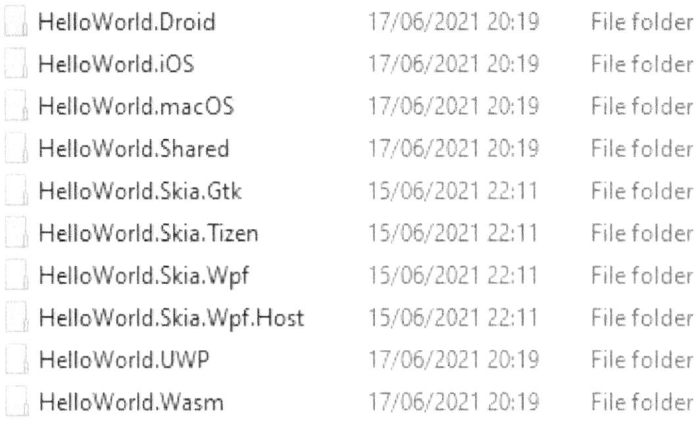

HelloWorld.Droid	17/06/2021 20:19	File folder
HelloWorld.iOS	17/06/2021 20:19	File folder
HelloWorld.macOS	17/06/2021 20:19	File folder
HelloWorld.Shared	17/06/2021 20:19	File folder
HelloWorld.Skia.Gtk	15/06/2021 22:11	File folder
HelloWorld.Skia.Tizen	15/06/2021 22:11	File folder
HelloWorld.Skia.Wpf	15/06/2021 22:11	File folder
HelloWorld.Skia.Wpf.Host	15/06/2021 22:11	File folder
HelloWorld.UWP	17/06/2021 20:19	File folder
HelloWorld.Wasm	17/06/2021 20:19	File folder

Figure 2.4 – HelloWorld project in File Explorer

In the root of the generated solution is a file called `.vsconfig`. This file contains a list of all the Visual Studio components required to work with the generated project. If you set your environment up as in *Chapter 1*, *Introducing Uno Platform*, then you'll have everything you need. But, if you see the prompt in *Figure 2.5*, click on the **Install** link and add the missing workloads:

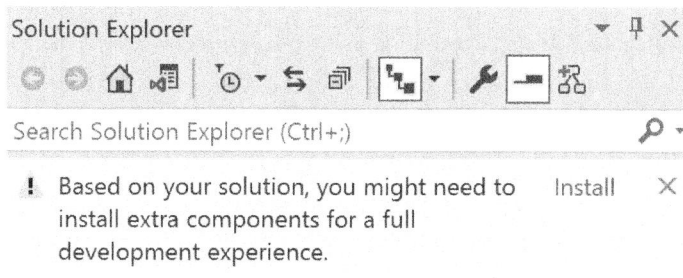

Figure 2.5 – Missing components warning in Visual Studio

Under the `Platforms` solution folder, you will find a `C#` project for every one of the supported platforms:

- `HelloWorld.Droid.csproj` for Android

- `HelloWorld.iOS.csproj` for iOS

- `HelloWorld.macOS.csproj` for macOS

- `HelloWorld.Skia.Gtk.csproj` for Linux with GTK

- `HelloWorld.Skia.Tizen.csproj` for Tizen

- `HelloWorld.Skia.Wpf.csproj`: Base project for Windows 7 and Windows 8

- `HelloWorld.Skia.Wpf.WpfHost.csproj`: Host for the `HelloWorld.Skia.Wpf` project on Windows 7 and Windows 8

- `HelloWorld.UWP.csproj` for Windows 10

- `HelloWorld.Wasm.csproj` for WebAssembly (WASM)

Those projects are also called **heads** for the respective platforms since they contain the platform-specific configuration files that are unique to the platform and are the projects that will be built for the specific platforms. Those projects don't contain a lot of code since any code in there is only for that specific platform. Most of your app's logic and XAML will, typically, not be put in the head projects but rather in the shared project. The heads are already configured for you and allow you to run your C# and XAML on those platforms. This includes creating a main activity for the Android head, starting a `UIApplication` for iOS, creating and displaying an `NSApplication` on macOS, or starting the application on WASM.

Some specific settings and configurations, such as permissions required by your app, will differ based on the platform. Some platforms allow you to use APIs without any restrictions. In contrast, other platforms are more prohibitive and require your app to specify those APIs beforehand or ask the user for permission, which is something you have to configure in the head project. As those configurations need to be done in the individual heads, the experience will differ based on the different platforms. We will only cover parts of those differences when configuring the platform heads in *Chapter 3*, *Working with Forms and Data*, (Mac, WASM, and UWP) and *Chapter 4*, *Mobilizing Your App*, (Android and iOS) as part of developing apps for those platforms.

In contrast to the head projects, the **shared project** is where almost all of your app's code will be, including your pages and views, the core logic of the app, and any assets such as resources or images that will be used on every platform. The shared project is referenced by all of the platform heads, so any code placed in there will be used on all of the platforms. If you are not familiar with C# shared projects, shared projects are nothing more than a list of files that will be included when compiling a project that references the shared project.

A newly created cross-platform app like our **Hello World** app already comes with a few files in the shared project:

- `App.xaml.cs`: This is the app's entry point; it will load the UI and navigate to `MainPage`. In here, you can also configure the logging of events by uncommenting the respective lines in the `InitializeLogging` function.
- `App.xaml`: This contains the list of common XAML resources such as resource dictionaries and theme resources.
- `MainPage.xaml.cs`: This file contains the C# code of your `MainPage`.
- `MainPage.xaml`: This is where you can put the UI of your `MainPage`.
- `Assets/SharedAssets.md`: This is a demo asset file that is included to show how assets work inside an Uno Platform app.
- `Strings/en/Resources.resw`: This is also a demo asset file that you can use to get started with localization inside your Uno Platform app.

Now that you are familiar with the project structure of your first Uno Platform app, let's dive into building and running your app.

Building and running your first Uno Platform app

Since you are familiar with the structure of an Uno Platform app, we can get to building and running your first Uno Platform app! In this section, we will go over the different ways of building and running your app.

Running and debugging your app with Visual Studio on Windows

Running your Uno Platform app from within Visual Studio is exactly the same as running a regular UWP, Xamarin.Forms, or WASM app. To build and run the app on a specific device or emulator, you can select the corresponding head from the startup project dropdown. Note that depending on the selected configuration, target platform, and architecture, not every project will be compiled to the expected output and might even not get compiled at all. For example, the UWP project always targets explicit architectures and as such, will compile to x86 when selecting the **Any CPU** architecture. That means not all combinations of target architecture and project will compile into what is specified but rather will fall back to a default architecture such as x86 in the case of UWP.

To run the UWP app, select the **HelloWorld.UWP** project as the startup project if it isn't already selected, by choosing **HelloWorld.UWP** from the startup project dropdown as shown in *Figure 2.6*:

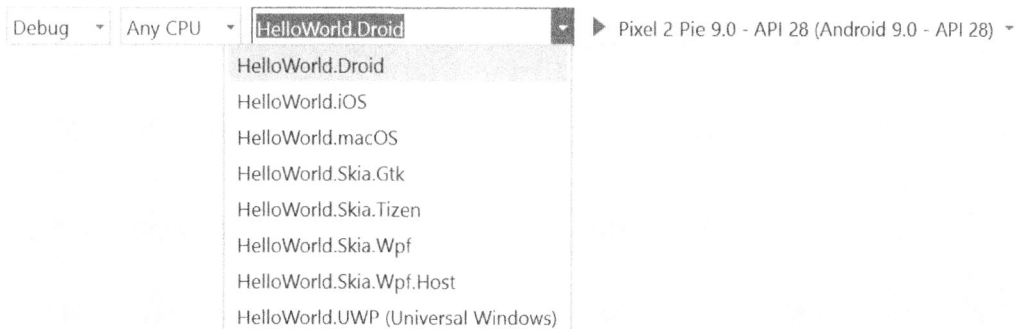

Debug ▾	Any CPU ▾	HelloWorld.Droid ▾	▶ Pixel 2 Pie 9.0 - API 28 (Android 9.0 - API 28) ▾
		HelloWorld.Droid	
		HelloWorld.iOS	
		HelloWorld.macOS	
		HelloWorld.Skia.Gtk	
		HelloWorld.Skia.Tizen	
		HelloWorld.Skia.Wpf	
		HelloWorld.Skia.Wpf.Host	
		HelloWorld.UWP (Universal Windows)	

Figure 2.6 – Configuration, architecture, startup project, and target machine options in Visual Studio

After that, select the correct architecture for your machine and the run configuration, debug, or release you want to run. Since we are going to debug the app in the next section, choose **Debug** for now. After that, you can choose the target device to deploy to, that is, the local machine, a connected device, or an emulator. To do that, use the dropdown to the right of the project list shown in *Figure 2.7*:

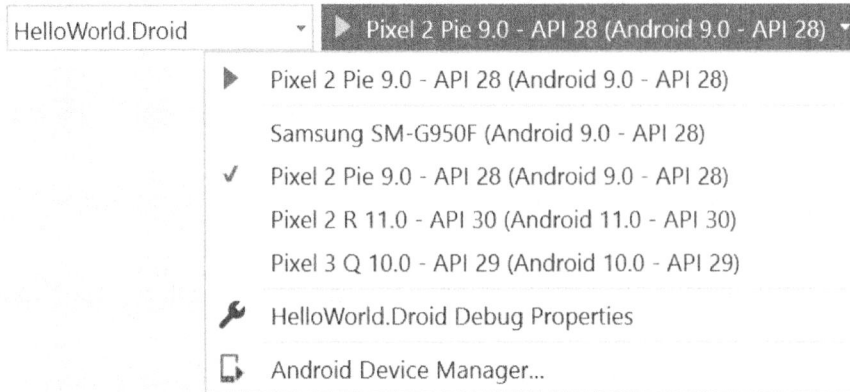

HelloWorld.Droid	▾	▶ Pixel 2 Pie 9.0 - API 28 (Android 9.0 - API 28) ▾
	▶	Pixel 2 Pie 9.0 - API 28 (Android 9.0 - API 28)
		Samsung SM-G950F (Android 9.0 - API 28)
	✓	Pixel 2 Pie 9.0 - API 28 (Android 9.0 - API 28)
		Pixel 2 R 11.0 - API 30 (Android 11.0 - API 30)
		Pixel 3 Q 10.0 - API 29 (Android 10.0 - API 29)
	🔧	HelloWorld.Droid Debug Properties
		Android Device Manager...

Figure 2.7 – List of Android emulators in Visual Studio

You can then start the project by clicking on the green arrow or hitting *F5*. The app will build, and you should be greeted by something like *Figure 2.8*:

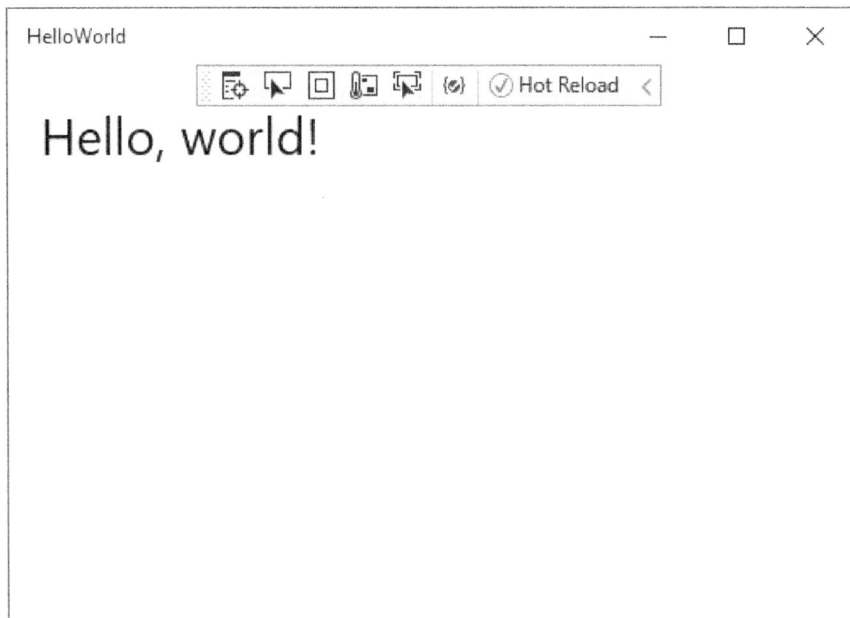

HelloWorld   —   □   ✕

Hello, world!

Figure 2.8 – Screenshot of the HelloWorld app running on Windows 10

Congratulations, you have just run your first Uno Platform app! Of course, running your app on Windows is not the only part of developing your cross-platform app. Running and debugging your app on Android, iOS, and other platforms is vital when writing cross-platform apps to ensure your apps work on all platforms supported.

For Android development, there are multiple different ways to try out and run your apps. One possibility is using an Android emulator, which comes with Visual Studio. For that, simply select the Android emulator from the target list dropdown as shown in *Figure 2.7*.

> **Note**
>
> If you haven't already added an Android emulator device image, you will only see **Android Emulator** as an option. To learn how to add and configure devices, the Visual Studio documentation (`https://docs.microsoft.com/en-us/xamarin/android/get-started/installation/android-emulator/device-manager`) covers creating new devices and configuring them for your needs.

If you have connected an Android phone to your computer, it will show up in the list of available target devices. An example of this can be seen with the Samsung device shown in *Figure 2.7*.

> **Note**
>
> For optimal development experience with Visual Studio, when editing C# or XAML files, ensure Visual Studio will use the UWP head for IntelliSense since, otherwise, IntelliSense might not work correctly. For this, when you have opened a C# or XAML file, select the UWP head from the dropdown below the tab name of the opened file.

Pairing Visual Studio for Windows with a Mac

For testing and debugging the iOS head, you can either directly develop on a Mac, which we will cover in the next section, or you can pair your Visual Studio for Windows with a Mac to remotely debug the iOS head.

The *Mobile development with .NET* workload in Visual Studio includes the software needed to connect to a Mac. However, there are three steps required to fully configure it:

1. Install **Xcode** and **Visual Studio for Mac** on the Mac and open these apps to ensure all dependencies are installed.
2. Enable **Remote login** on the Mac.
3. Connect to the Mac from Visual Studio.

Enabling remote login on the Mac requires the following:

1. Open the **Sharing** pane in **System Preferences**.

2. Check **Remote Login** and specify the users to **Allow access for:**.

3. Change any firewall settings as prompted.

To connect from Visual Studio, do the following:

-   Go to **Tools >iOS>Pair to Mac.**

-   If you're doing this for the first time, select **Add Mac…** and enter the Mac name or IP address, and then the username and password when prompted.

-   If the Mac is already listed, select it and click **Connect**.

The tool will check everything needed is installed and available on the Mac, and then it will open the connection.

If there's a problem, it will tell you what to do to address it.

> Note.
>
> More detailed instructions on pairing Visual Studio to a Mac and advice on addressing any problems you may encounter are available at `https://docs.microsoft.com/xamarin/ios/get-started/installation/windows/connecting-to-mac/`.

With Visual Studio now successfully paired to your Mac, you're able to debug the app from your Windows machine and see it running on the remoted iOS simulator.

Running and debugging your apps with Visual Studio for Mac

If you are primarily working on a Mac, using Visual Studio for Mac is the easiest way of developing your Uno Platform app.

Running your Uno Platform app using Visual Studio for Mac is the same as running other apps. You will need to select the correct head project in the startup project list (for example, `HelloWorld.macOS` or `HelloWorld.iOS`), select the correct target architecture to run the app for, and the device or emulator to run the app on.

Of course, in addition to running the app on your local machine, you can also run the Android or iOS app on an emulator. Any suitable devices that you can run the Android or iOS build of your app on will show up as targets in Visual Studio for Windows, including any emulators or simulators.

Since debugging the WASM build of your Uno Platform apps will happen outside of Visual Studio and Visual Studio for Mac, we will cover this in the next section.

Debugging the WASM head of your app

At the time of writing, debugging WASM from inside Visual Studio or Visual Studio for Mac is not well supported, however, there are alternative options. Because of this, the debugging experience for WASM will instead take place inside your browser when using Visual Studio for Windows or Visual Studio for Mac. For the best debugging experience, we recommend using the latest Canary build of Google Chrome. This is available from `https://www.google.com/chrome/canary/`. Since debugging WASM is still experimental, and as such will likely change, we highly recommend visiting the official documentation (`https://platform.uno/docs/articles/debugging-wasm.html`) to get the latest information. You can learn more about debugging the WASM head with Visual Studio here: `https://platform.uno/blog/debugging-uno-platform-webassembly-apps-in-visual-studio-2019/`.

Alternatively, you can use Visual Studio Code to debug the WASM version of your app. For an optimal experience, you should create your Uno Platform app with the `dotnet new` CLI. You must include the `-vscodeWasm` flag, as shown here, since it will add build configurations that you can use in Visual Studio Code:

```
dotnet new unoapp -o HelloWorld -ios=false -android=false
  -macos=false -uwp=false --vscodeWasm
```

Note that with the preceding `dotnet new` command, we opted out of the other heads since, at the time of writing, only the WASM version can be debugged with Visual Studio Code.

If you already have created your app, please follow the steps shown in the documentation at `https://platform.uno/docs/articles/get-started-vscode.html#updating-an-existing-application-to-work-with-vs-code`. This also works when heads for other platforms are already present in your project.

To start your app and debug it with Visual Studio, first restore NuGet packages using `dotnet restore`. After that, you will need to start the development server. To do this, open the **RUN AND DEBUG** panel shown in *Figure 2.9* by clicking on the triangle-bug icon on the left of Visual Studio Code:

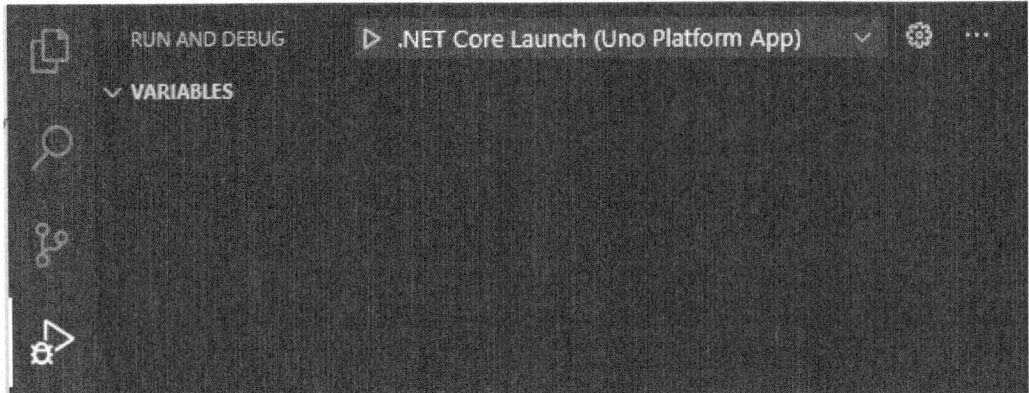

Figure 2.9 – RUN AND DEBUG view of Visual Studio Code

Click on the arrow, which will run the **.NET Core Launch** configuration, which builds the app and starts a development server. The development server will host your app. Check the terminal output to see on which URL you can visit the WASM app on your local machine, as shown in *Figure 2.10*:

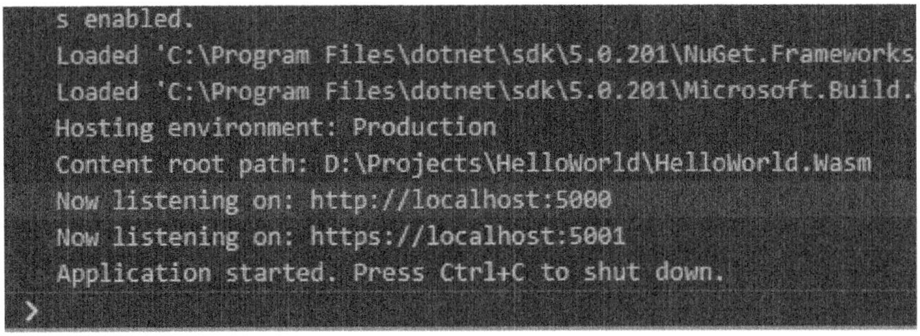

Figure 2.10 – Terminal output of the development server

If you just want to start the app and continue without debugging capabilities, you are done here. However, if you want to take advantage of the debugging and breakpoint support, you will also have to select the **.NET Core Debug Uno Platform WebAssembly in Chrome** configuration. After selecting the launch configuration in the **Run and Debug** panel, start it, which will start the debugging server. The debugging server then opens a browser window with your Uno Platform WASM app opened.

> **Note**
>
> By default, the debugging server will start using the latest stable release of Google Chrome. If you have no stable release of Google Chrome installed, the server will not start. If you wish to use the latest stable release of Edge instead, you can update the `.vscode/launch.json` file and change `pwa-chrome` to `pwa-msedge`.

After the debugging server has started and is ready for requests, it will open the website in Chrome or Edge depending on your configuration. Any breakpoints you place in Visual Studio Code will be respected by the browser and pause your WASM app, similar to how breakpoints would work with Visual Studio on non-WASM projects.

After successfully completing these steps, you can open your app in a browser of your choice and it will look like *Figure 2.11*:

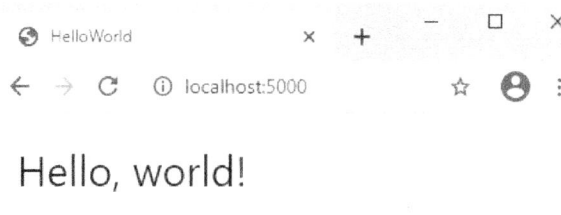

Figure 2.11 – HelloWorld app running in the browser

Now that we covered running and debugging your app, let's quickly cover two very helpful features for developing with Uno Platform: XAML Hot Reload and C# Edit and Continue.

XAML Hot Reload and C# Edit and Continue

To make development easier and faster, especially UI development, Uno Platform supports XAML Hot Reload and C# Edit and Continue when developing with Visual Studio. XAML Hot Reload allows you to modify the XAML code of your views and pages, and the running app will update in real time, while C# Edit and Continue allows you to modify C# code without having to restart your app for changes to be picked up.

Since the UWP head of your app is being built using the UWP toolchain, you can use XAML Hot Reload and C# Edit and Continue. Since at the time of writing, UWP is the only platform supporting both, we will use UWP to showcase it. Other platforms do not support C# Edit and Continue, but do, however, support XAML Hot Reload.

XAML Hot Reload

To try out XAML Hot Reload, open your **HelloWorld** project in Visual Studio, set the UWP head project as the startup project, and start it. Once it is started, open your `MainPage.xaml` file inside the shared project. The page's content will just be a `Grid` and a `TextBlock`:

```
<Grid Background="{ThemeResource
                    ApplicationPageBackgroundThemeBrush}">
    <TextBlock Text="Hello, world!"
        Margin="20" FontSize="30" />
</Grid>
```

Now let's change our page by replacing the text with **Hello from hot reload!**, save the file (*Ctrl* + *S*), and voilà, our app now looks like as shown in *Figure 2.12* without having restarted the app!

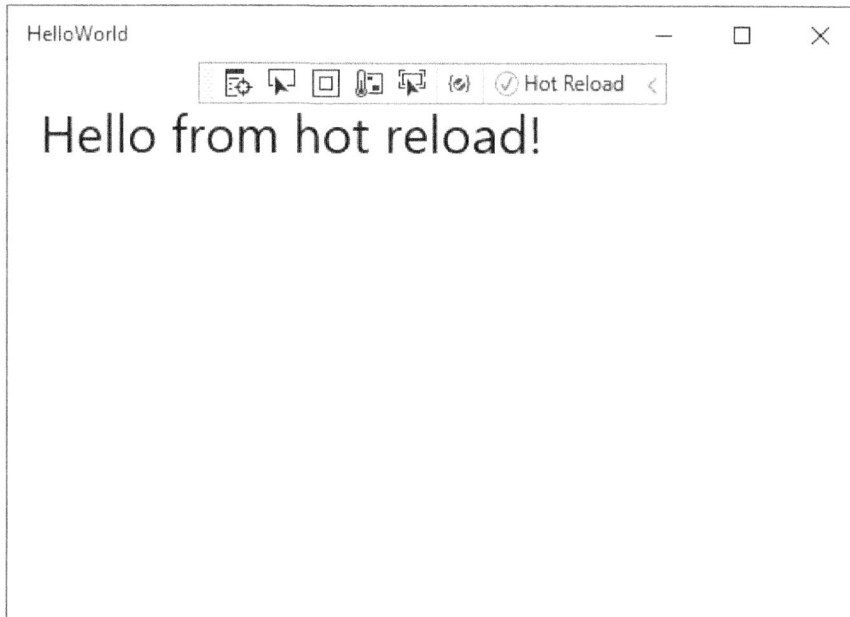

Figure 2.12 – Our HelloWorld app with XAML Hot Reload changes

XAML Hot Reload works on UWP, iOS, Android, and WebAssembly. However, not all types of changes are supported, for example, changing the event handler of controls is not supported by XAML Hot Reload and requires an app restart. In addition to that, updating `ResourceDictionary` files will also not update the app and will require an app restart.

C# Edit and Continue

Sometimes, you also need to make changes to your "*code-behind*", and that's where C# Edit and Continue will be your friend. Note that you will need to use the UWP head of your app since it is the only platform supporting C# Edit and Continue. Before we continue with trying out C# Edit and Continue, you will need to add a few things since our HelloWorld app doesn't contain much C# code yet. For that, first, you will need to close the debugger and the app since the following code changes are not supported by C# Edit and Continue. Update your page to contain a button with a `Click` event handler by changing your `MainPage` content to this:

```
<StackPanel Background="{ThemeResource
                ApplicationPageBackgroundThemeBrush}">

    <TextBlock x:Name="helloTextBlock"
            Text="Hello from hot reload!" Margin="20"
            FontSize="30" />
```

```
    <Button Content="Change text"
        Click="ChangeTextButton_Click"/>
</StackPanel>
```

Now, in your `MainPage` class, add the following code:

```
private void ChangeTextButton_Click(object sender,
                                         RoutedEventArgs e)
{
    helloTextBlock.Text = "Hello from code behind!";
}
```

When you run the app and click on the button, the text will change to **Hello from code behind!**. Now click the **Break all** button highlighted in *Figure 2.13* or press *Ctrl + Alt + Break*:

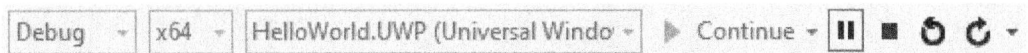

Figure 2.13 – Break all button

Your app is now paused and you can make changes to your C# code, which will be picked up when you resume your app by clicking on **Continue**. To see this, change the string inside the `Click` event handler to `Hello from C# Edit and Continue!`:

```
private void ChangeTextButton_Click(object sender,
                                         RoutedEventArgs e)
{
    helloTextBlock.Text =
        "Hello from C# Edit and Continue!";
}
```

Then resume the app. If you now click on the button, the text will now change to **Hello from C# Edit and Continue!**.

There are some limitations on the changes you can make with Edit and Continue though; not all code changes are supported, for example, changing the type of an object. For a full list of unsupported changes, please visit the official documentation (`https://docs.microsoft.com/en-us/visualstudio/debugger/supported-code-changes-csharp`). Note that at the time of writing, C# Edit and Continue only works on Windows for the UWP and the Skia heads.

Now that we have covered building and running your app, let's talk about conditional code, namely platform-specific C# and XAML.

Platform-specific XAML and C#

While Uno Platform allows you to run your app on any platform without having to worry about the underlying platform-specific API, there are still cases where you might want to write code that is specific to a platform, for example, accessing native platform APIs.

Platform-specific C#

Writing platform-specific C# code is similar to writing architecture-specific or runtime-specific C# code. Uno Platform ships with a set of compiler symbols that will be defined when your code is being compiled for a specific platform. This is achieved using preprocessor directives. Preprocessor directives will only be respected by the compiler if the symbol was set for the compilation, otherwise, the compiler will completely ignore the preprocessor directive.

At the time of writing, Uno Platform comes with the following preprocessor directives:

- `NETFX_CORE` for UWP
- `__ANDROID__` for Android
- `__IOS__` for iOS
- `HAS_UNO_WASM` (or `__WASM__`) for the web using WebAssembly
- `__MACOS__` for macOS
- `HAS_UNO_SKIA` (or `__SKIA__`) for Skia-based heads

Note that WASM and Skia have two different symbols available. Both are equally valid and have no difference except their name.

You can use those exactly like you would any other symbols, such as DEBUG, and you can even combine them, for example, if __ANDROID__ || __MACOS__. Let's try it out in our example from earlier and have the TextBlock element indicate whether we are on desktop, the web, or mobile using C# symbols:

```
private void ChangeTextButton_Click(object sender,
                                    RoutedEventArgs e)
{
#if __ANDROID__ || __IOS__
    helloTextBlock.Text = "Hello from C# on mobile!";
#elif HAS__UNO__WASM
    helloTextBlock.Text = "Hello from C# on WASM!";
#else
    helloTextBlock.Text = "Hello from C# on desktop!";
#endif
}
```

If you run the UWP head of your app and click the button, the text will then change to **Hello from C# on desktop!** since the UWP head is only compiled with the NETFX_CORE symbol being set. Now, if you run the app on an Android or iOS emulator (or device) and click on the button, it will display **Hello from C# on mobile**! since the Android and iOS heads are compiled with the __ANDROID__ or the __IOS__ symbols.

Platform-specific XAML

While platform-specific C# code is great, there are also cases where you need to render a control on a specific platform. This is where platform-specific XAML prefixes come in. XAML prefixes allow you to render controls only on specific platforms, similar to conditional namespaces for UWP.

There are, at the time of writing, the following XAML prefixes that you can use:

XAML Prefix	Platforms	Namespace URI
Win	UWP	http://schemas.microsoft.com/winfx/2006/xaml/presentation
android	Android	http://uno.ui/android
Ios	iOS	http://uno.ui/ios
Wasm	Web/Wasm	http://uno.ui/wasm
Macos	macOS	http://uno.ui/macos
Skia	Skia-based	http://schemas.microsoft.com/winfx/2006/xaml/presentation
xamarin	Android, iOS, macOS, Skia, and Wasm	http://uno.ui/xamarin
not_win	Android, iOS, macOS, Skia, and Wasm	http://uno.ui/not_win
not_android	iOS, macOS, Skia, UWP, and Wasm	http://schemas.microsoft.com/winfx/2006/xaml/presentation
not_ios	Android, macOS, Skia, UWP, and Wasm	http://schemas.microsoft.com/winfx/2006/xaml/presentation
not_wasm	Android, iOS, macOS, Skia, and UWP	http://schemas.microsoft.com/winfx/2006/xaml/presentation
not_macos	Android, iOS, Skia, UWP, and Wasm	http://schemas.microsoft.com/winfx/2006/xaml/presentation
not_skia	Android, iOS, UWP, and Wasm	http://schemas.microsoft.com/winfx/2006/xaml/presentation
netstdref	Wasm and Skia	http://uno.ui/netstdref
not_netstdref	Android, iOS, macOS, and UWP	http://uno.ui/not_netstdref

Figure 2.14 – Table of namespace prefixes, the supported platforms, and their namespace URIs

To include a specific XAML prefix in your XAML, you have to add `xmlns:[prefix-name]=[namespace URI]` at the top of the XAML file with all other namespace declarations. **Prefix-name** is the XAML prefix (column 1 in *Figure 2.14*) while **namespace URI** is the URI of the namespace (column 3 in *Figure 2.14*) the prefix should be used with.

For prefixes that will be excluded from Windows, you need to add the prefixes to the `mc:Ignorable` list. Those prefixes are `android`, `ios`, `wasm`, `macos`, `skia`, `xamarin`, `netstdref`, `not_netstdref`, and `not_win`, so all prefixes that are not in `http://schemas.microsoft.com/winfx/2006/xaml/presentation`.

Now let's try out a few platform XAML prefixes by updating our HelloWorld project to have a `TextBlock` element that only renders on WASM. For that, we will first add the prefix to our `MainPage.xaml` file (note that we have omitted some definitions):

```
<Page
    x:Class="HelloWorld.MainPage"
    ...
    xmlns:win="http://schemas.microsoft.com/winfx/2006/xaml/
            presentation"
    xmlns:android="http://uno.ui/android"
    xmlns:ios="http://uno.ui/ios"
    xmlns:wasm="http://uno.ui/wasm"
    xmlns:macos="http://uno.ui/macos"
    xmlns:skia="http://schemas.microsoft.com/winfx/2006/xaml/
            presentation"
    ...
    mc:Ignorable="d android ios wasm macos skia">
    ...
</Page>
```

Since the Android, iOS, WASM, macOS, and Skia XAML prefixes will be excluded on Windows, we need to add them to the `mc:Ignorable` list. This is because they are not part of the standard XAML specification and would result in errors otherwise. After adding them, we can add controls that will render only if the app is running on a specific platform, for example, WASM or iOS. To try that out, we will add a `TextBlock` element to welcome users on each platform as follows:

```
<StackPanel>
    <TextBlock x:Name="helloTextBlock"
        Text="Hello World!" Margin="20"
        FontSize="30" />
```

```
    <win:TextBlock Text="Welcome on Windows!"/>
    <android:TextBlock Text="Welcome on Android!"/>
    <ios:TextBlock Text="Welcome on iOS!"/>
    <wasm:TextBlock Text="Welcome on WASM!"/>
    <macos:TextBlock Text="Welcome on Mac OS!"/>
    <skia:TextBlock Text="Welcome on Skia!"/>
    <Button Content="Change test"
        Click="ChangeTextButton_Click"/>
</StackPanel>
```

Now, if you start the WASM head of your app and open the app in your browser (if it's not open already), the app will show the **Welcome on WASM!** TextBlock element, as shown on the left side of *Figure 2.15*. If you start the UWP head of your app now, the app will show **Welcome on Windows!** instead, as shown on the right side of *Figure 2.15*:

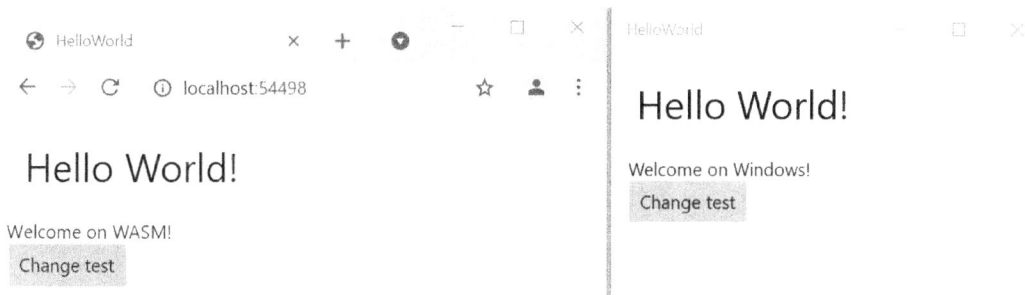

Figure 2.15 – HelloWorld app running using WASM (left) and using UWP (right)

If you are using the XAML prefixes in cross-targeted libraries such as the Cross Target Library (Uno Platform) project template, which is covered in the next section, the XAML prefixes behave slightly differently. Because of the way cross-targeted libraries work, the wasm and skia prefixes will always evaluate to false. An example of a cross-targeted library is the Cross-Runtime Library project type, which we'll cover in the next section. This is because both compile to .NET Standard 2.0 instead of the WASM or Skia heads. Instead of those prefixes, you can use the netstdref prefix with the namespace URI http://uno.ui/netstdref, which will evaluate to true if running on WASM or Skia. In addition to that, there is also the not_netstdref prefix with the namespace URI http://uno.ui/not_netstdref, which is the exact opposite of netstdref. Note that you will need to add both prefixes to the mc:Ignorable list. Now that you have learned about platform-specific code using C# compiler symbols and XAML prefixes, let's look into the other project types.

Going beyond the default cross-platform app structure

So far, we have created a cross-platform app that contains the heads for every platform. But there are also different project types that you can use to write your Uno Platform app, which we will cover in this section.

> **Note**
>
> The **Uno Platform Visual Studio solution templates** extension only contains a subset of the available Uno Platform types. If you haven't already installed the templates using the `dotnet` CLI, do this now by opening a terminal and running `dotnet new -i Uno.ProjectTemplates.Dotnet`, since we will use these in the remaining part of the chapter.

The multi-platform library project type

One of the most important project types besides the **Multi-Platform App (Uno Platform)** project type is the **Cross-Platform Library (Uno Platform)** type. The **Cross-Platform Library (Uno Platform)** project type allows you to write code that can be consumed by Uno Platform apps. The easiest way of getting to know the project type is by creating a new cross-platform library. We will do this by creating a new project inside our existing HelloWorld solution.

> **Note**
>
> To be able to use all the project templates installed with the `dotnet new` CLI, you will need to allow Visual Studio to include the `dotnet new` templates in the project type list. You can do this by opening the options under **Tools** > **Options** and opening the **Preview Features** section located under **Environment** by checking **Show all .NET Core templates in the New Project dialog**. After this, you will need to restart Visual Studio for the changes to take effect.

After enabling that option, restart Visual Studio and open the new project dialog by right-clicking on the solution in the solution view and clicking **Add** > **New Project**. The dialog will look like *Figure 2.16*:

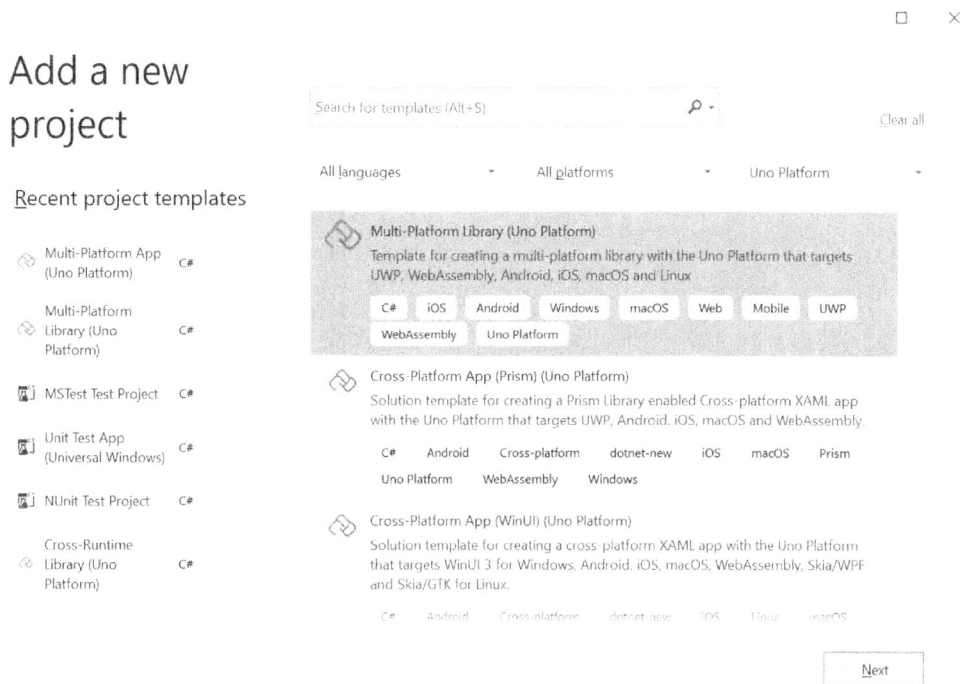

Figure 2.16 – The Add a new project dialog in Visual Studio

Next, select the **Multi-Platform Library (Uno Platform)** project (highlighted in *Figure 2.16*) and click **Next**. Now you will need to choose the name of your project. In this case, we will name the project `HelloWorld.Helpers`. After entering the name, click **Create**.

This will create a new cross-platform Uno Platform library in your solution. On disk, the library has its own folder named after itself and your solution view will look like *Figure 2.17*:

Figure 2.17 – HelloWorld solution view

Now let's add some code to our cross-platform library. We will rename the class Class1 to Greetings and introduce a new public static function called GetStandardGreeting that will return the string "Hello from a cross-platform library!":

```
public class Greetings
{
    public static string GetStandardGreeting()
    {
        return "Hello from a cross-platform library!";
    }
}
```

In addition to creating the library, you must also add a reference to it in each of the head projects you want to use the project in. The process of adding a reference to the library is the same for all heads, that's why we will only show you how to add the reference to the UWP head.

To add the reference to the UWP head, right-click the UWP project in Solution Explorer. Inside the context menu, you will find the **Add** category, which contains the **Reference…** option, which is also shown in *Figure 2.18*:

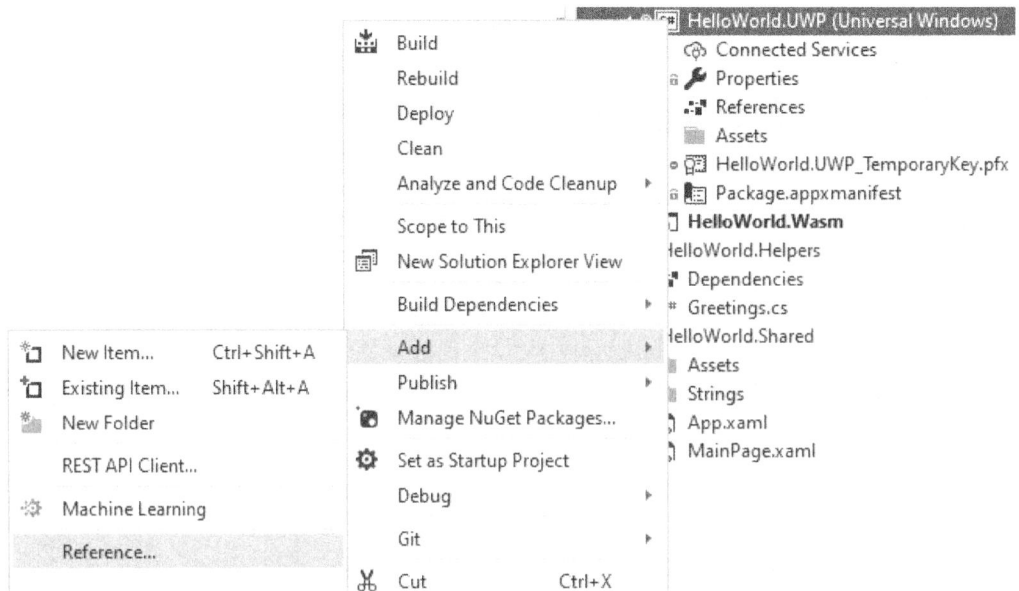

Figure 2.18 – Add | Reference… option for the UWP head

After clicking on **Reference...**, a new dialog where you can select the reference to add will open. In our case, you will need to select the project, as shown in *Figure 2.19*:

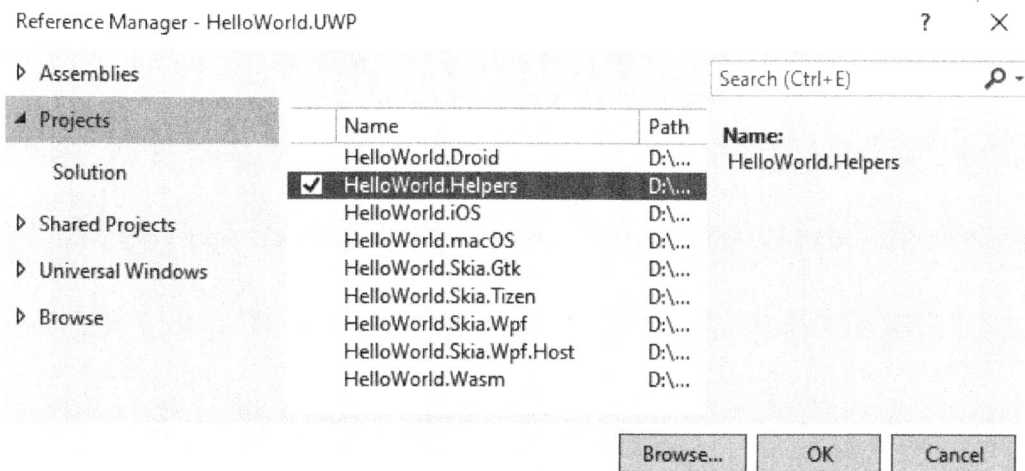

Figure 2.19 – Reference Manager for the UWP head

After checking the `HelloWorld.Helpers` project, click **OK** to save the changes. Now we can use our library in the UWP version of the app. Let's update our event handler from the platform's conditional code section to use the Greetings helper class as follows:

```
private void ChangeTextButton_Click(object sender,
                                RoutedEventArgs e)
{
#if __ANDROID__ || __IOS__
    helloTextBlock.Text = "Hello from C# on mobile!";
#elif __WASM__
    helloTextBlock.Text = "Hello from C# on WASM!";
#else
    helloTextBlock.Text=
        HelloWorld.Helpers.Greetings.GetStandardGreeting();
#endif
}
```

If you run the UWP version of the app now and click on the button, the app will display **Hello from a cross-platform library!**. However, if you are building the app using the macOS configuration, you will get a compiler error indicating that it is unable to find the `Helpers namespace` in the `HelloWorld namespace`. This is because we have not added a reference to the library from the macOS head yet. For any platform where you plan to use the library, you will need to add a reference in the platform's head. The procedure also applies to libraries being referenced as a NuGet package; you will need to add a reference to the NuGet package in every platform head that you want to use the library in. Unlike the Uno Platform app project, where most of the source code is inside a shared project, the **Cross-Platform Library** project type is a multi-targeted project.

Other project types

In addition to the Cross-Platform Library project type, there are other Uno Platform project templates. We will cover them broadly in this section. To be able to create them from Visual Studio, enable displaying `dotnet` new templates in Visual Studio as shown in the last section.

If you are already familiar with app development using XAML and the MVVM pattern, you might already know Prism (`https://prismlibrary.com/`), a framework *"for building XAML applications that are loosely coupled, maintainable, and testable."* Among the Uno Platform templates is also the **Cross-Platform App (Prism) (Uno Platform)** template, which will create a Prism Uno Platform app. Creating a Prism Uno Platform app is the same as creating a "normal" multi-platform Uno app.

In addition to the Uno Platform Prism app template, there is also an Uno Platform template for building apps for **WinUI 3**. However, you can create an Uno Platform app that uses a preview version of WinUI 3 for Windows 10. To create an Uno Platform app using WinUI 3, in the new project dialog, choose the **Cross-Platform App (WinUI) (Uno Platform)** template.

Another project type that will be useful, especially when developing libraries that will be shipped using NuGet, is the **Cross-Runtime Library (Uno Platform)** project type, which will create a Cross-Runtime Library. In contrast to the Cross-Platform Library, where Skia and WASM versions are not built separately and cannot be distinguished, the Cross-Runtime Library will compile the project separately for WASM and Skia, allowing the writing of WASM- and Skia-specific code using XAML prefixes and compiler symbols.

In addition to that, we also have the **Cross-Platform UI Tests Library**. The Cross- Platform UI Tests Library allows you to write UI tests that can be run on multiple platforms using a single code base. Since we will cover testing more thoroughly in *Chapter 7*, *Testing Your Apps*, we will cover that project type there.

Last but not least, we have the **Uno Platform WebAssembly Head for Xamarin.Forms** project type. The Uno Platform WebAssembly head for Xamarin.Forms allows bringing existing Xamarin.Forms apps to the web using WebAssembly and Uno Platform, which will be covered in *Chapter 8*, *Deploying Your Apps and Going Further*.

Summary

In this chapter, you learned how to create, build, and run your first Uno Platform app, and learned about the general solution structure and how platform heads work. We also covered building, running, and debugging your app on different platforms using Visual Studio and Visual Studio Code. In addition to that, you also learned about using XAML Hot Reload and C# Edit and Continue to make development easier.

In the next section, we will write apps for UnoBookRail, the company operating public transport in UnoBookCity. We will start off *Chapter 3*, *Working with Forms and Data*, by writing a task management app for UnoBookRail that allows entering, filtering, and editing data on the desktop and the web.

Section 2: Writing and Developing Uno Platform Apps

In the following four chapters, we'll look at four separate apps to show the different functionality available for the apps you build with Uno Platform. These apps are created for the same fictional business (UnoBookRail), which is part of the public transit authority for a fictional city (UnoBookCity).

The business is responsible for all the technology used as part of the light-rail network in the city. Light-rail networks are electrically powered trains that only carry passengers and exist in many cities worldwide. They are known by names including Metro, Rapid Transit, Subway, Tube, Underground, U-Bahn, and many more.

Don't worry, you don't need to know anything about these trains or how they work. The following figure shows a map of the network to give you an idea of what we're talking about. You'll see the main line heads west from the airport along the river. When it reaches the center of the city, it branches north and south along the coast.

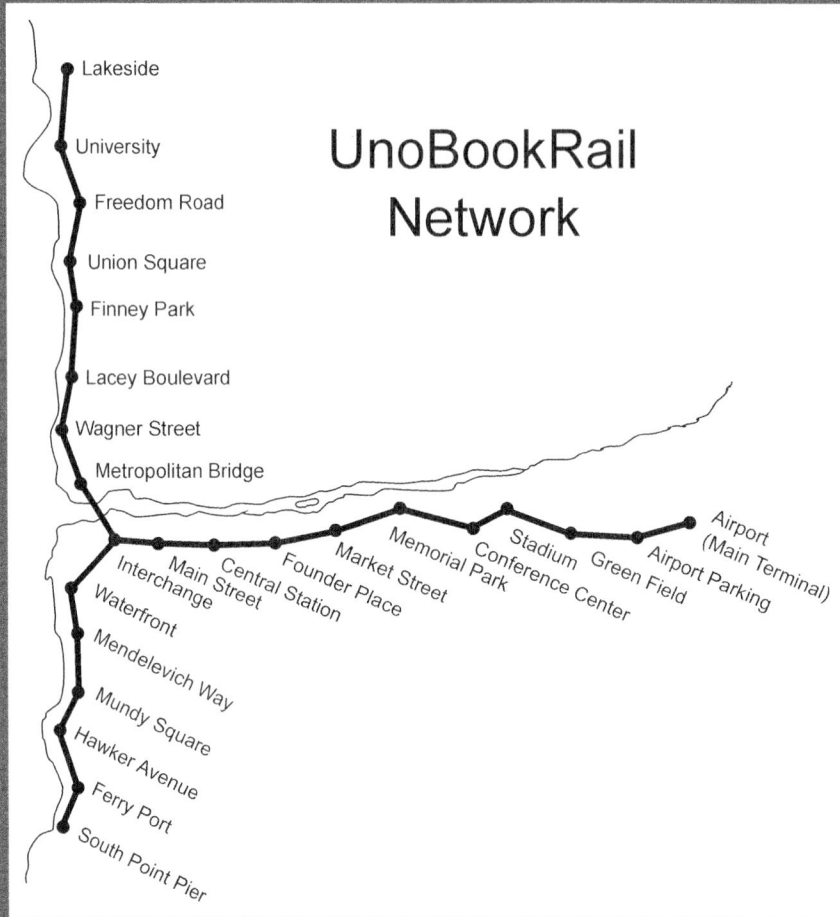

A map of the UnoBookRail network of stations

The four apps will show how Uno Platform can be used to create applications for different scenarios and show different functionality being used in appropriate scenarios.

In this section, we include the following chapters:

- *Chapter 3, Working with Forms and Data*
- *Chapter 4, Mobilizing Your App*
- *Chapter 5, Making Your App Ready for the Real World*
- *Chapter 6, Displaying Data in Charts and with Custom 2D Graphics*

3

Working with Forms and Data

In this chapter, we will write our first app for the fictional company UnoBookRail, which will be targeting desktops and the web. We will write a typical **line of business (LOB)** app that allows us to view, enter, and edit data. In addition to that, we will also cover how to export data in PDF format since this is a common requirement for LOB apps.

In this chapter, we'll cover the following topics:

- Writing a desktop-focused Uno Platform app

- Writing forms and validating user input

- Using the Windows Community Toolkit in your Uno Platform app

- Generating PDF files programmatically

By the end of this chapter, you'll have created a desktop-focused app that can also run on the web that displays data, allows you to edit the data, and also export the data in PDF format.

Technical requirements

This chapter assumes that you already have your development environment set up, as well as the project templates installed, as we covered in *Chapter 1*, *Introducing Uno Platform*. The source code for this chapter can be found at `https://github.com/ PacktPublishing/Creating-Cross-Platform-C-Sharp-Applications- with-Uno-Platform/tree/main/Chapter03`.

The code in this chapter makes use of the following library: `https://github.com/ PacktPublishing/Creating-Cross-Platform-C-Sharp-Applications- with-Uno-Platform/tree/main/SharedLibrary`.

Check out the following video to see the code in action: `https://bit.ly/3fWYRai`

Introducing the app

In this chapter, we will build the UnoBookRail **ResourcePlanner** app, which will be used internally, inside UnoBookRail. UnoBookRail employees will be able to use this app to manage any resources within UnoBookRail, such as trains and stations. In this chapter, we will develop the issue-managing part of the app. While a real version of this app would have a lot more features, in this chapter, we will only develop the following features:

- Creating a new issue
- Displaying a list of issues
- Exporting issues in PDF format

Since this application is a typical line of business app, the app will be targeting UWP, macOS, and WASM. Let's continue by creating the app.

Creating the app

Let's start by creating the solution for the app:

1. In Visual Studio, create a new project using the **Multi-Platform App (Uno Platform)** template.

2. Name the project **ResourcePlanner**. You can use a different name if you want, but in this chapter, we will assume the project is named **ResourcePlanner**.

3. Remove all the project heads except those for **UWP**, **macOS**, and **WASM**.

4. To avoid having to write more code than we need, download the shared library project from `https://github.com/PacktPublishing/Creating-Cross-Platform-C-Sharp-Applications-with-Uno-Platform/tree/main/SharedLibrary` and add a reference to it. To do this, right-click on the solution node in the **Solution Explorer** window, select **Add** > **Existing Project...**, navigate to the `UnoBookRail.Common.csproj` file, and click **Open**.

5. Now that we've added the project to the solution, we need to add a reference to the library in the platform-specific projects. For this, right-click the **UWP** project node in **Solution Explorer**, select **Add** > **Reference...** > **Projects**, check the **UnoBookRail.Common** entry, and click OK. *Repeat this process for the macOS and WASM projects.*

6. Lastly, add the following code before the closing linker tag in the `LinkerConfig.xml` file, inside the **ResourcePlanner.Wasm** project:

```
<assembly fullname="UnoBookRail.Common" />
```

This code is needed to bind objects from the **UnoBookRail.Common** library so that they work properly on WASM. The `LinkerConfig.xml` file tells the WebAssembly Linker to include the types in the compiled source code, even though the classes are not currently being used. If we don't specify these entries, the types that are defined in the assembly will not be included as the linker removes the code. This is because it doesn't find a direct reference to it. When using other packages or libraries, you may also need to specify entries for those libraries. For this chapter, though, the preceding entry is enough.

For our app, we will use the **Model-View-ViewModel** (**MVVM**) pattern. This means that our app will mostly be split into three areas:

- **Model**: The **Model** contains the data of your app and the business logic. For example, this would handle loading data from a database or running specific business logic.

- **ViewModel**: The **ViewModel** acts as the layer between the View and Model. It presents the app's data in a suitable way for the View, provides ways for the View to interact with the Model, and notifies the View of changes to the Model.

- **View**: The **View** represents data to the user and is responsible for what is being represented on the screen.

To make development easier, we will use the **Microsoft.Toolkit.MVVM** package, which we will add now. This package helps us write our ViewModels and takes care of the boilerplate code that is needed to support bindings with XAML:

1. First, right-click the solution node in the **Solution** view and select **Manage NuGet Packages for solution…**.

2. Now, search for **Microsoft.Toolkit.MVVM** and select the package from the list.

3. Select the **macOS**, **UWP**, and **WASM** projects from the project list and click **Install**.

4. Since we will use them later, also create three folders called **Models**, **ViewModels**, and **Views**. For this, right-click the **ResourcePlanner.Shared** shared project, select **Add** > **New Folder**, and name it **Models**. Repeat this process for **ViewModels** and **Views**.

Now that we've set up the project, let's start by adding the first pieces of code to our app. As is typical with line of business apps, we will be using the **MenuBar** control as the main way of switching views inside our app:

1. Start by creating a new class inside the **ViewModels** folder called **NavigationViewModel**.

2. Now, replace the code inside the `NavigationViewModel.cs` file with the following:

```csharp
using Microsoft.Toolkit.Mvvm.ComponentModel;
using Microsoft.Toolkit.Mvvm.Input;
using System.Windows.Input;
using Windows.UI.Xaml;
namespace ResourcePlanner.ViewModels
{
    public class NavigationViewModel :
        ObservableObject
    {
        private FrameworkElement content;
        public FrameworkElement Content
        {
            Get
            {
                return content;
            }
            Set
```

```
        {
            SetProperty(ref content, value);
        }
    }
    public ICommand Issues_OpenNewIssueViewCommand
        { get; }
    public ICommand Issues_ExportIssueViewCommand
        { get; }
    public ICommand Issues_OpenAllIssuesCommand {
        get; }
    public ICommand Issues_OpenTrainIssuesCommand
        { get; }
    public ICommand
        Issues_OpenStationIssuesCommand { get; }
    public ICommand Issues_Open OtherIssuesCommand
        { get; }
    public NavigationViewModel()
    {
        Issues_OpenNewIssueViewCommand =
            new RelayCommand(() => { });
        Issues_ExportIssueViewCommand =
            new RelayCommand(() => { });
        Issues_OpenAllIssuesCommand =
            new RelayCommand(() => { });
        Issues_OpenAllTrainIssuesCommand =
            new RelayCommand(() => { });
        Issues_OpenAllStationIssuesCommand =
            new RelayCommand(() =>{ });
        Issues_OpenAllOtherIssuesCommand =
            new RelayCommand(() =>{ });
    }
  }
}
```

This is the class that will handle navigating to different controls. As we implement
more views later in this chapter, we will update the Command objects so that
they point to the correct views.

3. Now, add the following code to the `MainPage` class:

```
using ResourcePlanner.ViewModels;
...
private NavigationViewModel navigationVM = new
NavigationViewModel();
```

This will add a `NavigationViewModel` object to the `MainPage` class that we can bind to in our XAML.

4. Finally, replace the content of your `MainPage.xaml` file with the following:

```
...
xmlns:muxc="using:Microsoft.UI.Xaml.Controls">
<Grid Background="{ThemeResource
    ApplicationPageBackgroundThemeBrush}">
    <Grid.RowDefinitions>
        <RowDefinition Height="Auto"/>
        <RowDefinition Height="*"/>
    </Grid.RowDefinitions>
    <muxc:MenuBar>
        <muxc:MenuBar.Items>
            <muxc:MenuBarItem Title="Issues">
                <MenuFlyoutItem Text="New"
                    Command="{x:Bind
                    navigationVM.Issues_
                    OpenNewIssueViewCommand}"/>
                <MenuFlyoutItem Text="Export to
                    PDF" Command="{x:Bind
                    navigationVM.Issues_
                    ExportIssueViewCommand}"/>
                <MenuFlyoutSeparator/>
                <MenuFlyoutItem Text="All"
                    Command="{x:Bind
                    navigationVM.Issues_
                    OpenAllIssuesCommand}"/>
                <MenuFlyoutItem Text="Train
                    issues" Command="{x:Bind
                    navigationVM.Issues_
                    OpenTrainIssuesCommand}"/>
```

```
                        <MenuFlyoutItem Text="Station
                            issues" Command="{x:Bind
                            navigationVM.Issues_
                            OpenStationIssuesCommand}"/>
                        <MenuFlyoutItem Text="Other
                            issues" Command="{x:Bind
                            navigationVM.Issues_
                            OpenOtherIssuesCommand}"/>
                    </muxc:MenuBarItem>
                    <muxc:MenuBarItem Title="Trains"
                        IsEnabled="False"/>
                    <muxc:MenuBarItem Title="Staff"
                        IsEnabled="False"/>
                    <muxc:MenuBarItem Title="Depots"
                        IsEnabled="False"/>
                    <muxc:MenuBarItem Title="Stations"
                        IsEnabled="False"/>
                </muxc:MenuBar.Items>
            </muxc:MenuBar>
            <ContentPresenter Grid.Row="1"
                Content="{x:Bind navigationVM.Content,
                    Mode=OneWay}"/>
        </Grid>
```

This code adds MenuBar, which users can use to navigate to different views. ContentPresenter, at the bottom, is used to display the content that was navigated to.

Now, if you start the app, you will see something similar to the following:

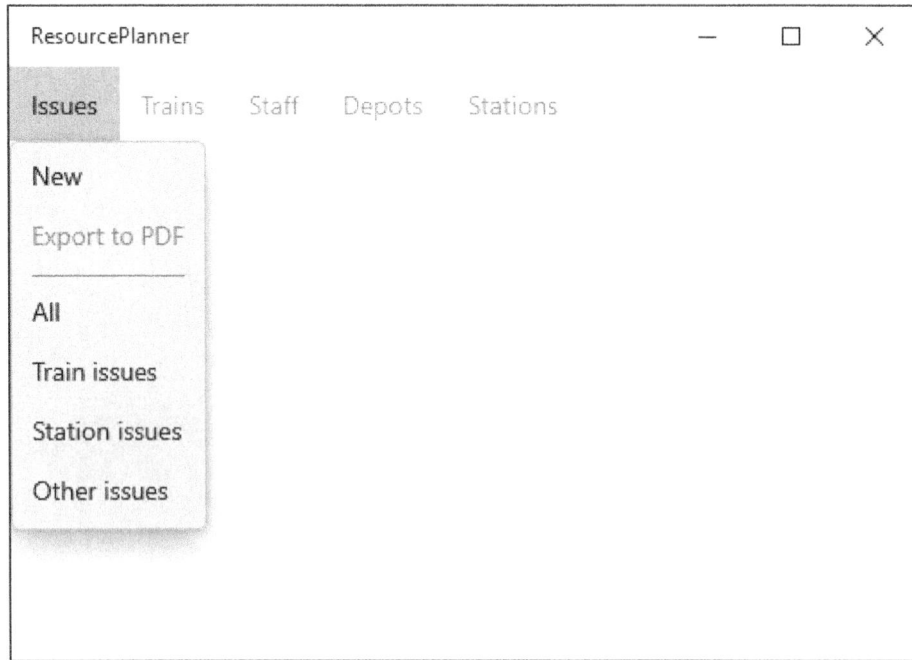

Figure 3.1 – Running the ResourcePlanner app with MenuBar navigation

In the next section, we will add our first view to the app, which will allow users to create new issues.

Entering and validating data

A typical requirement for line of business apps is to enter data and also provide input validation for said data. Uno Platform provides a variety of different controls to allow users to enter data, in addition to dozens of libraries that support Uno Platform.

> **Note**
>
> While at the time of writing, there is no built-in support for input validation, input validation is planned to be supported by Uno Platform. This is because neither UWP nor WinUI 3 fully support input validation right now. To learn more about the upcoming input validation support, take a look at the following issue in the WinUI repository: `https://github.com/microsoft/microsoft-ui-xaml/issues/179`. The progress that's being made on this as part of Uno Platform is being tracked through this issue: `https://github.com/unoplatform/uno/issues/4839`.

To make our development process easier, first, let's add a reference to the Windows Community Toolkit controls:

1. First, right-click the solution node in the **Solution** view and select **Manage NuGet Packages for solution…**.

2. Search for **Microsoft.Toolkit.UI.Controls** and select the package.

3. In the project list, select the **UWP** head and click **Install**.

4. Repeat *steps 2* and *3* for the **Microsoft.Toolkit.UI.Controls.DataGrid** package.

5. Now, search for **Uno.Microsoft.Toolkit.UI.Controls** and select the package.

> **Note**
>
> While the Windows Community Toolkit only supports UWP, thanks to the effort of the Uno Platform team, we can also use the Windows Community Toolkit inside our Uno Platform app on all the supported platforms. The Uno Platform team maintains Uno Platform-compatible versions of the Windows Community Toolkit packages based on the original packages and updates them accordingly.

6. From the project list, select the **macOS** and **WASM** heads and click **Install**.

7. Finally, repeat *steps 5* and *6* with the **Uno.Microsoft.Toolkit.UI.Controls. DataGrid** package.

This allows us to use the Windows Community Toolkit controls inside our app. Since we also want to use these controls on macOS and WASM, we also installed the Uno Platform versions of those two packages. Since we added the **Windows Community Toolkit** control packages, we can start creating the Create Issue view:

1. First of all, create the `IssueRepository.cs` class inside the `Models` folder and add the following code to it:

```
using System.Collections.Generic;
using UnoBookRail.Common.Issues;
namespace ResourcePlanner.Models
{
    public class IssuesRepository
    {
        private static List<Issue> issues = new
            List<Issue>();
        public static List<Issue> GetAllIssues()
```

```
        {
            return issues;
        }
        public static void AddIssue(Issue issue)
        {
            issues.Add(issue);
        }
    }
}
```

This is the model that will collect issues. In a real-world app, this code would communicate with a database or API to persist issues, but for simplicity, we will only save them in a list.

2. Next, create the `CreateIssueViewModel.cs` class inside the `ViewModels` folder and use the following code from GitHub: `https://github.com/PacktPublishing/Creating-Cross-Platform-C-Sharp-Applications-with-Uno-Platform/blob/main/Chapter03/ResourcePlanner.Shared/ViewModels/CreateIssueViewModel.cs`

Now that we've created the necessary Model and ViewModel, we will continue by adding the user interface to create a new issue.

For the user interface, we will implement input validation as this is typical for data entry forms in a line of business app. For this, we will implement the following behavior: if the user clicks on the **Create Issue** button, we will validate the data using a function in code behind. If we determine that the data is valid, we will create a new issue; otherwise, we will show an error message below every field that failed our custom validation using code behind. In addition to that, we will validate an input field every time the entered input changes.

Let's continue by creating the user interface:

1. Create a new `UserControl` inside the `Views` folder named `CreateIssueView.xaml` and replace the XAML with the following:

```
<UserControl
    x:Class="ResourcePlanner.Views.CreateIssueView"
    xmlns="http://schemas.microsoft.com/winfx/2006
        /xaml/presentation"
    xmlns:x="http://schemas.microsoft.com/
        winfx/2006/xaml"
```

```
xmlns:local="using:ResourcePlanner.Views"
xmlns:d="http://schemas.microsoft.com/
         expression/blend/2008"
xmlns:mc="http://schemas.openxmlformats.org/
         markup-compatibility/2006"
xmlns:wctcontrols="using:Microsoft.Toolkit.
                    Uwp.UI.Controls"
xmlns:wctui="using:Microsoft.Toolkit.Uwp.UI"
xmlns:ubrcissues="using:UnoBookRail.Common.Issues"
mc:Ignorable="d"
d:DesignHeight="300"
d:DesignWidth="400">
<StackPanel Orientation="Vertical" Padding="20">
    <TextBlock Text="Create new issue"
        FontSize="24"/>
    <Grid ColumnSpacing="10">
        <Grid.ColumnDefinitions>
            <ColumnDefinition Width="200"/>
            <ColumnDefinition Width="200"/>
        </Grid.ColumnDefinitions>
        <Grid.RowDefinitions>
            <RowDefinition />
            <RowDefinition />
        </Grid.RowDefinitions>
        <TextBox x:Name="TitleTextBox"
            Header="Title"
            Text="{x:Bind createIssueVM.Title,
                Mode=TwoWay}"
            HorizontalAlignment="Stretch"
            TextChanged="FormInput_TextChanged"/>
        <TextBlock x:Name="titleErrorNotification"
            Grid.Row="1"Foreground="{ThemeResource
                SystemErrorTextColor}"/>
        <ComboBox Header="Type" Grid.Column="1"
            ItemsSource="{wctui:EnumValues
                Type=ubrcissues:IssueType}"
```

```
                    HorizontalAlignment="Stretch"
                    SelectedItem="{x:Bind
                            createIssueVM.IssueType,
                            Mode=TwoWay}"/>
            </Grid>
            <TextBox Header="Description"
                    Text="{x:Bind createIssueVM.Description,
                            Mode=TwoWay}"
                    MinWidth="410" MaxWidth="800"
                    HorizontalAlignment="Left"/>
            <Button Content="Create new issue"
                    Margin="0,20,0,0" Width="410"
                    HorizontalAlignment="Left"
                    Click="CreateIssueButton_Click"/>
        </StackPanel>
    </UserControl>
```

This is a basic UI that allows users to enter a title and description and lets the user choose the issue's type. Note that we have a `TextBlock` control below the text inputs so that we can show error messages to the user if the provided input is not valid. In addition to that, we have also added a `TextChanged` listener to `Title` to be able to update the error message when the text changes.

2. Now, replace the content of the `CreateIssueView.xaml.cs` file with the following code:

```
using ResourcePlanner.ViewModels;
using Windows.UI.Xaml;
using Windows.UI.Xaml.Controls;
namespace ResourcePlanner.Views
{
    public sealed partial class CreateIssueView :
        UserControl
    {
        private CreateIssueViewModel createIssueVM;
        public CreateIssueView(CreateIssueViewModel
            viewModel)
        {
```

```
        this.createIssueVM = viewModel;
        this.InitializeComponent();
}
private void FormInput_TextChanged(object
    sender, TextChangedEventArgs args)
{
        EvaluateFieldsValid(sender);
}
private bool EvaluateFieldsValid(object
    sender)
{
        bool allValid = true;
        if(sender == TitleTextBox || sender ==
            null)
        {
            if (TitleTextBox.Text.Length == 0)
            {
                allValid = false;
                titleErrorNotification.Text =
                    "Title must not be empty.";
            }
            Else
            {
                titleErrorNotification.Text = "";
            }
        }
        return allValid;
}


private void CreateIssueButton_Click(object
    sender, RoutedEventArgs args)
{
        if (EvaluateFieldsValid(null))
        {
            createIssueVM.CreateIssueCommand.
                Execute(null);
```

```
            }
         }
      }
   }
```

With this code, we now have input validation that's run when the text of an input field changes or when the user clicks on the **Create Issue** button. Only if all the input fields (right now, this is only the **Title** input field) are valid will we create an issue and execute `CreateIssueCommand` on our ViewModel.

3. Finally, inside the `NavigationViewModel.cs` file, replace the creation of the `Issues_OpenNewIssueViewCommand` object with the following code and add the necessary `using` statement. That way, when the command is invoked, `CreateIssueView` will be displayed:

```
Issues_OpenNewIssueViewCommand = new RelayCommand(() =>
{
    Content = new CreateIssueView(new
        CreateIssueViewModel(this));
});
```

Now, if you start the app and click on the **New Issue** option from the **Issue** dropdown, you will see something similar to the following *Figure 3.2*:

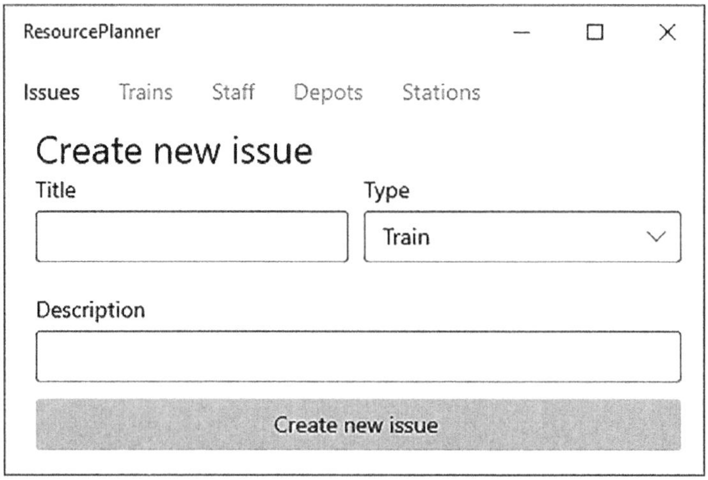

Figure 3.2 – Create new issue interface

If you try to click on the **Create new issue** button, you will see a short message below the title input field that states "**Title must not be empty**". Upon entering text into the **Title** field, the message will disappear. While we have added simple inputs, we will now add more input options using the Windows Community Toolkit.

Using Windows Community Toolkit controls

So far, users can only enter a title and description and choose the issue's type. However, we also want to allow users to input specific data based on the issue's. For this, we will use one of the controls the Windows Community Toolkit provides: **SwitchPresenter**. The **SwitchPresenter** control allows us to render a certain part of the UI based on a property that's been set, similar to how a switch case in C# works.

Of course, **SwitchPresenter** is not the only control that's available from the Windows Community Toolkit; there are many more, such as **GridSplitter**, **MarkdownTextBlock**, and **DataGrid**, which we will use in the *Displaying data using DataGrid* section. Since we've already installed the necessary packages earlier in this chapter, we will add the controls to our user interface. Let's get started:

1. Add the following XAML code below the description `TextBox` control inside `CreateIssueView.xaml`:

```xaml
<wctcontrols:SwitchPresenter Value="{x:Bind
createIssueVM.IssueType, Mode=OneWay}">
    <wctcontrols:SwitchPresenter.SwitchCases>
        <wctcontrols:Case Value="{x:Bind
            ubrcissues:IssueType.Train}">
            <StackPanel Orientation="Horizontal"
                Spacing="10">
                <StackPanel MinWidth="410"
                    MaxWidth="800">
                    <TextBox x:Name=
                        "TrainNumberTextBox"
                        Header="Train number"
                        Text="{x:Bind
                            createIssueVM.TrainNumber,
                            Mode=TwoWay}"
                        HorizontalAlignment="Stretch"
                        TextChanged=
                            "FormInput_TextChanged"/>
```

```
        <TextBlock x:Name=
            "trainNumberErrorNotification"
            Foreground="{ThemeResource
                SystemErrorTextColor}"/>
        </StackPanel>
    </StackPanel>
</wctcontrols:Case>
<wctcontrols:Case Value="{x:Bind
    ubrcissues:IssueType.Station}">
    <StackPanel MinWidth="410" MaxWidth="800"
        HorizontalAlignment="Left">
        <TextBox x:Name="StationNameTextBox"
        Header="Station name" Text="{x:Bind
            createIssueVM.StationName,
            Mode=TwoWay}"
        HorizontalAlignment="Stretch"
        TextChanged=
            "FormInput_TextChanged"/>
        <TextBlock x:Name=
            "stationNameErrorNotification"
            Foreground="{ThemeResource
                SystemErrorTextColor}"/>
    </StackPanel>
</wctcontrols:Case>
<wctcontrols:Case Value="{x:Bind
    ubrcissues:IssueType.Other}">
    <StackPanel MinWidth="410" MaxWidth="800"
        HorizontalAlignment="Left">
        <TextBox x:Name="LocationTextBox"
            Header="Location" Text="{x:Bind
                createIssueVM.Location,
                    Mode=TwoWay}"
            HorizontalAlignment="Stretch"
            TextChanged=
                "FormInput_TextChanged"/>
        <TextBlock x:Name=
            "locationErrorNotification"
            Foreground="{ThemeResource
                SystemErrorTextColor}"/>
```

```
            </StackPanel>
          </wctcontrols:Case>
      </wctcontrols:SwitchPresenter.SwitchCases>
  </wctcontrols:SwitchPresenter>
```

This allows us to display specific input fields, depending on the issue type that's selected by the user. This is because `SwitchPresenter` renders a specific `Case` based on the `Value` property that's been set. Since we bind it to the `IssueType` property of our ViewModel, any time the user changes the issue type, it will update accordingly. Note that this binding only works if we specify the mode to be `OneWay` since the default binding mode of `x:Bind` is `OneTime` and, as such, wouldn't update.

2. Now, add the following code before the return statement of the `EvaluateFields` function inside `CreateIssueViewModel.xaml.cs`:

```
if (sender == TrainNumberTextBox || sender == null)
{
    if (TrainNumberTextBox.Text.Length == 0)
    {
        if (createIssueVM.IssueType ==
            UnoBookRail.Common.Issues.IssueType.Train)
        {
            allValid = false;
        }
        trainNumberErrorNotification.Text =
            "Train number must not be empty.";
    }
    else
    {
        trainNumberErrorNotification.Text = "";
    }
}
if (sender == StationNameTextBox || sender == null)
{
    if (StationNameTextBox.Text.Length == 0)
    {
        if (createIssueVM.IssueType ==
            UnoBookRail.Common.Issues.IssueType.Station)
```

```
        {
            allValid = false;
        }
        stationNameErrorNotification.Text =
            "Station name must not be empty.";
    }
    else
    {
        stationNameErrorNotification.Text = "";
    }
}
if (sender == LocationTextBox || sender == null)
{
    if (LocationTextBox.Text.Length == 0)
    {
        if (createIssueVM.IssueType ==
            UnoBookRail.Common.Issues.IssueType.Other)
        {
            allValid = false;
        }
        locationErrorNotification.Text =
            "Location must not be empty.";
    }
    else
    {
        locationErrorNotification.Text = "";
    }
}
```

Now, our input validation will also take the newly added input fields into account. Note that we will only block the creation of an issue if input that does not meet the validation process is relevant to the issue. For example, if the issue type is Train, we will ignore whether the location text is passing validation or not and users can create a new issue, regardless of whether the location input passes the validation stage.

Now, if you start the app and navigate to the **Create new issue** view, you will see something similar to the following *Figure 3.3*:

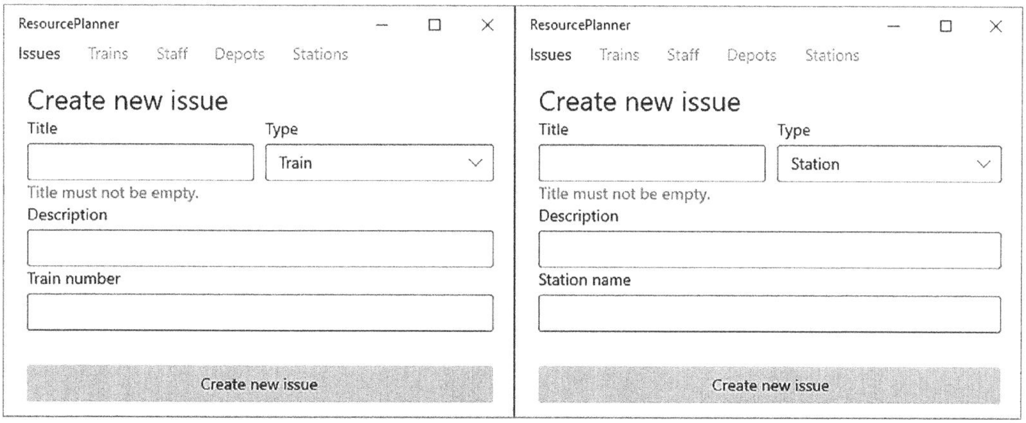

Figure 3.3 – Updated issue creation view. Left: Issue Train type selected; right: Issue Station type selected

When you change the issue type, you will notice that the form will change and show the correct input field, depending on the issue type. While we allow users to create a new issue, we currently have no way of displaying them. In the next section, we will change this by adding a new view to show the list of issues.

Displaying data using DataGrid

Since UnoBookRail employees will use this app to manage existing issues, it is important for them to view all the issues to easily get an overview of their current status. While there is no built-in UWP and Uno Platform control that makes this easy to implement, luckily, the Windows Community Toolkit contains the right control for this case: **DataGrid**.

The **DataGrid** control allows us to render data as a table, specify which columns to display, and allows users to sort the table based on a column. Before we start using the **DataGrid** control, though, we need to create the ViewModel and prepare the views:

1. First, create a new class named `IssueListViewModel.cs` inside the `ViewModels` Solution folder and add the following code to it:

    ```
    using System.Collections.Generic;
    using UnoBookRail.Common.Issues;
    namespace ResourcePlanner.ViewModels
    {
        public class IssueListViewModel
        {
    ```

```
        public readonly IList<Issue> Issues;
        public IssueListViewModel(IList<Issue> issues)
        {
            this.Issues = issues;
        }
    }
}
```

Since we only want to show a subset of issues, such as when navigating to the train issues list, the list of issues to display will be passed as a constructor parameter.

2. Now, create a new `UserControl` inside the `Views` folder named `IssueListView.xaml`.

3. Finally, inside the `NavigationViewModel` class constructor, replace the creation of the `Issues_OpenAllIssuesCommand`, `Issues_OpenTrainIssuesCommand`, `Issues_OpenTrainIssuesCommand`, and `Issues_OpenTrainIssuesCommand` objects with the following code:

```
Issues_OpenAllIssuesCommand = new RelayCommand(() =>
{
    Content = new IssueListView(new IssueListViewModel
        (IssuesRepository.GetAllIssues()), this);
});
Issues_OpenTrainIssuesCommand = new RelayCommand(() =>
{
    Content = new IssueListView(new IssueListViewModel
        (IssuesRepository.GetAllIssues().Where(issue
            => issue.IssueType ==
                IssueType.Train).ToList()), this);
});
Issues_OpenStationIssuesCommand = new RelayCommand(() =>
{
    Content = new IssueListView(new IssueListViewModel
        (IssuesRepository.GetAllIssues().Where(issue
            => issue.IssueType ==
                IssueType.Station).ToList()), this);
});
Issues_OpenOtherIssuesCommand = new RelayCommand(() =>
{
```

```
        Content = new IssueListView(new IssueListViewModel
            (IssuesRepository.GetAllIssues().Where(issue
            => issue.IssueType ==
                IssueType.Other).ToList()), this);
    });
```

This allows the user to navigate to the issue list when the user clicks on the corresponding elements from the navigation, while also ensuring that we only show the issues in the list that are relevant to the navigation option. Note that we have chosen to create the commands using inline lambdas. However, you can also declare functions and use them to create the `RelayCommand` objects.

Now that we've added the necessary ViewModel and updated `NavigationViewModel` to allow us to navigate to the issue list view, we can continue writing the UI of our issue list view.

Displaying data with the DataGrid control

Before we implement the issue list view, let's quickly cover the basic features of DataGrid that we will use. There are two ways to get started with DataGrid:

- Let DataGrid auto-generate the columns. This has the disadvantage that the column headers will use the property names unless you change them inside `AutoGeneratingColumn`. While they are good to get started with the DataGrid control, they are often not the best choice. Also, using this method, you can't choose which columns to show; instead, it will show all columns.

- Specify which properties to include by manually specifying the columns you want. This option has the advantage that we can control which properties to include and also specify the column name. Of course, this also means that we have to ensure that our bindings are correct, which is a potential cause of bugs.

Specifying the columns of a DataGrid can be done by setting the DataGrid's `Columns` property and providing a collection of `DataGridColumn` objects. For certain data types, there are already built-in columns you can use, such as `DataGridTextColumn` for text-based data. Every column allows you to customize the header being displayed by specifying the `Header` property and whether users can sort the column through the `CanUserSort` property. For more complex data where there is no built-in `DataGridColumn` type, you can also implement your own `DataGridColumn object`. Alternatively, you can also use `DataGridTemplateColumn`, which allows you to render cells based on a specified template. For this, you can specify a `CellTemplate object`, which will be used to render cells, and a `CellEditTemplate object`, which will be used to let users edit the current cell's value.

In addition to specifying columns, the DataGrid controls also have more features you can customize. For example, the DataGrid allows you to select rows and customize the row and cell backgrounds. Now, let's continue by writing our issue list.

Now that we've covered the basics of DataGrid, let's continue by writing our issue list display interface:

1. For this, add the following code to the `IssueListView.xaml.cs` file:

```csharp
using Microsoft.Toolkit.Uwp.UI.Controls;
using ResourcePlanner.ViewModels;
using UnoBookRail.Common.Issues;
using Windows.UI.Xaml.Controls;
namespace ResourcePlanner.Views
{
    public sealed partial class IssueListView :
        UserControl
    {
        private IssueListViewModel issueListVM;
        private NavigationViewModel navigationVM;
        public IssueListView(IssueListViewModel
            viewModel, NavigationViewModel
                navigationViewModel)
        {
            this.issueListVM = viewModel;
            this.navigationVM = navigationViewModel;
            this.InitializeComponent();
        }
        private void IssueList_SelectionChanged(object
            sender, SelectionChangedEventArgs e)
        {
            navigationVM.SetSelectedIssue((sender as
                DataGrid).SelectedItem as Issue);
        }
    }
}
```

This allows us to create a binding from the DataGrid to the list issues. Note that we will also add a `SelectionChanged` handler function so that we can notify `NavigationViewModel` whether an issue has been selected. We're doing this since some options only make sense if an issue is selected. One of these options is the **Export to PDF** option, which we will implement in the *Exporting issues in PDF format* section.

2. Add the following XAML namespace definition to the `IssueListView.xaml` file:

    ```
    xmlns:wct="using:Microsoft.Toolkit.Uwp.UI.Controls"
    ```

3. Now, replace `Grid` inside the `IssueListView.xaml` file with the following XAML:

    ```
    <wct:DataGrid
        SelectionChanged="IssueList_SelectionChanged"
        SelectionMode="Single"
        AutoGenerateColumns="False"
        ItemsSource="{x:Bind
            issueListVM.Issues,Mode=OneWay}">
        <wct:DataGrid.Columns>
            <wct:DataGridTextColumn Header="Title"
                Binding="{Binding Title}"
                IsReadOnly="True" CanUserSort="True"/>
            <wct:DataGridTextColumn Header="Type"
                Binding="{Binding IssueType}"
                IsReadOnly="True" CanUserSort="True"/>
            <wct:DataGridTextColumn Header="Creator"
                Binding="{Binding OpenedBy.FormattedName}"
                IsReadOnly="True" CanUserSort="True"/>
            <wct:DataGridTextColumn Header="Created on"
                Binding="{Binding OpenDate}"
                IsReadOnly="True" CanUserSort="True"/>
            <wct:DataGridCheckBoxColumn Header="Open"
                Binding="{Binding IsOpen}"
                IsReadOnly="True" CanUserSort="True"/>
            <wct:DataGridTextColumn Header="Closed by"
                Binding="{Binding ClosedBy.FormattedName}"
                IsReadOnly="True" CanUserSort="True"/>
            <wct:DataGridTextColumn Header="Closed on"
                Binding="{Binding CloseDateReadable}"
                IsReadOnly="True" CanUserSort="True"/>
    ```

```
        </wct:DataGrid.Columns>
    </wct:DataGrid>
```

Here, we added columns for the most important fields of our issue. Note that we only allow the title to be changed since the other fields would require more logic than what can easily be displayed as part of the DataGrid table layout. Since `x:Bind` is not supported in this case, we are using `Binding` to bind the properties to the columns.

Now, if you start the app and create an issue, you will see something similar to the following *Figure 3.4*:

Figure 3.4 – DataGrid showing a demo issue

In this section, we only covered the basics of using the Windows Community Toolkit DataGrid control. If you wish to learn more about the DataGrid control, the official documentation contains hands-on examples covering the different APIs that are available for it. You can find out more here: `https://docs.microsoft.com/en-us/windows/communitytoolkit/controls/datagrid`. Now that we can display the list of existing issues, we will continue by writing a PDF export for issues. As part of this, we will also learn how to write a custom Uno Platform control that we will only use for the web.

Exporting issues in PDF format

In addition to being able to view data inside a line of business app, often, it is desired to be able to be export data, for example, as a PDF, so that you can print it or send it via email. For this, we will write an interface that allows users to export a given issue to PDF. Since there are no built-in APIs for this, we will use the **iText** library for this. Note that if you want to use the library in your application, you either need to follow the AGPL license or buy a commercial license for the library. However, before we can write the code to generate the PDF, we will need to prepare the project:

1. First, we need to install the **iText** NuGet package. For this, right-click the solution and search for **iText**. Select the package. Then, from the project list, select the **macOS**, **UWP**, and **WASM** heads and click **Install**.

2. Now, create a class named `ExportIssueViewModel.cs` inside the `ViewModels` folder with the following code:

```
using iText.Kernel.Pdf;
using iText.Layout;
using iText.Layout.Element;
using Microsoft.Toolkit.Mvvm.Input;
using System;
using System.IO;
using System.Runtime.InteropServices.WindowsRuntime;
using System.Windows.Input;
using UnoBookRail.Common.Issues;
namespace ResourcePlanner.ViewModels
{
    public class ExportIssueViewModel
    {
        public readonly Issue Issue;
        public ICommand SavePDFClickedCommand;
        public ExportIssueViewModel(Issue issue)
        {
            Issue = issue;
            SavePDFClickedCommand =
                new RelayCommand(async () => { });
        }
    }
}
```

Note that we are adding those `using` statements now as we will need them later in this section.

3. Now, create a new `UserControl` named `ExportIssueView.xaml` inside the **Views** folder.

4. Replace the code inside `ExportIssueView.xaml.cs` with the following:

```
using ResourcePlanner.ViewModels;
using Windows.UI.Xaml.Controls;
namespace ResourcePlanner.Views
{
    public sealed partial class ExportIssueView :
```

```
        UserControl
    {

        private ExportIssueViewModel exportIssueVM;
        public ExportIssueView(ExportIssueViewModel
            viewModel)
        {
            this.exportIssueVM = viewModel;
            this.InitializeComponent();
        }
    }
}
```

5. Replace the code inside `ExportIssueView.xaml` with the code from GitHub:

    ```
    https://github.com/PacktPublishing/Creating-Cross-
    Platform-C-Sharp-Applications-with-Uno-Platform/blob/main/
    Chapter03/ResourcePlanner.Shared/Views/ExportIssueView.
    xaml
    ```

6. Lastly, replace the creation of `Issue_ExportIssueViewCommand` in the `NavigationViewModel.cs` file with the following code:

    ```
    Issues_ExportIssueViewCommand = new RelayCommand(() =>
    {
        Content = new ExportIssueView(new
            ExportIssueViewModel(this.selectedIssue));
    });
    ```

Now that we've added the necessary interface, we will continue by writing the code for exporting an issue as a PDF. Since the behavior on the desktop will be different compared to that on the web, we will cover the desktop version first.

Exporting on desktop

Since we've already written the user interface to allow users to export issues, the only thing left is to update `ExportIssueViewModel` to generate the PDF and provide users with a way to access it. On the desktop, we will write the PDF file to the local filesystem and open it. Since the app is also a UWP app, we will write the file to the app's local folder. Now, let's update `ExportIssueViewModel`:

1. First, create a new function called `GeneratePDF` inside the `ExportIsseuViewModel` class with the following code:

    ```
    public byte[] GeneratePDF()
    {
        byte[] bytes;
        using (var memoryStream = new MemoryStream())
        {
            bytes = memoryStream.ToArray();
        }
        return bytes;
    }
    ```

2. Now, add the following code before the assignment inside the `using` block:

    ```
    var pdfWriter = new PdfWriter(memoryStream);
    var pdfDocument = new PdfDocument(pdfWriter);
    var document = new Document(pdfDocument);
    document.Close();
    ```

    This creates a new **iText** `PdfWriter` and **iText** `PdfDocument` that will be written to the byte array using the `MemoryStream` object.

3. After adding `PDFWriter`, `PDFDocument`, and `Document`, add the following code to write the header of the document:

    ```
    var header = new Paragraph("Issue export: " +
        Issue.Title)
        .SetTextAlignment(
            iText.Layout.Properties.TextAlignment.CENTER)
        .SetFontSize(20);
    document.Add(header);
    ```

This creates a new paragraph with the text "**Issue export:**" and the issue's title. It also sets the text alignment and font size to make it easier to distinguish as the header of the document.

4. Since we also want to export information about the issue, add the following code before the call to `document.Close()`:

```
var issueType = new Paragraph("Type: " + Issue.
IssueType);
document.Add(issueType);
switch (Issue.IssueType)
{
    case IssueType.Train:
        var trainNumber = new Paragraph("Train number: "
            + Issue.TrainNumber);
        document.Add(trainNumber);
        break;
    case IssueType.Station:
        var stationName = new Paragraph("Station name: "
            + Issue.StationName);
        document.Add(stationName);
        break;
    case IssueType.Other:
        var location = new Paragraph("Location: " +
            Issue.Location);
        document.Add(issueType);
        break;
}
var description = new Paragraph("Description: " + Issue.
Description);
document.Add(description);
```

This will add the necessary paragraph to the PDF document based on the issue's type. In addition to that, we will add the issue's description to the PDF document.

> **Note**
>
> Due to a bug in **iText**, running this code may create
> a `NullReferenceException` when adding the first element to the
> document. Unfortunately, at the time of writing this book, there is no known
> workaround. This will only occur when the debugger is attached and will not
> cause any issues when the app is running in production. When running the app
> with the debugger attached, you can click **Continue** via the toolbar to continue
> debugging the app.

5. Lastly, replace the creation of `SavePDFClickedCommand` with the
    following code:

```
SavePDFClickedCommand = new RelayCommand(async () =>
{
#if !__WASM__
    var bytes = GeneratePDF();
    var tempFileName =
        $"{Path.GetFileNameWithoutExtension
            (Path.GetTempFileName())}.pdf";
    var folder = Windows.Storage.ApplicationData.
        Current.TemporaryFolder;
    await folder.CreateFileAsync(tempFileName,
        Windows.Storage.CreationCollisionOption.
            ReplaceExisting);
    var file = await
        folder.GetFileAsync(tempFileName);
    await Windows.Storage.FileIO.WriteBufferAsync
        (file, bytes.AsBuffer());
    await Windows.System.Launcher.LaunchFileAsync
        (file);
#endif
});
```

This will create a PDF, save it to the `apps` temporary folder, and open it with the
default PDF handler.

> **Note**
>
> In this chapter, we are writing the file to a temporary folder and opening it using the default PDF viewer. Depending on your application and use case, `FileSavePicker` and other file pickers can be a very good fit. You can learn more about `FileSavePicker` and the other file pickers that are available here: `https://platform.uno/docs/articles/features/windows-storage-pickers.html`.

To try the issue export out, start the app and create a new issue. After that, select the issue from the issue list and click **Export to PDF** from the **Issues** dropdown at the top. Now, if you click on **Create PDF**, the PDF will be created. Shortly after that, the PDF will be opened in your default PDF viewer. The PDF should look something like this:

Issue export: Yearly maintenance

Type: Train

Train number: TR-128875

Description: This is the yearly maintenance job for train TR-128875. Use maintenance procedure UM-17a.

Figure 3.5 – Demo issue export PDF

Since we cannot write a file to the user's local filesystem when the app is running on the web using WASM, in the next section, we will update our app to provide a download link on WASM instead of the **Create PDF** button by writing a custom HTML-element control.

Exporting on the web with a download link

While the key feature of Uno Platform is to run code that runs on all platforms, it also allows developers to write custom controls that are platform-specific. You can use this to take advantage of platform-specific controls. In our case, we will use this to create an HTML `a-tag` to provide a download link for the WASM version of our app. We will do this using the `Uno.UI.Runtime.WebAssembly.HtmlElement` attribute:

1. First, create a new class called `WasmDownloadElement.cs` inside the `Views` folder with the following code:

    ```
    using System;
    using System.Collections.Generic;
    using System.Text;
    using Windows.UI.Xaml;
    ```

```
using Windows.UI.Xaml.Controls;
namespace ResourcePlanner.Views
{
#if __WASM__
    [Uno.UI.Runtime.WebAssembly.HtmlElement("a")]
    public class WasmDownloadElement : ContentControl
    {
    }
#endif
}
```

This will be our a -tag, which we will use to allow users to download the issue-export PDF. Since we only want this control on WASM, we have placed it inside the #if __WASM__ preprocessor directive.

2. To be able to customize the MIME type of the download and the name of the downloaded file, add the following code to the WasmDownloadElement class:

```
public static readonly DependencyProperty
MimeTypeProperty = DependencyProperty.Register(
    "MimeType", typeof(string),
        typeof(WasmDownloadElement), new
        PropertyMetadata("application/octet-stream",
        OnChanged));
public string MimeType
{
    get => (string)GetValue(MimeTypeProperty);
    set => SetValue(MimeTypeProperty, value);
}
public static readonly DependencyProperty
FileNameProperty = DependencyProperty.Register(
    "FileName", typeof(string),
        typeof(WasmDownloadElement), new
        PropertyMetadata("filename.bin", OnChanged));
public string FileName
{
    get => (string)GetValue(FileNameProperty);
    set => SetValue(FileNameProperty, value);}
private string _base64Content;
```

```csharp
public void SetBase64Content(string content)
{
    _base64Content = content;
    Update();
}
private static void OnChanged(DependencyObject
dependencyobject, DependencyPropertyChangedEventArgs
args)
{
    if (dependencyobject is WasmDownloadElement wd)
    {
        wd.Update();
    }
}
private void Update()
{
    if (_base64Content?.Length == 0)
    {
        this.ClearHtmlAttribute("href");
    }
    else
    {
        var dataUrl =
            $"data:{MimeType};base64,{_base64Content}";
        this.SetHtmlAttribute("href", dataUrl);
        this.SetHtmlAttribute("download", FileName);
    }
}
```

While this is a lot of code, we are only creating two DependencyProperty fields on the WasmDownloadElement class, namely MimeType and FileName, and allowing them to set the content that will be downloaded. The rest of the code handles setting the correct attributes on the underlying control.

3. Lastly, add the following code to the constructor of `ExportIssueView`, after the call to `this.InitializeComponent()`:

```
#if __WASM__
    this.WASMDownloadLink.MimeType =
        "application/pdf";
    var bytes = exportIssueVM.GeneratePDF();
    var b64 = Convert.ToBase64String(bytes);
    this.WASMDownloadLink.SetBase64Content(b64);
#endif
```

This will set the correct MIME type on the download link and set the correct content to download. Note that we defined the `WASMDownloadLink` element earlier in this chapter, inside the `ExportIssueView.xaml` file.

To test this, start the WASM head of your app. Once it has loaded, create an issue, then select it from the issue list and click **Export to PDF** via the **Issues** option. Instead of the **Create PDF** button, you should now see the **Download PDF** option, as shown in *Figure 3.6*:

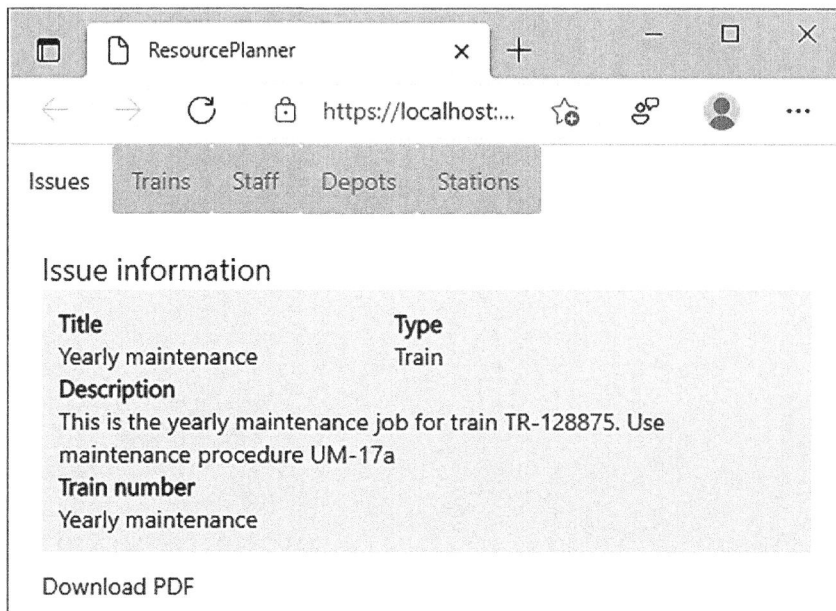

Figure 3.6 – Exporting a PDF on WASM

Once you click the link, the PDF export will be downloaded.

Summary

In this chapter, we built a desktop app that works on Windows, macOS, and on the web using WASM. We covered how to write a data input form with input validation and how to use the Windows Community Toolkit. After that, we learned how to display data using the Windows Community Toolkit DataGrid control. Lastly, we covered how to export data in PDF format and provided a download link by writing a custom HTML control.

In the next chapter, we'll build a mobile app instead. While it will also be designed to be used by employees of UnoBookRail, the main focus will be running the app on a mobile device. Among other things, we'll use this app as an opportunity to look at working with unreliable connectivity and using device capabilities such as a camera.

4

Mobilizing Your App

This chapter will show you how to develop apps with Uno Platform for mobile devices. Such apps can be quite different from ones that run on a desktop device or the web and bring their own challenges that you must take into account.

In this chapter, we'll cover the following topics:

- Building for mobile devices running iOS and Android
- Working with remote data in occasionally connected environments
- Styling the app for the platform it is running on
- Using the capabilities of the device that the app is running on

By the end of this chapter, you'll have created a mobile app that runs on Android and iOS devices, looks different on each platform, and communicates with a remote server to retrieve and send data.

Technical requirements

This chapter assumes that you already have your development environment set up, as well as the necessary project templates installed, as we covered in *Chapter 1, Introducing Uno Platform*. The source code for this chapter can be found at `https://github.com/PacktPublishing/Creating-Cross-Platform-C-Sharp-Applications-with-Uno-Platform/tree/main/Chapter04`.

The code in this chapter makes use of the following library: `https://github.com/PacktPublishing/Creating-Cross-Platform-C-Sharp-Applications-with-Uno-Platform/tree/main/SharedLibrary`.

This chapter also retrieves data from a remote web server that you can recreate with the code at `https://github.com/PacktPublishing/Creating-Cross-Platform-C-Sharp-Applications-with-Uno-Platform/tree/main/WebApi`.

Check out the following video to see the code in action: `https://bit.ly/3jKGRkI`

Introducing the app

The app we'll be building in this chapter is called **Network Assist**. It's an application that will be made available to all staff. It is particularly useful to those working at stations in a public-facing capacity. The real version of this app would have many features, but we're only going to implement two:

- Showing when the next trains will arrive at each station

- Recording and reporting details of events happening around the network.

As this application will be used by staff members as they perform their jobs across the network, it will be built to run on Android and iOS devices.

> **What does "mobile" mean?**
>
> It's easy to think of "mobile" as only being about the device an app is on, but to do so is limiting. "Mobile" can be a helpful shorthand for "Android and iOS devices." However, it's essential to remember more than phones (or tablets) are mobile. It's also the person who is using the device who is mobile. Considering the people who will be using the application is often more important than the device that it will be running on. The device is just one factor to consider. A person may use multiple devices as part of a process, thereby requiring the experience to be mobile as they move between devices – perhaps starting a task on one device and finishing it on another.
>
> The reason we're building the Network Assist app as a mobile one is primarily because the people who will use it will be travelling around all day. It's because the person is mobile that we're building a "mobile" app, that runs on a "mobile" device.

Rather than spending a lot of time explaining the functionality in advance, let's get on with building the app. We'll expand on the requirements as we write the code.

Creating the app

We'll start by creating the solution for the app:

1. In Visual Studio, create a new project with the **Multi-Platform App (Uno Platform)** template.

2. Call the project `NetworkAssist`. You can use a different name, but you'll need to adjust all subsequent code snippets accordingly.

3. Remove all the platform head projects *except* for the **Android**, **iOS**, and **UWP** ones.

> **Always keep the UWP head in the solution**
>
> Even if you're not going to release a UWP version of an app, there are two reasons to keep the UWP head in the solution. Firstly, this can be helpful when diagnosing any compilation errors, to check if the code has a fundamental problem or if the issue is related to the Uno-specific tooling. Secondly, and more importantly, Visual Studio can provide additional tooling and IntelliSense when the UWP head is selected. By having the UWP head in the project, your Uno Platform development experience will be more straightforward.

4. To avoid the need to write more code than necessary, we'll add a reference to the shared library project. Right-click on the solution node in **Solution Explorer**, select **Add > Existing Project...**, navigate to the `UnoBookRail.Common.csproj` file, and click **Open**.

5. For each of the platform-specific projects, we need to add a reference to the common library project. Right-click on the **Android** project node in **Solution Explorer** and select **Add > Reference... > Projects**. Then, check the entry for **UnoBookRail.Common** and click **OK**. Now, *repeat this process for the iOS and UWP projects.*

With the basic solution structure now ready, we can add some functionality to the main page.

Creating the main page

As this will be a simple application, we will put all the functionality on a single page. The requirement for the design is that the app has tabs or buttons at the bottom of the screen to enable switching between the different areas of functionality. We'll put the different pieces of functionality in separate controls and change the control that's shown based on the button (or tab) the user presses.

This is appropriate because the user does not need to navigate backward through the tabs they have viewed already.

Allowing for camera notches, cutouts, and safe areas

Before we add any of our own content, you may wish to run the app to check that everything compiles and can be debugged without issue. Depending on the device or simulator you run the app on, you may see something like the left-hand side of *Figure 4.1*, which shows the default app running on an iPhone 12 simulator. In this figure, you can see that the **Hello, World!** text overlaps (or crashes into) the time and goes behind the camera notch.

If you don't have a device that allows you to test this, some emulators are available that have this notch. Other emulators will have a configurable option to allow testing with and without the cutout. Look under **Settings > System > Developer Options > Simulate a display with a cutout**:

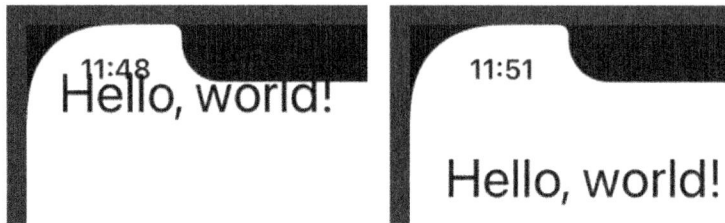

Figure 4.1 – Before and after screenshots showing content allowing for the status bar and camera notch

Our app won't have the **Hello, World!** text, but we don't want our content to be obscured. Fortunately, Uno Platform comes with a helper class that will allow space for camera notches, regardless of the device they are on or the position they are in.

To use this helper class, we need to do the following:

1. Add `xmlns:toolkit="using:Uno.UI.Toolkit"` to the `Page` element at the root of `MainPage.xaml`.

2. Add `toolkit:VisibleBoundsPadding.PaddingMask="All"` to the `Grid` element inside the `Page` element. By setting a value of `All`, the helper will provide the appropriate space if the device is turned sideways, and the notch will be shown at the side of the screen.

When you run the app now, you will see something like the right-hand side image in *Figure 4.1*, which demonstrates how adequate space has been added to the layout. This keeps the status bar or camera notch from obscuring our content.

Now that we have taken care of allowing notches on the screen, we can implement the functionality we need for the app.

Implementing the main page's content

As we only have one page in the app, we'll implement it now:

1. Replace the existing contents of Grid with the following:

```
<Grid.RowDefinitions>
    <RowDefinition Height="*" />
    <RowDefinition Height="Auto" />
</Grid.RowDefinitions>
<CommandBar VerticalAlignment="Bottom" Grid.Row="1">
    <CommandBar.PrimaryCommands>
        <AppBarButton Icon="Clock" Label="Arrivals"
            Click="ShowArrivals" />
        <AppBarButton Label="Quick Report"
            Click="ShowQuickReport">
            <AppBarButton.Icon>
                <FontIcon Glyph="&#xE724;" />
            </AppBarButton.Icon>
        </AppBarButton>
    </CommandBar.PrimaryCommands>
</CommandBar>
```

The top row of the grid will contain the controls for the different elements of functionality. The bottom row will host the buttons for selecting the different controls.

We're using a CommandBar as this is the UWP control that's best suited for providing buttons for selecting areas of functionality within the app. This is only an approximation of how we want things to look on iOS and Android, and we'll address those shortly.

> **Note**
>
> XAML provides multiple ways of doing things that all produce comparable results. With the code in this chapter, we've used the simplest approach to provide a consistent output on all platforms.

2. We now need custom controls for displaying the different pieces of functionality. Start by right-clicking on the **Shared** project and selecting **Add** > **New Folder**. Name it `Views` so that it matches the convention for where to store UI-related controls.

   If you wish, you can move the `MainPage` files into the `Views` folder, but it doesn't matter for the functionality of this app.

3. In the new folder, right-click and select **Add** > **New Item…**, choose the **User Control (Uno Platform UWP)** option, and call it `ArrivalsControl`. Repeat this to add a control named `QuickReportControl`.

4. We'll now add the controls to `MainPage.xaml`. Declare a new XML namespace alias at the page level, with the value of `xmlns:views="using:Network Assist.Views"`. After the opening of the `Grid` tag and before `CommandBar`, add the following to create instances of our new controls:

```
<views:ArrivalsControl x:Name="Arrivals"
Visibility="Visible" />
<views:QuickReportControl x:Name="QuickReport"
Visibility="Collapsed" />
```

5. In the code-behind file (`MainPage.xaml.cs`), we need to add the methods to handle the `Click` events referenced in the XAML for the AppBarButtons:

```
public void ShowArrivals(object sender, RoutedEventArgs
args)
{
    Arrivals.Visibility = Visibility.Visible;
    QuickReport.Visibility = Visibility.Collapsed;
}
public void ShowQuickReport(object sender,
RoutedEventArgs args)
{
    Arrivals.Visibility = Visibility.Collapsed;
    QuickReport.Visibility = Visibility.Visible;
}
```

We'll use click events and code-behind here as the logic is tightly coupled to the UI and won't benefit from having coded tests. It's possible and acceptable to use ICommand implementations and bindings to control when each control is shown, but it is up to you to implement it that way if you wish.

MVVM and Code-Behind

In this chapter, we will use a combination of code-behind files and the **Model-View-ViewModel** (**MVVM**) pattern. There are three reasons for this. Firstly, it allows us to keep the code shorter and simpler, so that it is easier for you to follow along. Secondly, it avoids the need to explain a specific MVVM framework or implementation, and we can instead focus on the code that's relevant to the application. Finally, it demonstrates that Uno Platform doesn't force you to work in a specific way. You can use the coding style, pattern, or framework you prefer.

With the main page up and running, we can now add the functionality for displaying details of upcoming arrivals.

Showing upcoming arrival details

The requirements for showing upcoming arrivals are as follows:

- A list of stations is displayed, and when one is selected, the arrival times of the next three trains in each direction are shown.

- The data can be refreshed to ensure the latest information is always available.

- The time when the last piece of data was retrieved is displayed.

- Prompts are shown if no station is selected or there's a problem retrieving data.

- The app indicates when it is retrieving data.

You can see an example of the final functionality we'll create by the end of this chapter in the following figure:

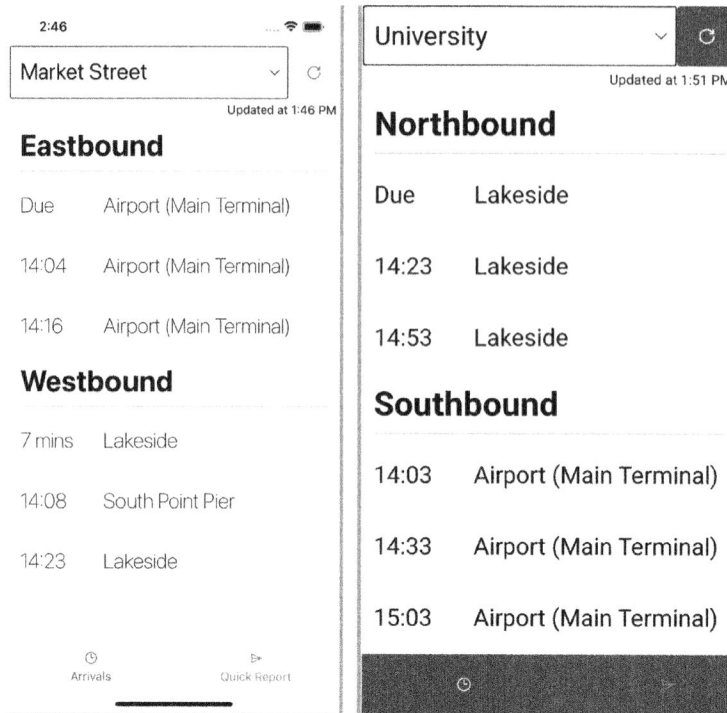

Figure 4.2 – Upcoming arrival details shown on an iPhone (left) and on an Android device (right)

This user control for showing the upcoming arrivals is going to be the most complicated piece of UI in the app. It may seem like a lot of steps, but each one is simple:

1. Start by adding two column definitions, and four row definitions to `Grid` in `ArrivalsControl.xaml`:

```
<Grid.ColumnDefinitions>
    <ColumnDefinition Width="*" />
    <ColumnDefinition Width="Auto" />
</Grid.ColumnDefinitions>
<Grid.RowDefinitions>
    <RowDefinition Height="Auto" />
    <RowDefinition Height="Auto" />
    <RowDefinition Height="Auto" />
    <RowDefinition Height="*" />
</Grid.RowDefinitions>
```

2. The top row will contain a `ComboBox` control for selecting the station and a `Button` element to request that the data be refreshed:

```
<ComboBox x:Name="StationList"
    HorizontalAlignment="Stretch"
    VerticalAlignment="Stretch"
    ItemsSource="{x:Bind VM.ListOfStations}"
    SelectedItem="{x:Bind VM.SelectedStation,
        Mode=TwoWay}"
    SelectionChanged="OnStationListSelectionChanged"
    SelectionChangedTrigger="Always">
    <ComboBox.ItemTemplate>
        <DataTemplate x:DataType="network:Station">
            <TextBlock Text="{x:Bind Name}"
                FontSize="26" />
        </DataTemplate>
    </ComboBox.ItemTemplate>
</ComboBox>
<Button Grid.Column="1"
    Width="60"
    Height="60"
    Command="{x:Bind VM.RefreshCommand}">
    <SymbolIcon Symbol="Refresh" />
</Button>
```

The data template refers to a data type we are yet to add, but we can add the namespace alias now as `xmlns:network="using:UnoBookRail.Common.Network"`.

3. The next two rows will use `TextBlocks` to show the time when data was last retrieved and if there was a problem retrieving data:

```
<TextBlock
    Grid.Row="1"
    Grid.ColumnSpan="2"
    Margin="4"
    HorizontalAlignment="Stretch"
    HorizontalTextAlignment="Right"
    Text="{x:Bind VM.DataTimestamp, Mode=OneWay}" />
```

```xml
<TextBlock
    Grid.Row="2"
    Grid.ColumnSpan="2"
    Margin="4"
    HorizontalAlignment="Stretch"
    HorizontalTextAlignment="Right"
    Foreground="Red"
    TextWrapping="WrapWholeWords"
    Text="Connectivity issues: data may not be up to
        date!"
    Visibility="{x:Bind VM.ShowErrorMsg,
        Mode=OneWay}"/>
```

4. `ListView` will use a couple of data templates that we'll define at the control level. Add the following after the opening `UserControl` tag:

```xml
<UserControl.Resources>
    <DataTemplate x:Key="HeaderTemplate">
        <Grid HorizontalAlignment="Stretch"
            Background="{ThemeResource
                ApplicationPageBackgroundThemeBrush}">
        <TextBlock
            Margin="0"
            FontWeight="Bold"
            Style="{StaticResource
                SubheaderTextBlockStyle}"
            Text="{Binding Platform}" />
        </Grid>
    </DataTemplate>
    <DataTemplate x:Key="ItemTemplate">
        <Grid Margin="0,10">
          <Grid.ColumnDefinitions>
            <ColumnDefinition Width="100" />
            <ColumnDefinition Width="*" />
          </Grid.ColumnDefinitions>
          <TextBlock
            Margin="0,10"
                Style="{StaticResource TitleTextBlockStyle}"
```

```
            Text="{Binding DisplayedTime}" />
        <TextBlock
            Grid.Column="1"
            Margin="0,10"
            Style="{StaticResource TitleTextBlockStyle}"
            Text="{Binding Destination}" />
    </Grid>
  </DataTemplate>
</UserControl.Resources>
```

5. The fourth, and last, row contains a `ListView` that shows the upcoming arrival times:

```
<ListView Grid.Row="3"
    Grid.ColumnSpan="2"
    ItemTemplate="{StaticResource ItemTemplate}"
    ItemsSource="{x:Bind VM.ArrivalsViewSource}"
    SelectionMode="None">
    <ListView.GroupStyle>
        <GroupStyle HeaderTemplate="{StaticResource
            HeaderTemplate}" />
    </ListView.GroupStyle>
</ListView>
```

6. The fourth row also contains a `Grid` that hosts other informational controls that are displayed over or instead of the `ListView` as appropriate:

```
<Grid Grid.Row="3" Grid.ColumnSpan="2">
    <TextBlock HorizontalAlignment="Stretch"
        VerticalAlignment="Center"
        HorizontalTextAlignment="Center"
        Style="{StaticResource
                SubheaderTextBlockStyle}"
        Text="Select a station" TextWrapping="NoWrap"
        Visibility="{x:Bind VM.ShowNoStnMsg,
            Mode=OneWay}" />
    <ProgressRing Width="100" Height="100"
        IsActive="True" IsEnabled="True"
        Visibility="{x:Bind VM.IsBusy, Mode=OneWay}"
```

```
        />
    </Grid>
```

7. We've added quite a lot of XAML here. The first step to seeing how it looks is to wire up a ViewModel so that we can access the relevant properties and commands. Change the contents of ArrivalsControlxaml.cs to the following:

```
public sealed partial class ArrivalsControl : UserControl
{
    private ArrivalsViewModel VM { get; set; }
    public ArrivalsControl()
    {
        InitializeComponent();
        VM = new ArrivalsViewModel();
    }
    private async void OnStationListSelectionChanged
        (object sender, SelectionChangedEventArgs e)
    {
        if ((sender as ComboBox).SelectedItem is
            Station selectedStn)
        {
            await VM.LoadArrivalsDataAsync
                (selectedStn.Id);
        }
    }
}
```

Here, we created an instance of the ViewModel (named VM to help keep the code concise) in the constructor, and it's this class that contains most of the logic.

The code-behind also includes a method to handle the SelectionChanged event on the ComboBox. This is currently necessary as a workaround for a bug due to the order that ComboBox events are raised in. The bug is logged at https://github.com/unoplatform/uno/issues/5792. Once fixed, it should be possible to bind to a Command on the ViewModel to perform the equivalent functionality.

8. Add the following `using` declarations to the top of the file so that the compiler can find the types we just added:

```
using NetworkAssist.ViewModels;
using UnoBookRail.Common.Network;
```

9. We're now ready to create a ViewModel that will contain the remaining logic for the functionality. We'll start by creating a folder called `ViewModels`. Within that folder, create a class called `ArrivalsViewModel`.

10. To avoid writing common code that's needed when following the MVVM pattern, add a reference to the `Microsoft.Toolkit.Mvvm` NuGet package *in each of the platform head projects*:

```
Install-Package Microsoft.Toolkit.Mvvm -Version 7.0.2
```

11. Update the `ArrivalsViewModel` class so that it inherits from `Microsoft.Toolkit.Mvvm.ComponentModel.ObservableObject`.

12. `ArrivalsViewModel` will use types from different places, so we need to reference the following namespaces:

```
using Microsoft.Toolkit.Mvvm.Input;
using System.Collections.ObjectModel;
using System.Threading.Tasks;
using System.Windows.Input;
using UnoBookRail.Common.Network;
using Windows.UI.Xaml.Data;
```

13. Start by adding the following fields to the class:

```
private static DataService _data = DataService.Instance;
private List<Station> _listOfStations;
private ObservableCollection<StationArrivalDetails>
_arrivals =
    new ObservableCollection<StationArrivalDetails>();
private Station _selectedStation = null;
private string _dataTimestamp;
private bool _isBusy;
private bool _showErrorMsg;
```

14. Our `ViewModel` requires the following properties as they were referenced in the bindings of the XAML we defined previously. They will use the backing fields we just added:

```
public List<Station> ListOfStations
{
    get => _listOfStations;
    set => SetProperty(ref _listOfStations, value);
}
public bool ShowErrorMsg
{
    get => _showErrorMsg;
    set => SetProperty(ref _showErrorMsg, value);
}
public Station SelectedStation
{
    get => _selectedStation;
    set {
        if (SetProperty(ref _selectedStation, value))
        {
            OnPropertyChanged(nameof(ShowNoStnMsg));
        }
    }
}
public ObservableCollection<StationArrivalDetails>
Arrivals
{
    get => _arrivals;
    set => SetProperty(ref _arrivals, value);
}
public string DataTimestamp
{
    get => _dataTimestamp;
    set => SetProperty(ref _dataTimestamp, value);
}
public bool IsBusy
{
```

```
    get => _isBusy;
    set => SetProperty(ref _isBusy, value);
}
public IEnumerable<object> ArrivalsViewSource => new
CollectionViewSource()
{
    Source = Arrivals,
    IsSourceGrouped = true
}.View;
public bool ShowNoStnMsg => SelectedStation == null;
public ICommand RefreshCommand { get; }
public ICommand SelectionChangedCommand { get; }
```

15. We'll use the constructor to initialize the list of stations and the commands:

```
public ArrivalsViewModel()
{
    ListOfStations = _data.GetAllStations();
    RefreshCommand = new AsyncRelayCommand(async () =>
        { await LoadArrivalsDataAsync(); });
    SelectionChangedCommand = new AsyncRelayCommand(
        async () => { await LoadArrivalsDataAsync();
            });
}
```

16. Now, add the method that handles retrieving and displaying the data:

```
public async Task LoadArrivalsDataAsync(int stationId =
0)
{
  if (stationId < 1)
  {
    // if no value passed use the previously selected
    // Id.
    stationId = SelectedStation?.Id ?? 0;
  }
  else
  {
    // We've changed station so clear current details
```

```
      Arrivals.Clear();
   DataTimestamp = string.Empty;
   ShowErrorMsg = false;
 }
  if (stationId > 0)
  {
   IsBusy = true;
   try {
     var arr = await
        _data.GetArrivalsForStationAsync(stationId);
     ShowErrorMsg = false;
     if (arr.ForStationId == stationId)
     {
        DataTimestamp =
           $"Updated at {arr.Timestamp:t}";
        Arrivals.Clear();
        if (!string.IsNullOrEmpty(
           arr.DirectionOneName))
        {
          var d1details = new StationArrivalDetails
             (arr.DirectionOneName);
          d1details.AddRange(arr.DirectionOneDetails);
          Arrivals.Add(d1details);
        }
        if (!string.IsNullOrEmpty(
           arr.DirectionTwoName))
        {
          var d2details = new StationArrivalDetails(
             arr.DirectionTwoName);
          d2details.AddRange(arr.DirectionTwoDetails);
          Arrivals.Add(d2details);
        }
     }
   }
   catch (Exception exc) {
     // Log this or take other appropriate action
     ShowErrorMsg = true;
```

```
        }
        finally {
            IsBusy = false;
        }
    }
}
```

17. You may have noticed that the data was retrieved from a singleton `DataService` class. We'll start by creating a simple version of this that we'll expand upon later. Common convention suggests putting this class in a directory called `Services`, though you could put this in the `ViewModels` folder as well:

```csharp
using System.Linq;
using System.Threading.Tasks;
using UnoBookRail.Common.Network;

public class DataService
{
    private static readonly Lazy<DataService> ds =
        new Lazy<DataService>(() => new
            DataService());
    private static readonly Lazy<Stations> stations =
        new Lazy<Stations>(() => new Stations());
    public static DataService Instance => ds.Value;
    private DataService() { }
    public List<Station> GetAllStations() =>
        stations.Value.GetAll().OrderBy(s =>
            s.Name).ToList();
    public async Task<Arrivals>
        GetArrivalsForStationAsync(int stationId)
    {
        return await Task.FromResult(
            stations.Value.GetNextArrivals(stationId));
    }
}
```

This class is currently getting all its data from the shared library, but we'll change this later. This is also why the `GetArrivalsForStationAsync` method may seem overly complex.

18. Now that we have the `DataService` class, we can retrieve the arrival details, but we need to do a little bit more work to display them. There is one more class we need. This is `StationArrivalDetails`, and it allows us to group the information by the platform and direction the train is traveling in. Create this in the `ViewModels` directory:

```
using UnoBookRail.Common.Network;

public class StationArrivalDetails :
List<ArrivalDetail>
{
    public StationArrivalDetails(string platform)
    {
        Platform = platform;
    }
    public string Platform { get; set; }
}
```

> **CollectionViewSource with grouped data in Uno**
>
> Displaying grouped lists with Uno Platform is more complicated than on UWP. If you've previously used a `CollectionViewSource` in a UWP app, you've probably defined it in XAML and not as an `IEnumerable<object>`. Unfortunately, it's necessary to define our `CollectionViewSource` as an `IEnumerable<IEnumerable>` for Uno Platform to correctly render all the groups and headers on Android and iOS. Without doing this, we'd see the group headings missing on iOS and only the first group's contents on Android.

We now have a working app, but there are two improvements we'll make in the next two sections. There, we'll improve the look of the app and use some native controls, but before that, we'll switch to use "as live" data from a remote source and not data that ships with the app.

Retrieving remote data

Very few apps only work with the data that they ship with. The value the **Network Assist** provides is based on giving real-time information. There is a lot more value in knowing when trains will actually arrive rather than just when they are scheduled to arrive. To gather this information, the app must connect to a remote source of real-time data.

Most mobile applications connect to external data sources, and the most common way to do this is over HTTP(S). If you're only developing an application that runs on desktop, you might be able to assume that a connection is always available. For mobile apps, it's necessary to consider the device as being **occasionally connected**.

As it's impossible to assume that an app will have a connection available or that it will be fast, it's necessary to account for this when designing an app. These issues apply to all mobile apps and are not something unique to developing with Uno Platform. The correct way to handle the occasional connectivity and availability of data will vary by application. It's too big an issue for us to fully cover here but important to bring up. At a minimum, accounting for occasional connectivity means needing to consider retrying failed connection requests and managing data. The code we wrote previously in the LoadArrivalsDataAsync method already does a crude form of caching, by not getting rid of the current information when refreshing the data until a successful request is made and newer data is available to display. While the information shown in the app can become outdated very quickly, it's considered more appropriate for the app to show something that it acknowledges is a few minutes out of date than to show nothing.

In another app, it may be more appropriate to save data in a file or database so that it can be retrieved and shown when remote data is not available. *Chapter 5*, *Making Your App Ready for the Real World*, shows how you may do this using an SQLite database.

We'll look at how the app can handle failures in connecting to the remote data shortly, but first, we'll look at how to connect to the remote data.

Connecting to a remote data source

The GitHub repository for this book at `https://github.com/PacktPublishing/Creating-Cross-Platform-C-Sharp-Applications-with-Uno-Platform` includes a **WebAPI** project that will return train arrival data for the app.

You can choose to run the code and access it via your local machine, or you can connect to the version available at `https://unobookrail.azurewebsites.net/`. If you're connecting to the hosted version, note that it bases data on the local time for the server, and this may be different from where you are. If the server continually says there is a long time until the next train as it's the early hours of the morning where the server is, you'll see more varied data if you run the project yourself:

1. We'll use `System.Net.Http.HttpClient` to connect to the server. To be able to do this, we must add package references to `System.Net.Http` in the *Android and iOS* projects:

    ```
    Install-Package System.Net.Http -Version 4.3.4
    ```

2. As the data that's returned by the API is in JSON format, we'll also add a reference to the `Newtonsoft.Json` library in *all platform projects* so that we can deserialize the responses:

    ```
    Install-Package Newtonsoft.Json -Version 12.0.3
    ```

3. We're now ready to retrieve remote data. The changes will all be in the `DataService.cs` file. Start by adding an instance of an `HttpClient`. We will use this for all requests:

    ```
    using System.Net.Http;
    private static readonly HttpClient _http = new
    HttpClient();
    ```

4. To connect to the server, we need to specify where it is. As we will eventually be making multiple requests, it's sensible to define the server domain in a single place. We'll do this by **adding a property** to return this value:

    ```
    public static string WebApiDomain {
        get
        {
    #if __ANDROID__
                    return "https://10.0.2.2:44302";
    #else
                    return "https://localhost:44302";
    #endif
            // Or connect to the hosted version
            //return
                "https://unobookrail.azurewebsites.net";
    ```

```
        }
    }
```

Note that we're using the `__ANDROID__` constant, which is available to the `#if` preprocessor directive. See *Chapter 2, Writing Your First Uno Platform App*, for more on this.

If you're connecting to a locally hosted WebAPI instance from an Android emulator, it's necessary to use the IP address of `10.0.2.2` to connect. This is a special IP address that the emulator uses to refer to the host machine. You can use conditional compilation to specify this, as in the preceding snippet. If you're connecting to an external server, you can set the address directly and don't need any conditional code.

5. We can now update the `GetArrivalsForStationAsync` method to get the live data. *Replace* the current implementation with the following:

```
using Newtonsoft.Json;


public async Task<Arrivals> GetArrivalsForStationAsync(int
stationId)
{
   var url = $"{WebApiDomain}/stations/?stationid=
      {stationId}";
   var rawJson = await _http.GetStringAsync(url);
   return JsonConvert.DeserializeObject<Arrivals>
      (rawJson);
}
```

If you run the app now, the data will come from the remote location. You might notice that data retrieval is no longer instantaneous and that a busy indicator is shown while waiting. We added the code for showing the progress indicator in the original version of the app but haven't seen it displayed until now. This highlights another potential issue when working with data that takes time to retrieve. *It is crucial to keep the user informed when something is happening.* We're using a `ProgressRing` here to indicate that something is happening. Without this, the user may be wondering if anything is happening and become frustrated or press the refresh button repeatedly.

At this point, we've retrieved data from a remote source and kept the user informed while this is happening, but we need to do more for when things go wrong. So, we'll look at that next.

Using Polly to handle exceptions and retry requests

The need to handle exceptions and retry failed requests is common across almost all applications. Fortunately, many solutions exist to handle some of the complexity for us. **Polly** (`https://github.com/App-vNext/Polly`) is a popular, open source library for handling transient errors that we'll use in our app. Let's take a look:

1. We'll start by adding a reference to the `Polly.Extensions.Http` package to *all the platform projects*:

   ```
   Install-Package Polly.Extensions.Http -Version 3.0.0
   ```

   This extends the standard Polly capabilities and simplifies handling HTTP-related faults.

2. We'll now update the `GetArrivalsForStationAsync` method again so that it uses a Polly **policy** when making the request:

   ```
   using Polly;
   using Polly.Extensions.Http;


   public async Task<Arrivals> GetArrivalsForStationAsync(int
   stationId)
   {
       var url = $"{WebApiDomain}/stations/?stationid=
           {stationId}";
       var policy = HttpPolicyExtensions
                       .HandleTransientHttpError()
                       .WaitAndRetryAsync(3, attempt =>
                           TimeSpan.FromSeconds(Math.Pow(
                               attempt, 2)));
       using (var response = await policy.ExecuteAsync(
           async () => await _http.GetAsync(url)))
       {
           if (response.IsSuccessStatusCode)
           {
               var rawJson = await
                   response.Content.ReadAsStringAsync();
               return JsonConvert.DeserializeObject<Arrivals>
                   (rawJson);
           }
       }
   }
   ```

```
        return default;
    }
```

There are three important parts to the code.

The first is the call to `HandleTransientHttpError`. This tells Polly to retry the request if the HTTP response is a server error (HTTP 5xx) or a timeout error (HTTP 408).

The call to `WaitAndRetryAsync` tells Polly to retry up to three times. We also specify a delay between each request using an **exponential backoff strategy**. We wait 1 second before the first reattempt, 4 seconds before the second, and 9 seconds before the final attempt. Such a strategy gives the server time to recover any error and avoids overloading it with multiple repeated requests in quick succession.

The final piece of code that's of interest is the way the policy is used. We call `policy.ExecuteAsync` and pass it the action we wish to apply the policy to.

3. If the request fails for a reason not covered by our policy, the code we created earlier causes a message to be shown at the top of the screen, as shown in the following screenshot, that indicates the problem. Other applications may need to log or report such problems differently, but it's rarely appropriate to do nothing:

Updated at 2:55 PM

Connectivity issues: data may not be up to date!

Figure 4.3 – App showing a message to indicate a connectivity problem

We now have an app that provides useful data from a remote source, and in a reliable way. The final thing we want to do is improve how it looks on different platforms.

Making your app look like it belongs on each platform

So far, everything in the app has used the default styling provided by Uno Platform. Because Uno Platform bases everything on UWP and WinUI, our apps have been styled based on the Fluent Design system as this is the default on Windows. This is fine if we want our apps to look this way, but what if we want our apps to use the default styles for Android or iOS? Fortunately, Uno Platform has a solution for us. It provides libraries in the **Material** and **Cupertino** styles that we can apply to our apps. While these are native for Android and iOS devices, respectively, they can be used anywhere.

We'll now use the resources these libraries provide to apply the Material Design styling to the Android version of our app, and the Cupertino styles to the iOS version.

Applying Material styles to the Android version of the app

Let's get started:

1. We'll start by adding a reference to the Uno.Material package to the *Android project*. Note that this is a prerelease package, so enable this if you're searching via the UI:

    ```
    Install-Package Uno.Material -Version 1.0.0-dev.790
    ```

2. While the Uno.Material library knows how to style controls, it doesn't contain all the assets and references to use them. For this, *add* the Xamarin. AndroidX.Lifecycle.LiveData and Xamarin.AndroidX.AppCompat. AppCompatResources packages *to the Android project*:

    ```
    Install-Package Xamarin.AndroidX.AppCompat.
    AppCompatResources -Version 1.2.0.5

    Install-Package Xamarin.AndroidX.Lifecycle.LiveData
    -Version 2.3.1
    ```

3. To use the styles in the Android library, we must add them to the styles available in the app by referencing them in App.xaml:

    ```
    <Application
        x:Class="NetworkAssist.App"
        xmlns="http://schemas.microsoft.com/winfx/2006/
               xaml/presentation"
        xmlns:x="http://schemas.microsoft.com/winfx/2006/
                 xaml"
        xmlns:android="http://uno.ui/android"
        xmlns:local="using:NetworkAssist"
        xmlns:mc="http://schemas.openxmlformats.org/
                  markup-compatibility/2006"
        mc:Ignorable="android">
        <Application.Resources>
            <ResourceDictionary>
                <ResourceDictionary.MergedDictionaries>
    ```

```
            <XamlControlsResources xmlns=
            "using:Microsoft.UI.Xaml.Controls" />
            <android:MaterialColors xmlns=
                "using:Uno.Material" />
            <android:MaterialResources xmlns=
                "using:Uno.Material" />
        </ResourceDictionary.MergedDictionaries>
      </ResourceDictionary>
    </Application.Resources>
  </Application>
```

4. Some controls will pick up Material styling automatically, while others will need to have the styles applied directly. To show this, we'll apply a specific style to the refresh `Button`.

    In `ArrivalsControl.xaml`, *add the Android namespace alias* to the top of the file. We will only use this when running on Android. Then, apply the style to the `Button` element:

    ```
    xmlns:android="http://uno.ui/android"
    mc:Ignorable="d android">

    <Button
        Grid.Column="1"
        Width="60"
        Height="60"
        android:Style="{StaticResource
            MaterialContainedButtonStyle}"
        Command="{x:Bind VM.RefreshCommand}">
        <SymbolIcon Symbol="Refresh" />
    </Button>
    ```

    The preceding code has improved how the `Button` control looks on the arrivals control, but it hasn't improved the buttons in `CommandBar` at the bottom of the shell page. Let's address this now.

5. Rather than using the Windows `CommandBar`, the Material Design system has a separate control that is more appropriate for showing navigation-related buttons at the bottom of the screen. This is called `BottomNavigationBar`. We'll start by adding this to `MainPage.xaml` and wrapping the existing `CommandBar` in a `Grid` that will only be shown on Windows:

```
xmlns:android="http://uno.ui/android"
xmlns:win="http://schemas.microsoft.com/winfx/2006/xaml/
           presentation"
mc:Ignorable="d android">


<android:Grid Grid.Row="1" >
    <material:BottomNavigationBar
        xmlns:material="using:Uno.Material.Controls">
        <material:BottomNavigationBar.Items>
            <material:BottomNavigationBarItem
                Click="ShowArrivals">
                <material:
                    BottomNavigationBarItem.Icon>
                    <SymbolIcon Symbol="Clock" />
                </material:
                    BottomNavigationBarItem.Icon>
            </material:BottomNavigationBarItem>
            <material:BottomNavigationBarItem
                Click="ShowQuickReport">
                <material:BottomNavigationBarItem.Icon>
                    <FontIcon Glyph="&#xE724;" />
                </material:BottomNavigationBarItem.Icon>
            </material:BottomNavigationBarItem>
        </material:BottomNavigationBar.Items>
    </material:BottomNavigationBar>
</android:Grid>
<win:Grid Grid.Row="1">
    <CommandBar />
        // All XAML for this control notshown
</win:Grid>
```

This new control will use the same images and `Click` events as before. It's only the control that's displaying them that we're changing.

> **Note**
>
> After adding the `Xamarin.AndroidX` packages, you may get a compilation error related to a file called `abc_vector_test.xml`. This error is due to compatibility inconsistencies between different preview versions of the packages and Visual Studio. This error can be addressed by opening the **Properties** section of the **Android** project, selecting **Android Options**, and unchecking the **Use incremental Android packaging system (aap2)** option. This may lead to a separate build warning and slightly slower builds, but the code will now compile. Hopefully, future updates that are made to these packages will help us avoid this issue.

6. If you run the app now, you'll see that the button and navigation bar are purple. This is part of a color scheme defined in the `Uno.Material` library. You can use your own color scheme by including a `ResourceDictionary` that provides different values for the predefined Material colors. Then, you can reference this when you add the resources shown in *step 2*. A guide to doing this can be found at `https://platform.uno/docs/articles/features/uno-material.html#getting-started`.

Now that we've improved the app's look on Android, let's do the same for iOS.

Applying Cupertino styles to the iOS version of the app

Let's get started:

1. A separate package includes the Cupertino styles, so we must add a reference to `Uno.Cupertino` *in the iOS project*:

```
Install-Package Uno.Cupertino -Version 1.0.0-dev.790
```

As with the Material package in the previous section, we need to load the resources from this package in `App.xaml` by adding the following:

```
xmlns:ios="http://uno.ui/ios"
mc:Ignorable="android ios">
<Application.Resources>
    <ResourceDictionary>
        <ResourceDictionary.MergedDictionaries>
            <XamlControlsResources xmlns=
                "using:Microsoft.UI.Xaml.Controls" />
```

```
        <android:MaterialColors xmlns=
            "using:Uno.Material" />
        <android:MaterialResources xmlns=
            "using:Uno.Material" />
        <ios:CupertinoColors xmlns=
            "using:Uno.Cupertino" />
        <ios:CupertinoResources xmlns=
            "using:Uno.Cupertino" />
    </ResourceDictionary.MergedDictionaries>
    </ResourceDictionary>
</Application.Resources>
```

2. This package doesn't include a native tab bar control (a `UITabBar`) yet, but we can easily create something that matches Apple's Human Interface Guidelines.

   Add the following to `MainPage.xaml`, after the `win:Grid` element:

```
xmlns:converters="using:UnoBookRail.NetworkAssist.
Converters"
xmlns:ios="http://uno.ui/ios"
mc:Ignorable="d android ios">


<ios:Grid Grid.Row="1">
    <Grid.ColumnDefinitions>
        <ColumnDefinition Width="*" />
        <ColumnDefinition Width="*" />
    </Grid.ColumnDefinitions>
    <Grid.Resources>
        <converters:CupertinoButtonColorConverter
            x:Key="CupertinoBtnColor" />
    </Grid.Resources>
    <Button Click="ShowArrivals"
        HorizontalAlignment="Center"
            Foreground="{Binding ElementName=Arrivals,
                Path=Visibility, Converter={
                    StaticResource CupertinoBtnColor},
                        ConverterParameter=Visible,
                            Mode=OneWay}">
        <StackPanel>
            <SymbolIcon
```

```
                    Symbol="Clock"
                    Width="25"
                    Height="25"
                    HorizontalAlignment="Center" />
                <TextBlock>Arrivals</TextBlock>
            </StackPanel>
        </Button>
        <Button
            Grid.Column="1"
            Click="ShowQuickReport"
            HorizontalAlignment="Center"
                Foreground="{Binding ElementName=
                    QuickReport, Path=Visibility,
                        Converter={StaticResource
                            CupertinoBtnColor},
                                ConverterParameter=Visible,
                                    Mode=OneWay}">
            <StackPanel>
                <FontIcon
                    Glyph="&#xE724;"
                    Width="25"
                    Height="25"
                    HorizontalAlignment="Center" />
                <TextBlock>Quick Report</TextBlock>
            </StackPanel>
        </Button>
    </ios:Grid>
```

We're using the same icons and Click events that we did previously, but we're using a new converter for ForegroundColor of the Buttons. For this, you'll need to *create a folder* called Converters and *create a file* called CupertinoButtonColorConverter.cs containing the following code:

```
using Windows.UI.Xaml.Data;

public class CupertinoButtonColorConverter :
IValueConverter
{
```

```
public object Convert(object value, Type targetType,
    object parameter, string language)
{
    if (value?.ToString() == parameter?.ToString())
    {
        return App.Current.Resources[
            "CupertinoBlueBrush"];
    }
    else
    {
        return App.Current.Resources[
            "CupertinoSecondaryGrayBrush"];
    }
}
public object ConvertBack(object value, Type
    targetType, object parameter, string language)
    => throw new NotImplementedException();
}
```

3. As with the Android project, the Cupertino styles won't be automatically applied to the buttons in the app. However, rather than applying styles to each `Button` element directly, we can create an *implicit style* that will be applied to all the `Button` elements throughout the app. To do this, *modify* `App.xaml` to add the style, as follows:

```
<Application.Resources>
    <ResourceDictionary>
        <ResourceDictionary.MergedDictionaries>
            <XamlControlsResources xmlns=
                "using:Microsoft.UI.Xaml.Controls" />
            <android:MaterialColors xmlns=
                "using:Uno.Material" />
            <android:MaterialResources xmlns=
                "using:Uno.Material" />
            <ios:CupertinoColors xmlns=
                "using:Uno.Cupertino"  />
            <ios:CupertinoResources xmlns=
                "using:Uno.Cupertino" />
```

```
        </ResourceDictionary.MergedDictionaries>
        <ios:Style TargetType="Button"
            BasedOn="{StaticResource
                CupertinoButtonStyle}" />
    </ResourceDictionary>
</Application.Resources>
```

Implicit styles can be used for any platform so, if you wanted, you could do a similar thing in the Android version of the app.

We now have an app that looks like it belongs on each platform, and it can display content we retrieve from an external server. Now, let's look at how we can use the device's capabilities to create data and send it to a remote source.

Accessing device capabilities

The final piece of functionality we'll add to the app is different from what we've done so far. So far we've looked at consuming data, but we'll now look at creating it.

The requirement from the company for this part of the app is that it provides a way for staff to capture information whenever an incident occurs. An "incident" could be anything that the business may need to record or know about. It could be something minor such as a customer tripping while on company property to a major accident. All these incidents have something in common: that it's beneficial to capture details when they happen rather than relying on people remembering details later. The goal is that giving staff a way to capture an image or some text as quickly and simply as possible will increase the amount of information that's captured. The software will augment the captured information with the time and location of the incident and add who recorded it. This will be aggregated and further documented in a separate backend system.

Let's create a simple way of meeting these requirements as a way of demonstrating how Uno Platform provides a way to use UWP APIs on different platforms:

1. To use the camera and get the location of the device, we need to indicate that the app will require the permissions that are necessary to do this. The way we specify permissions is done slightly differently on each platform.

   On Android, open the project's **Properties** window and select **Android Manifest**. Under the list of **Required permissions**, select **ACCESS_COARSE_LOCATION**, **ACCESS_FINE_LOCATION**, **CAMERA**, **READ_EXTERNAL_STORAGE**, and **WRITE_EXTERNAL_STORAGE**.

On **iOS**, right-click on `info.plist` and open it with **Generic PList Editor**. Double-clicking on the file will open the manifest editor, but this does not provide us with a way to add the required new properties. Now, add properties for **Privacy - Camera Usage Description**, **Privacy - Photo Library Usage Description**, **Privacy - Location Usage Description**, and **Privacy - Location When In Use Usage Description**. To add a new property, go to the bottom of the list, click the + symbol, and select it from the dropdown. For each of these properties, you should add a description in the **Value** column that explains why that permission is needed. These descriptions will be displayed when the permission is requested.

On Windows, open `Package.appxmanfiest`, go to **Capabilities**, and check the option for **Location**. You do not need to specify any permissions to use the camera when accessing it through `CameraCaptureUI`.

2. We can create the UI by adding the following to `Grid` in `QuickReportControl.xaml`:

```
xmlns:android="http://uno.ui/android"
mc:Ignorable="d android">


<Grid.RowDefinitions>
    <RowDefinition Height="Auto" />
    <RowDefinition Height="*" />
    <RowDefinition Height="Auto" />
    <RowDefinition Height="2*" />
</Grid.RowDefinitions>
<Button HorizontalAlignment="Right"
        Click="SendClicked"
        Margin="15,0"
        android:Style="{StaticResource
            MaterialContainedButtonStyle}">
            Send</Button>
<Image Grid.Row="1" x:Name="ImageToInclude" />
<Button x:Name="TakePictureButton" Grid.Row="1"
    Click="CaptureImageClicked"
    VerticalAlignment="Center"
    HorizontalAlignment="Center"
```

```
    android:Style="{StaticResource
        MaterialContainedSecondaryButtonStyle}">
    <SymbolIcon Symbol="Camera" Height="50" Width="50" />
</Button>
<TextBlock Grid.Row="2" Text="What do you have to
report?" />
<TextBox x:Name="EnteredText" Grid.Row="3"
    AcceptsReturn="True" />
<Grid x:Name="BusyOverlay" Grid.RowSpan="4"
    Visibility="Collapsed" >
    <Grid Background="{ThemeResource
        ApplicationPageBackgroundThemeBrush}"
            Opacity="0.5" />
    <ProgressRing
        Width="100"
      Height="100"
      IsActive="True"
      IsEnabled="True"/>
</Grid>
```

This XAML is very simple. The only new thing is that we've used different styling for the Button elements on Android. This is to highlight the importance of each button.

3. In QuickReportControl.xaml.cs, let's add the code to handle what happens when the user clicks on the button to add a photo:

```
using Windows.Media.Capture;
using Windows.UI.Xaml.Media.Imaging;

Windows.Storage.StorageFile capturedPhoto;

private async void CaptureImageClicked(object sender,
RoutedEventArgs e)
{
    try
    {
```

```
            var captureUI = new CameraCaptureUI();
            capturedPhoto = await
                captureUI.CaptureFileAsync(
                    CameraCaptureUIMode.Photo);
            if (capturedPhoto == null)
            {
                return;
            }
            else
            {
                var source = new BitmapImage(new
                    Uri(capturedPhoto.Path));
                ImageToInclude.Source = source;
                TakePictureButton.Visibility =
                    Visibility.Collapsed;
            }
        }
        catch (Exception ex)
        {
            // Log the exception as appropriate
        }
    }
```

This code is simple: we create an instance of CameraCaptureUI and call
CaptureFileAsync to ask it to capture a photograph. When that returns
successfully (it isn't canceled by the user), we display the image on the screen
and store it in a field to send it to the server later.

4. We'll now create a method to encapsulate the logic to retrieve the device's location:

```
using Windows.Devices.Geolocation;
using System.Threading.Tasks;

private async Task<string> GetLocationAsync()
{
    try
    {
```

```
            var accessStatus = await
                Geolocator.RequestAccessAsync();
            switch (accessStatus)
            {
                case GeolocationAccessStatus.Allowed:
                    var geolocator = new Geolocator();
                    var pos = await
                        geolocator.GetGeopositionAsync();
                    return $"{pos.Coordinate.Latitude},
                        {pos.Coordinate.Longitude},
                            {pos.Coordinate.Altitude}";
                case GeolocationAccessStatus.Denied:
                    return "Location access denied";
                case GeolocationAccessStatus.Unspecified:
                    return "Location Error";
            }
        }
        catch (Exception ex)
        {
            // Log the exception as appropriate
        }
        return string.Empty;
}
```

5. The final step is to add the event handler for the **Send** button:

```
using System.Net.Http;
using System.IO;
using Windows.UI.Popups;


private async void SendClicked(object sender,
RoutedEventArgs e)
{
    var url = $"{ViewModels.DataService.WebApiDomain}/
        QuickReports/Create";
    BusyOverlay.Visibility = Visibility.Visible;
```

```
try
{
    var http = new HttpClient();
  var formContent =
      new MultipartFormDataContent();
  if (capturedPhoto != null)
  {
      var fileContent = new StreamContent(await
        capturedPhoto?.OpenStreamForReadAsync());
      formContent.Add(fileContent, "imageFile",
          "capturedFile");
  }
  formContent.Add(new StringContent(await
      GetLocationAsync()), "location");
  formContent.Add(new StringContent(
      EnteredText.Text), "information");
  var response = await http.PostAsync(new
      Uri(url), formContent);
  var serverResponse = await
      response.Content.ReadAsStringAsync();
  if (serverResponse == "success")
  {
      EnteredText.Text = string.Empty;
      capturedPhoto = null;
      ImageToInclude.Source = null;
      TakePictureButton.Visibility =
          Visibility.Visible;
      var msgDlg = new MessageDialog("Quick
          report submitted", "Thank you");
      await msgDlg.ShowAsync();
  }
  else
  {
```

```
            throw new HttpRequestException(
                "Unsuccessful upload");
        }
    }
    catch (Exception ex)
    {
        // Log or retry the request as appropriate.
        var msgDlg = new MessageDialog("Failed to
            upload quick report");
        await msgDlg.ShowAsync();
    }
    finally
    {
        BusyOverlay.Visibility = Visibility.Collapsed;
    }
}
```

This code shows a busy (Activity) indicator while uploading the image, location, and any entered text in the server. The same WebAPI we've been using throughout this chapter can receive such uploads and returns a message stating "success" when valid data is submitted. The app checks for this and displays an appropriate message to the user.

Note

You may think it will be more convenient to allow the user to speak to the app and record their voice. This is a sensible suggestion and something that could easily be added in the future. We're not including it here as most devices have built-in capabilities to use speech to text to enter details. It can be quicker and easier to use the existing functionality of a device rather than duplicating what's already there.

With this final piece of functionality now complete, our app is finished. You can see how it looks when run in the following figure:

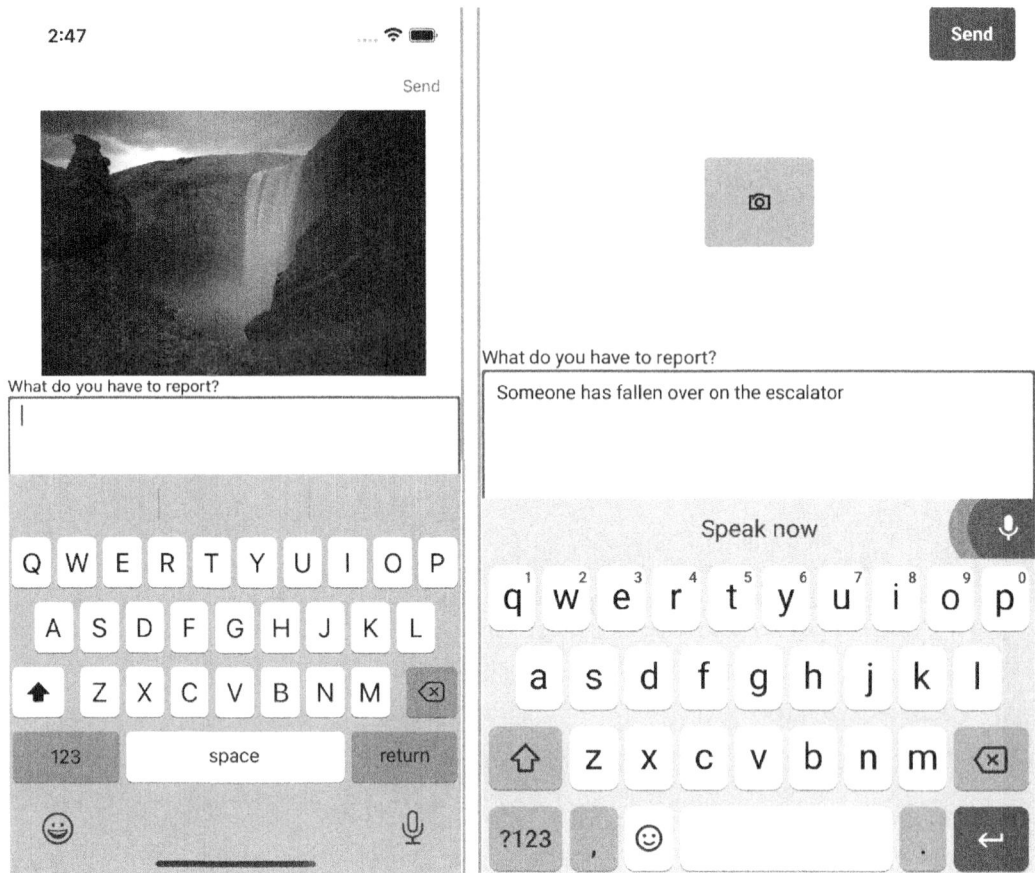

Figure 4.4 – The Quick Report screen running on an iPhone (left) and showing a selected image, and an Android device (right) showing the entry of some dictated text

Summary

In this chapter, we built an app that works on both iOS and Android devices. This allowed you to learn what it means to create "mobile" apps, work with remote data, apply native platform theming to apps, and use native device capabilities.

In the next chapter, we'll build another mobile app. This will be different from the ones we've made so far in that it is intended to be used by customers rather than the company's staff. Among other things, we'll use this app as an opportunity to look at accessibility, localization, and using an SQLite database.

5

Making Your App Ready for the Real World

In the last chapter, we covered writing your first mobile app using Uno Platform that was targeted toward employees of UnoBookRail. We will also write a mobile app in this chapter; however, we will focus on making it ready for customers. In this chapter, you will write an app that persists user preferences and larger sets of data on a device. In addition, you will also learn how to make your app more visually appealing to users with a custom app icon and how to write apps that can be used by people using assistive technology.

To do that, we'll cover the following topics in this chapter:

- Introducing the app
- Persisting data locally using the `ApplicationData` API and SQLite
- Making your app ready for customers
- Localizing your app
- Using a custom app icon and splash screen
- Making your app accessible for all users

By the end of this chapter, you'll have created a mobile app running on iOS and Android that is ready for customers and is also localized and accessible.

Technical requirements

This chapter assumes that you already have your development environment set up, including installing the project templates, as was covered in *Chapter 1, Introducing Uno Platform*. The source code for this chapter is at `https://github.com/ PacktPublishing/Creating-Cross-Platform-C-Sharp-Applications- with-Uno-Platform/tree/main/Chapter05`.

The code in this chapter makes use of the library from `https://github.com/ PacktPublishing/Creating-Cross-Platform-C-Sharp-Applications- with-Uno-Platform/tree/main/SharedLibrary`.

Check out the following video to see the code in action: `https://bit.ly/3AywuqQ`

Introducing the app

In this chapter, we will build the UnoBookRail DigitalTicket app, an app targeting UnoBookRail's customers that want to get from A to B using UnoBookRail. While the real version of this app would have a lot of features, in this chapter, we will only develop the following features:

- Booking tickets for journeys between two stations of the UnoBookRail network
- Viewing all booked tickets as well as QR codes for the ticket
- Localization of the app and letting users choose the language being used for the app

As part of this, we will also ensure that our app is accessible and allow more people of different levels of ability to use our app. Let's start now by creating the app and adding the first bit of content.

Creating the app

First of all, we need to set up the solution for our app:

1. Start by creating a new app using the **Multi-Platform App (Uno Platform)** template.
2. Name the project `DigitalTicket`. Of course, you can use a different name; however, in this chapter, we will assume the app is named DigitalTicket and uses the respective namespace.

3. Remove all platform heads except the **Android**, **iOS**, and **UWP** ones. Note that we also remove the WASM head even if there might be a benefit to providing this functionality on the web. While WASM works reasonably well on mobile devices, it is not ideal, and for simplicity, we will continue without the WASM version of the app.

4. Add the UnoBookRail shared library to the solution since we will need its functionality later. To do this, right-click on the solution file, select **Add | Existing Project…**, navigate to the `UnoBookRail.Common.csproj` file, and click **Open**.

5. Reference the shared library project in every head project. To do this, right-click on the head project, select **Add | Reference… | Projects**, check **UnoBookRail. Common**, and click **OK**. Since we need a reference to the library in every head, repeat this process for every head, that is, Android, iOS, and UWP.

Since our app will also follow the **Model-View-Viewmodel** (**MVVM**) pattern and we want to avoid having to write boilerplate code for this, we will also use the `Microsoft. Toolkit.MVVM` package, which you will also need to add a reference to:

1. Right-click the solution node in the solution view and select **Manage NuGet Packages for solution…**.

2. Search for `Microsoft.Toolkit.MVVM` and select the **NuGet** package.

3. Select the Android, iOS, and UWP heads in the project list and click **Install**.

Similar to the previous chapter, we will also need to modify our app to leave space for camera notches to avoid the content of our app being occluded:

1. For this, add the following namespace to the `MainPage.xaml` file: `xmlns:toolkit="using:Uno.UI.Toolkit"`.

2. After this, add `toolkit:VisibleBoundsPadding.PaddingMask="All"` to the grid inside our `MainPage.xaml` file.

Creating the main navigation and booking process

Since our app will contain different features, we will split up the functionality of our app into different pages that we will navigate to. Inside `MainPage`, we will have our navigation and the code related to that:

1. First, start by creating a views folder by right-clicking **DigitalTicket.Shared** and clicking **Add | New Folder**, naming it `Views`.

2. Now, add the following three pages inside the **Views** folder by right-clicking the folder, clicking **Add** | **New Item…**, and selecting **Blank Page**: `JourneyBookingPage.xaml`, `OwnedTicketsPage.xaml`, and `SettingsPage.xaml`.

3. Since we will need it later, create a `Utils` folder and add a `LocalizedResources` class to it with the following code:

```
public static class LocalizedResources
{
    public static string GetString(string key) {
        return key;
    }
}
```

For now, this class will just return the string so we can reference the class and not have to update the code later. Later in this chapter, though, we will update the implementation to return the localized version for the keys provided.

4. After that, create a `ViewModels` folder in your shared project and create a `NavigationViewModel` class.

5. Add the following to your `NavigationViewModel` class:

```
using DigitalTicket.Views;
using Microsoft.Toolkit.Mvvm.ComponentModel;
using Microsoft.UI.Xaml.Controls;
using System;
namespace DigitalTicket.ViewModels
{
    public class NavigationViewModel :
        ObservableObject
    {
        private Type pageType;
        public Type PageType
        {
            get
            {
                return pageType;
            }
            set
```

```
        {
            SetProperty(ref pageType, value);
        }
    }
    public void NavigationView_SelectionChanged(
        NavigationView navigationView,
            NavigationViewSelectionChangedEventArgs
              args)
    {
        if (args.IsSettingsSelected)
        {
            PageType = typeof(SettingsPage);
        }
        else
        {
            switch ((args.SelectedItem as
                NavigationViewItem).Tag.ToString())
            {
                case "JourneyPlanner":
                    PageType =
                        typeof(JourneyBookingPage);
                    break;
                case "OwnedTickets":
                    PageType =
                        typeof(OwnedTicketsPage);
                    break;
            }
        }
    }
}
```

This code will expose the type of page MainPage should navigate to and provide a selection changed listener to update that whenever the selection of the app's navigation changes. To determine the correct page type, we will use the Tag property of the selected item.

6.   Now, replace the content of `MainPage` with this:

```
...
xmlns:muxc="using:Microsoft.UI.Xaml.Controls">
<Grid toolkit:VisibleBoundsPadding.PaddingMask=
    "All">
    <muxc:NavigationView x:Name="AppNavigation"
        PaneDisplayMode="LeftMinimal"
        IsBackButtonVisible="Collapsed"
        Background="{ThemeResource
            ApplicationPageBackgroundThemeBrush}"
        SelectionChanged="{x:Bind
            navigationVM.NavigationView_
                SelectionChanged, Mode=OneTime}">
        <muxc:NavigationView.MenuItems>
            <muxc:NavigationViewItem
                x:Name="JourneyBookingItem"
                Content="Journey Booking"
                Tag="JourneyPlanner"/>
            <muxc:NavigationViewItem
                Content="Owned tickets"
                Tag="OwnedTickets"/>
            <muxc:NavigationViewItem Content="All
                day tickets - soon"
                Tag="AllDayTickets"
                IsEnabled="False"/>
            <muxc:NavigationViewItem
                Content="Network plan - soon"
                IsEnabled="False"/>
            <muxc:NavigationViewItem
                Content="Line overview - soon"
                IsEnabled="False"/>
        </muxc:NavigationView.MenuItems>
        <Frame x:Name="ContentFrame"
            Padding="0,40,0,0"/>
    </muxc:NavigationView>
</Grid>
```

This is the main navigation of our app. We use the `NavigationView` control for this, which allows us to easily have a side pane that can be opened using a hamburger button. Inside that, we provide the different navigation options and set the `Tag` property to be used by `NavigationViewModel`. Since we only allow the journey booking and the list of owned tickets in this chapter, we disable the other options for now.

7. Replace your `MainPage` class with the following:

```
using DigitalTicket.ViewModels;
using DigitalTicket.Views;
using System;
using Windows.UI.Xaml.Controls;
using Windows.UI.Xaml.Navigation;
namespace DigitalTicket
{
    public sealed partial class MainPage : Page
    {
        public NavigationViewModel navigationVM = new
            NavigationViewModel();
        public MainPage()
        {
            InitializeComponent();
            if (navigationVM.PageType is null)
            {
                AppNavigation.SelectedItem =
                    JourneyBookingItem;
                navigationVM.PageType =
                    typeof(JourneyBookingPage);
                navigationVM.PageTypeChanged +=
                    NavigationVM_PageTypeChanged;
            }
        }
        protected override void OnNavigatedTo(
            NavigationEventArgs e)
        {
            base.OnNavigatedTo(e);
            if (e.Parameter is Type navigateToType)
```

```
                {
                    if (navigateToType ==
                        typeof (SettingsPage))
                    {
                        AppNavigation.SelectedItem =
                            AppNavigation.SettingsItem;
                    }
                    navigationVM.PageType =
                        navigateToType;
                    ContentFrame.Navigate (navigateToType);
                }
            }
            private void NavigationVM_PageTypeChanged(
                object sender, EventArgs e)
            {
                ContentFrame.Navigate (
                    navigationVM.PageType);
            }
        }
    }
```

With this, MainPage will create the necessary view models once it is created and update the displayed content based on that. MainPage also listens to the OnNavigatedTo event to update the displayed item based on the arguments passed to it. Lastly, we also listen to the NavigationViewModels property changed event.

Note that we are overriding the OnNavigatedTo function to be able to allow navigating to MainPage and, within MainPage, to a specific page. While we don't need this right now, we will use this later. Let's continue by filling the journey booking page with some content:

1. Create the JourneyBookingOption class inside the ViewModels folder.

2. Add the following code to the JourneyBookingOption class:

```
using DigitalTicket.Utils;
using UnoBookRail.Common.Tickets;
namespace DigitalTicket.ViewModels
```

```
{
    public class JourneyBookingOption
    {
        public readonly string Title;
        public readonly string Price;
        public readonly PricingOption Option;
        public JourneyBookingOption(PricingOption
            option)
        {
            Title = LocalizedResources.GetString(
                option.OptionType.ToString() + "Label");
            Price = option.Price;
            Option = option;
        }
    }
}
```

Since this is a data object that will be used to display the options, it only contains properties. Since the title will be displayed inside the app and needs to be localized, we use the `LocalizedResources.GetString` function to determine the correct value.

3. Now create the `JourneyBookingViewModel` class inside the `ViewModels` folder and add the code as seen on GitHub (`https://github.com/ PacktPublishing/Creating-Cross-Platform-C-Sharp- Applications-with-Uno-Platform/blob/main/Chapter05/ DigitalTicket.Shared/ViewModels/JourneyBookingViewModel. cs`). Note that a few lines are commented out, and that's because we will need those lines later; however, right now we haven't added the necessary code yet.

4. Update `JourneyBookingPage.xaml.cs` and `JourneyBookingPage.xaml` so they are as seen on GitHub.

5. Copy the following entries into the `Strings.resw` file inside the `Strings/en` folder. Note that you don't have to copy the `Comments` column word by word, as it is only there to provide guidance and context for the other two columns:

Name	Value	Comments
BookTicketButton.Content	Book	Text of button at the bottom of the journey booking page to book a ticket
BookTicketDialogBookButton. Content	Book ticket	Text of button to confirm booking of a ticket
BookTicketDialogCancelButton. Content	Cancel	Text of button to cancel booking process
BookTicketDialogHeader.Text	Confirm ticket booking	Header text of book ticket dialog
BookTicketDialogInformation. Text	You are about to book the ticket listed below. Your account will be charged with the price listed below.	Explanation text for the book ticket dialog
EndPointLabel.Text	Destination	Label for destination station selection ComboBox
StartPointLabel.Text	Start	Label for start station selection ComboBox
TicketBookedInfoBar.Title	Ticket booked successfully!	Title of the book process confirmation InfoBar

As you might notice, some controls have the `x:Uid` property set, which is why the entries inside the `Strings.resw` file are needed. We will cover how these things work in the *Localizing your app* section; for now, we will only add the code and corresponding entries to our resources file. Now, if you start the app, you should be greeted by something as shown in *Figure 5.1*:

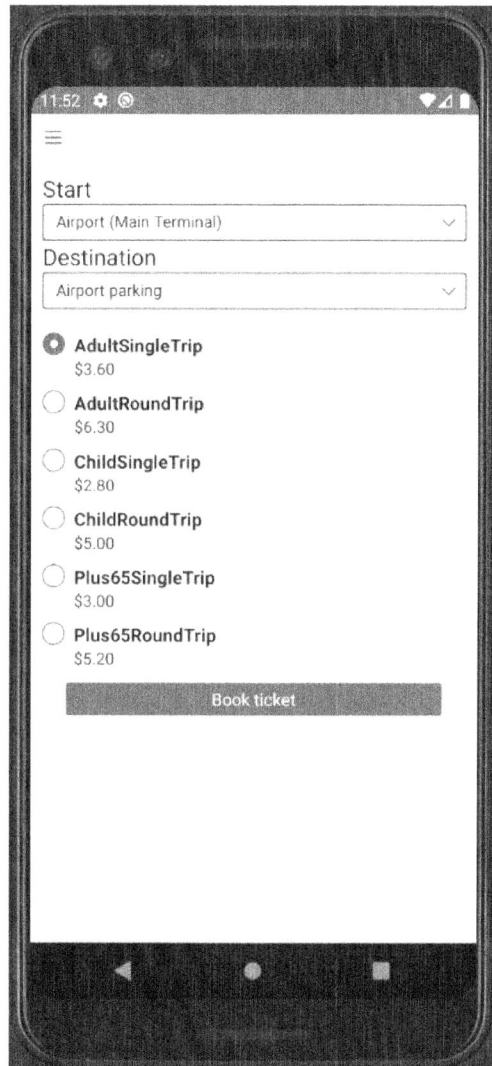

Figure 5.1 – Journey booking page on Android

Now your users are able to configure their journey, select the ticket, and book it, albeit with less-than-ideal ticket names. We will fix this in the *Localizing your app* section. For simplicity, we will not deal with the actual payment and assume that payment information is associated with the user's account.

In this section, we added the initial code and navigation of our app. We also added the journey booking page, even though it currently doesn't actually book the tickets, which we will change later. In the next section, we will cover how to persist data locally on the user's device using two different methods, the `ApplicationData` API and SQLite.

Persisting data locally using the ApplicationData API and SQLite

While in a lot of cases data can be fetched from the internet, as we have seen in *Chapter 4, Mobilizing Your App*, there is often a need to persist data on users' devices. This might be the case for data that needs to be available even when there is no internet connection or data that is device-specific such as settings. We will start by persisting small chunks of data using the ApplicationData API.

Storing data using the ApplicationData API

Since we will localize our app, we also want to give the users the possibility to choose the language of the app. To do this, first create a Models folder inside our shared project and add a SettingsStore class. Now, add the following code to the SettingsStore class:

```
using Windows.Storage;
public static class SettingsStore
{
    private const string AppLanguageKey =
        "Settings.AppLanguage";
    public static void StoreAppLanguageOption(string
        appTheme)
    {
        ApplicationData.Current.LocalSettings.Values[
            AppLanguageKey] = appTheme.ToString();
    }
    public static string GetAppLanguageOption()
    {
        if (ApplicationData.Current.LocalSettings.Values.
            Keys.Contains(AppLanguageKey))
        {
            return ApplicationData.Current.LocalSettings.
                Values[AppLanguageKey].ToString();
        }
        return "SystemDefault";
    }
}
```

To access the app's default local application storage, we use the `ApplicationData.Current.LocalSettings` object. The `ApplicationData` API also allows you to access different ways of storing data, for example, you can use it to access the app's local folder using `ApplicationData.Current.LocalFolder`. In our case, though, we will use `ApplicationData.Current.LocalSettings` to persist data. The `LocalSettings` object is an `ApplicationDataContainer` object, which you can use just like a dictionary. Note, though, that the `LocalSettings` object only supports simple data types such as strings and numbers. Now that we have added a way to store which language to display the app in, we will need to let users change the language:

1. First, create a new class named `SettingsViewModel` inside our `ViewModels` folder. You can find the code for this class here: `https://github.com/PacktPublishing/Creating-Cross-Platform-C-Sharp-Applications-with-Uno-Platform/blob/main/Chapter05/DigitalTicket.Shared/ViewModels/SettingsViewModel.cs`.

2. Now, we update our settings page to include the UI to change the app's language. To do this, replace the `Grid` element inside `SettingsPage.xaml` with the following:

```
<StackPanel Padding="10,0,10,10">
    <ComboBox x:Name="LanguagesComboBox"
        Header="Choose the app's language"
        SelectedIndex="{x:Bind
            settingsVM.SelectedLanguageIndex,
                Mode=TwoWay}"/>
</StackPanel>
```

3. In addition to this, we will also need to update `SettingsPage.xaml.cs`. Note that we will set the `ItemsSource` of `ComboBox` in code-behind to ensure that `ItemsSource` will be set after the `ComboBox` has been created and is ready so that the `ComboBox` will update correctly. To do this, add the following code:

```
using DigitalTicket.ViewModels;

...

private SettingsViewModel settingsVM = new
SettingsViewModel();
public SettingsPage()
{
    InitializeComponent();
    LanguagesComboBox.ItemsSource =
        settingsVM.LanguageOptions;
}
```

4. Finally, to ensure that the selected language will be respected on the app's start, add
    the following code inside the OnLaunched function of App.xaml.cs and add
    imports for DigitalTicket.Models and DigitalTicket.ViewModels:

```
ApplicationLanguages.PrimaryLanguageOverride =
SettingsViewModel.GetPrimaryLanguageOverrideFromLanguage(
SettingsStore.GetAppLanguageOption());
```

Now that we have added the language option, let's try it out. If you start the app now
and navigate to the settings page using the navigation on the left, you should see
something like on the left side of *Figure 5.2*. Now, if you select the **Deutsch** option
(German) and open the navigation, you will notice that the first item is now **Reise
buchen**, as shown on the right side of *Figure 5.2*. This is because SettingsViewModel
reloads MainPage and all other pages after setting the ApplicationLanguages.
PrimaryLanguageOverride property. We will talk more about this property in the
Localizing your app section and also update the app so that all text currently visible also
updates based on the language chosen:

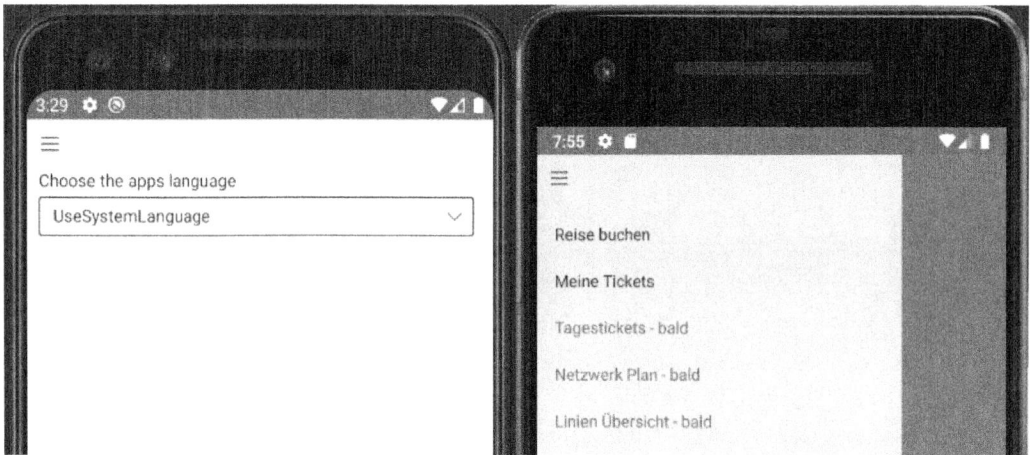

Figure 5.2 – Left: Settings page; Right: Navigation after switching language to German

Using SQLite to store data

While the `ApplicationData` API is good for storing small chunks of data, if you want to persist larger datasets of data, the `ApplicationData` API is not ideal since there are space limitations for the entries stored using the `ApplicationData.Current.LocalSettings` object. Namely, object keys can only be 255 characters in length and the entries can only be 8 kilobytes in size on UWP. Of course, this doesn't mean that you can't store larger or more complex datasets in your app. This is where **SQLite** comes in. Of course, SQLite is not the only way to store data; there are plenty of alternatives. For example, you could write your data to files and parse them yourself. In this chapter, however, we will use SQLite due to its ease of use and integration. There are different **C#** libraries available to include SQLite in your app and interact with SQLite databases. Since we want to store the SQLite database on mobile Android and iOS devices (and UWP), we will use the `sqlite-net-pcl` library as this library works on every platform supported by our app. `sqlite-net-pcl` includes a platform-independent implementation of SQLite and allows us to easily serialize objects into SQLite databases.

Let's start by adding a reference to `sqlite-net-pcl` to our app. To do this, right-click the solution in the solution view, click **Manage NuGet packages for Solution…**, and search for `sqlite-net-pcl`. Since at the time of writing this book the latest stable release is version **1.7.335**, select that version and select the Android, iOS, and UWP heads in the project list. Then, click **Install**. Now we need to add code to create, load, and write the SQLite database:

1. First of all, we need to add a class whose objects we want to persist using SQLite. For this, add a new class called `OwnedTicket` inside the `ViewModels` folder. You can find the source code for this class on GitHub here: `https://github.com/PacktPublishing/Creating-Cross-Platform-C-Sharp-Applications-with-Uno-Platform/blob/main/Chapter05/DigitalTicket.Shared/ViewModels/OwnedTicket.cs`.

   There are two important things to know:

   Since every SQLite table needs a primary key, we added the `DBId` property with the PrimaryKey and `AutoIncrement` attributes. Using these properties, we let `sqlite-net-pcl` manage the primary keys for us and we don't have to deal with this.

When passing objects to `sqlite-net-pcl` to persist them into a SQLite database, only properties will be persisted. Since we don't want to persist `ShowQRCodeCommand` (and actually can't), this is only a field, not a property.

2. Now create the `OwnedTicketsRepository` class inside the `Models` folder and add the following code to it:

```
using DigitalTicket.ViewModel;
using SQLite;
using System;
using System.IO;
using System.Threading.Tasks;
using Windows.Storage;
namespace DigitalTicket.Models
{
    public class OwnedTicketsRepository
    {
        const string DBFileName = "ownedTickets.db";
        private static SQLiteAsyncConnection database;
        public async static Task InitializeDatabase()
        {
            if(database != null)
            {
                return;
            }
            await ApplicationData.Current.LocalFolder.
                CreateFileAsync(DBFileName,
                CreationCollisionOption.OpenIfExists);
            string dbPath = Path.Combine(
                ApplicationData.Current.LocalFolder
                    .Path, DBFileName);
            database =
                new SQLiteAsyncConnection(dbPath);
            database.CreateTableAsync<
                OwnedTicket>().Wait();
        }
        public static Task<int> SaveTicketAsync(
            OwnedTicket ticket)
        {
```

```
        if (ticket.DBId != 0)
        {
            // Update an existing ticket.
            return database.UpdateAsync(ticket);
        }
        else
        {
            // Save a new ticket.
            return database.InsertAsync(ticket);
        }
    }
  }
}
```

The `InitializeDatabase` function handles creating the file for our SQLite database and creating the table if it does not exist, but also loads the existing database if the file already exists. Inside the `SaveTicketsAsync` function, we update and save the passed ticket to the database or update the ticket if it already existed in the database.

3. Update `App.xaml.cs` to include the following code at the start of the `OnLaunched` function and change the `OnLaunched` function to be async:

    ```
    await OwnedTicketsRepository.InitializeDatabase();
    ```

    This will initialize the SQLite connection when the app starts since creating the connection on demand is not ideal, especially when loading the owned tickets page.

4. Now update `JourneyBookingViewModel` to save the ticket to `OwnedTicketsRepository`. To do this, remove the current creation of `BookJourney` and uncomment the `using` statements at the top of the file and the code inside the `JourneyBookingViewModel` constructor.

Now let's talk about the steps we just did. First of all, we created our `OwnedTicket` object, which we will write to SQLite and also load from SQLite in the next section.

We then added `OwnedTicketsRepository`, which we use to interact with our SQLite database. Before any requests can be made to the SQLite database, we first need to initialize it, for which we will need a file to write the SQLite database into. Using the following code, we ensure that the file we want to write our database to exists:

```
await ApplicationData.Current.LocalFolder.
CreateFileAsync(DBFileName, CreationCollisionOption.
OpenIfExists);
```

After that, we create a `SQLiteAsyncConnection` object for our database. The `SQLiteAsyncConnection` object will handle all communication to SQLite, including creating tables and saving and loading data. Since we also need a table to write our data to, we use `SQLiteAsyncConnection` to create a table for our `OwnedTickets` objects if the table doesn't already exist within our SQLite database. To ensure that those steps will be done before any request to our database has been made, we call `OwnedTicketsRepository.InitializeDatabase()` inside our app constructor.

The last step was to update our `JourneyBookingViewModel` class to also persist data to the SQLite database. While we only add new items to our database, we still need to watch whether you are updating existing entries or adding a new entry, which is why the `SavedTicketAsync` function ensures we are only creating items if there is no ID present.

Loading data from SQLite

Now that we have covered how to persist data, of course, we also need to load the data; otherwise, we wouldn't need to persist the data in the first place. Let's change this by adding an overview of all the tickets booked by the user. Since UnoBookRail customers will need to present their tickets when boarding a train or when tickets are checked, we also want to be able to display a QR code for every ticket. Since we will use `ZXing.Net.Mobile` for this, please add that **NuGet** package to your solution now, namely the Android, iOS, and UWP heads. Note that at the time of writing, version **2.4.1** was the latest stable release and we will use that version for this chapter.

Before we want to display all tickets, we first need to load them from our SQLite database. To do this, add the following method to our `OwnedTicketsRepository` class:

```
using System.Collections.Generic;
...
static Task<List<OwnedTicket>> LoadTicketsAsync()
{
    //Get all tickets.
    return database.Table<OwnedTicket>().ToListAsync();
}
```

Thanks to `sqlite-net-pcl`, this is all we need to do. The library handles the rest for us, including reading the table and converting the rows into `OwnedTicket` objects.

Now that we can also load tickets, we can update the `OwnedTicketsPage` class we created at the beginning of this chapter to display all the tickets booked by the user. In our app, this means that we will only display the tickets that have been booked on this device. In a real app, we would also access the tickets from a remote server and download them to the device; however, we won't do this since it is out of scope for this chapter:

1. Before we update our owned tickets page, first add an `OwnedTicketsViewModel` class inside the `ViewModels` folder. The source code for the class is available here: `https://github.com/PacktPublishing/Creating-Cross-Platform-C-Sharp-Applications-with-Uno-Platform/blob/main/Chapter05/DigitalTicket.Shared/ViewModels/OwnedTicketsViewModel.cs`.

2. Now, update `OwnedTicketsPage.xaml` and `OwnedTicketsPage.xaml.cs`. You can find the source code for those two files on GitHub: `https://github.com/PacktPublishing/Creating-Cross-Platform-C-Sharp-Applications-with-Uno-Platform/tree/main/Chapter05/DigitalTicket.Shared/Views`.

Now, if you start the app and navigate to the owned tickets page, you should see an empty page. If you have already booked a ticket, you should see something like on the left side of *Figure 5.3*. If you click on the small, wide, gray box below the ticket, you should see something like on the right side of *Figure 5.3*:

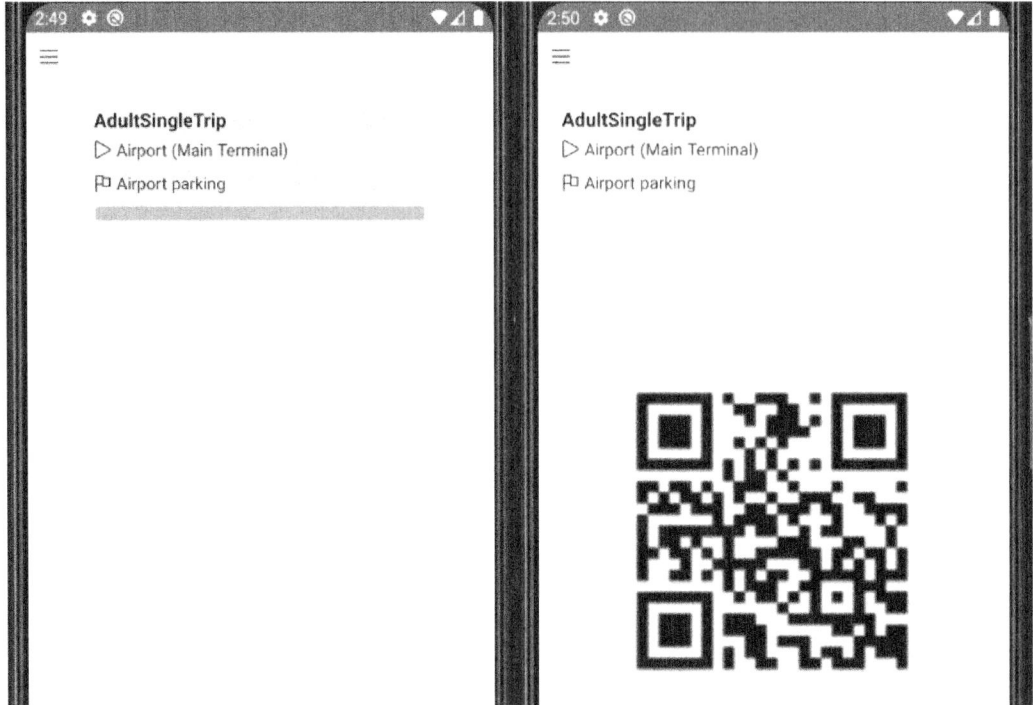

Figure 5.3 – Left: List of owned tickets with a single ticket; Right: Owned ticket and the QR code of the booked ticket

Of course, this is not the final UI yet; users should see text indicating that they haven't booked a ticket yet instead of a blank screen. Right now, though, it is expected that the text is missing and buttons don't have labels either since they are using x:Uid instead of having the Text or Content property set. In the next section, we will look at what x:Uid is and update our app so that all the labels are being displayed correctly.

Making your app ready for customers

In this section, we will update our app to be ready for our customers, including localization support to make the app easier to use for our customers. After adding localization support, we will update the icon and splash screen of our app so it is more easily recognizable for our users.

Localizing your app

If you are developing an app targeting customers, being able to provide translations for customers in their native tongue is very important, especially for apps that are targeted toward customers from different countries. In the previous section, we already added the x:Uid property and added entries to the Strings.resw file; however, there are also other ways to localize resources, which we will cover later. We will start localizing text with x:Uid.

Using x:Uid to localize your UI

Using x:Uid and resource files (.resw files) is the easiest way to localize your app, especially since adding new translations, for example, for a new language, is very easy. But how do you localize your app using x:Uid and .resw files?

The x:Uid property can be added to any elements of your XAML code. In addition to setting the x:Uid property on controls you would like to provide translations for, you also need to add those translations. This is where the .resw files come in. In a nutshell, resw files are XML documents that contain the necessary entries. The easiest way of thinking about them, though, is as a list of entries with three properties that is often represented as a table. Those properties (or columns) are as follows:

- **Name**: The name you can use to find the resource. This path will also be used to determine which property on which control to set.

- **Value**: The text being set or the text being returned when looking up this resource.

- **Comment**: You can use this column to provide comments explaining the row. This is especially useful when translating the app into a new language since you can use the comment to find out what the best translation would be. See the **Comment** column in *Figure 5.4* for how they might be used.

When opening a .resw file in Visual Studio, the representation will look as in *Figure 5.4*:

Name	Value	Comment
BookTicketButton.Content	Book ticket	Text of button at the bottom of the journey
BookTicketDialogBookButton.Content	Book ticket	Text of button to confirm booking of a ticket
BookTicketDialogCancelButton.Content	Cancel	Text of button to cancel booking process
BookTicketDialogHeader.Text	Confirm ticket booking	Header text of book ticket dialog
BookTicketDialogInformation.Text	You are about to book the ticket listed	Explanation text for the book ticket dialog
EndPointLabel.Text	Destination	Label for destination-station selection ComboBox
StartPointLabel.Text	Start	Label for start-station selection ComboBox
TicketBookedInfoBar.Title	Ticket booked successfully!	Title of the book process confirmation InfoBar

Figure 5.4 – View of the .resw file in Visual Studio

When using the x:Uid property in combination with .resw files, you need to watch how you write the name entries for the resources. The name entry needs to start with the x:Uid value of the control followed by a dot (.) and the name of the property that should be set. So, in the preceding example, if we wanted to localize the text of the TextBlock element, we would add an entry with the name value being ButtonTextBlock.Text since we want to set the Text property of the TextBlock element.

"But how does localization work with this?" you might ask. After all, we have only added a single entry; how would it know which language to pick? This is why the folder in which you place your .resw files is important. Inside your project, you need to have a Strings folder. In that folder, for every language you want to localize your app to, you need to have a folder with the **IETF BCP 47 tag** of the language. So, for example, for *British English*, you would create a folder named en-GB while for *German (Germany)*, you would create a folder called de-DE. Inside the folders that you create for every language you want to support, you need to place your .resw files for the localization to work properly. Note that if a certain language is not available, the resource lookup will try to find the next best match. You can learn more about this procedure here since your Uno Platform app will behave the same on every platform: https://docs.microsoft.com/windows/uwp/app-resources/how-rms-matches-lang-tags.

Important note

Be careful how you name those folders. The resource lookup will be done based on the folder's name. If the folder's name has a typo or does not adhere to the IETF BCP 47 standard, the resource lookup might fail and your users will be greeted with missing labels and texts or a mix of languages as resource lookup will fall back to languages where the texts have been translated.

We already have a folder for the English text resources; however, we also want to support German translations. To do this, create a new folder inside the Strings folder named de-DE. Now, add a new .resw file with the name Resources.resw and add the following entries:

Name	Value
BookTicketButton.Content	Ticket kaufen
BookTicketDialogBookButton.Content	Ticket kaufen
BookTicketDialogCancelButton.Content	Abbrechen
BookTicketDialogHeader.Text	Bestätige Ticketkauf
BookTicketDialogInformation.Text	Du bist im Begriff dieses Ticket zu kaufen. Dein Account wird mit dem unten gelisteten Betrag belastet.
EndPointLabel.Text	Ziel Haltestelle
StartPointLabel.Text	Start Haltestelle
TicketBookedInfoBar.Title	Ticket erfolgreich gekauft!

If you start the app now and switch to German as the app's language, you will see that the journey booking page is now localized. If your device's language was already set to German, instead of showing the page in English, it should now be displayed in German, even if you don't switch to the German option now.

Accessing resources from code-behind

Using x:Uid is not the only way to localize your app, though; we will now see how you can access a resource from code-behind. This is useful, for example, when you want to localize the items in a collection, for example, the list of owned tickets in our app. To access string resources, you can use the ResourceLoader class. We added the LocalizedResources class at the start of the chapter; however, until now, it hasn't accessed any resources. Update LocalizedResources now by adding the following import and replacing the GetString function with the following code:

```
using Windows.ApplicationModel.Resources;
...
private static ResourceLoader cachedResourceLoader;
public static string GetString(string name)
{
    if (cachedResourceLoader == null)
    {
        cachedResourceLoader =
            ResourceLoader.GetForViewIndependentUse();
    }
```

```
    if (cachedResourceLoader != null)
    {
        return cachedResourceLoader.GetString(name);
    }
    return null;
}
```

Since we will be using the loaded resource often, we are caching the value to avoid having to call `GetForViewIndependentUse` as it is expensive.

Now that we have covered how `x:Uid` works and how you can access localized resources from code-behind, let's update the rest of our app to be localized. Start by adding the necessary entries to our `.resw` files. The following is the table of entries you need for the `MainPage.xaml` file and their English and German entries:

Name	Value for English resources	Value for German resources
JourneyBookingItem.Content	Journey booking	Reise buchen
OwnedTicketsItem.Content	Owned tickets	Meine Tickets
AllDayTicketsItem.Content	All-day tickets – soon	Tagestickets – bald
NetworkPlanItem.Content	Network plan – soon	Netzwerk Plan – bald
LineOverViewItemItem.Content	Line overview – soon	Linien Übersicht – bald

Now, replace the `NavigationViewItems` property inside the `MainPage.xaml` file with the following:

```
<muxc:NavigationViewItem x:Name="JourneyBookingItem"
x:Uid="JourneyBookingItem" Tag="JourneyPlanner"/>

<muxc:NavigationViewItem x:Uid="OwnedTicketsItem"
Tag="OwnedTickets"/>

<muxc:NavigationViewItem x:Uid="AllDayTicketsItem"
Tag="AllDayTickets" IsEnabled="False"/>

<muxc:NavigationViewItem x:Uid="NetworkPlanItem"
IsEnabled="False"/>

<muxc:NavigationViewItem x:Uid="LineOverViewItemItem"
IsEnabled="False"/>
```

To update the rest of the app to be localized, please view the source code on GitHub. You can also find the updated `Resources.resw` files for English and German there. Note that we chose to not localize the station names as localizing street and place names might lead to confusion for customers.

> **Important note**
>
> You can also localize other resources such as images or audio files. To do that, you need to put them inside correctly named folders. For example, if you want to localize an image called `Recipe.png`, you need to put the localized version of the image for a language inside the `Assets/[language identifier]` folder, where `language identifier` is the IETF BCP 47 identifier of the language the image is for. You can learn more about customizing and localizing resources here: `https://docs.microsoft.com/windows/uwp/app-resources/images-tailored-for-scale-theme-contrast`.

In this section, we covered how to localize your app using `x:Uid` and resources file. As your app becomes larger and more languages are provided, using the multilingual app toolkit might be helpful. It allows you to check more easily which language keys are not translated and integrates into Visual Studio. You can learn more about this here: `https://developer.microsoft.com/en-us/windows/downloads/multilingual-app-toolkit/`.

Customizing your app's appearance

When publishing an app to the store, you want your app to be recognizable to users and convey your brand. However, so far, all the apps we developed have used the standard Uno Platform app icon. Luckily, Uno Platform allows us to change our app's icon and lets us set the splash image for our app.

Updating your app's icon

One of the most important things to make your app recognizable by users is having an icon for your app. Updating the icon for your app is easy. You can find the image we will use here: `https://github.com/PacktPublishing/Creating-Cross-Platform-C-Sharp-Applications-with-Uno-Platform/blob/main/Chapter05/DigitalTicket.Shared/Assets/AppIcon.png`.

Updating the Android app's icon

To update the app icon for the Android app, you just need to replace the `Icon.png` file inside the drawable folder of the Android project with your desired app logo. Note that you also need to select the correct image in the project properties. For this, double-click the **Properties** node inside the Android project. Inside the Android Manifest section, from the **Application icon** dropdown, select the icon you desire; for example, if you named your icon `Appicon`, you would select the **@drawable/Appicon** option. Alternatively, you can update the `android:icon` entry in the `AndroidManifest.xml` file inside the **Properties** node.

Updating the iOS app's icon

Updating the icon of our iOS app requires a bit more work. For the iOS app, you will need your app's icon in different sizes depending on the device the app is installed on. To see the list of dimensions and to update the app icon of the iOS app, simply expand the **Assets Catalog** node of the iOS project and double-click on the **Media** entry inside there. Inside the **AppIcons** tab, you select the images for the different devices and categories, and dimensions. It is not required to provide an image for every single dimension; however, you should provide at least one icon for every category.

Updating the icon of the UWP app

The easiest way to update the app icon of the UWP head is using the **Visual Assets** tab of the `Package.appxmanifest` file. For this, double-click `Package.appxmanifest` and select the **App icon** option inside the **Visual Assets** tab. To update the app's icon, choose the source image, select the destination folder, and click **Generate**. This will generate the app's icon in different sizes and as such, update your app's icon to the image specified.

Updating the icon of the other projects

While our app won't be available on other platforms and we removed the heads for the respective platforms, you might want to update the icon for the other platforms in other projects:

- **macOS**: Replace the images inside the `Assets/xcassets/AppIcon.appiconset` folder. If you rename the images, be sure to also update the `Contents.json` file.

- **Skia-based projects**: Right-click the project in Visual Studio and select **Properties**. Inside the **Application** tab, you can select a new icon using the **Browse** button in the **Resources** section.

- **WASM**: To update the icon being displayed in a browser, add your icon as `favicon.ico` inside the project's **Assets** folder.

Customizing your app's splash screen

Updating your app's icon is not the only way to make your app more recognizable. In addition to the app's icon, you can also customize the splash screen of your app. Note that at the time of writing this, only Android, iOS, UWP, and WASM apps support setting a splash screen. As with the icon, you can find the image resources for this on GitHub.

Updating the Android splash screen

To add a splash screen to the Android app, you will first need to add your splash screen image. In our case, we will name it `SplashScreen.png`. After this, add the following entry to the `Resource/values/Styles.xml` file:

```
<item name="android:windowBackground">@drawable/splash</item>
```

Then, you need to add the `splash.xml` file inside `Resources/drawable` and add the following code:

```xml
<?xml version="1.0" encoding="utf-8"?>
    <layer-list xmlns:android=
        "http://schemas.android.com/apk/res/android">
    <item>
        <!-- background color -->
        <color android:color="#008cff"/>
    </item>
    <item>
    <!-- splash image -->
        <bitmap android:src="@drawable/splashscreen"
                android:tileMode="disabled"
                android:gravity="center" />
    </item>
</layer-list>
```

Updating the iOS app's splash screen

As with any iOS app, the launch screen needs to be a storyboard. Uno Platform makes it easy to have a single image displayed as a launch screen. All it takes are these simple steps:

1. In Solution Explorer, select the iOS project and press the **Show All Files** button.

2. You'll now be able to see a file called **LaunchScreeen.storyboard**. Right-click on this and select **Include In Project**. This will now automatically be used when you launch the app.

If you run the app, you'll see the Uno Platform logo displayed when you launch the app. You can easily change this by replacing the images.

3. In the **Resources** folder, you'll find files named `SplashScreen@2x.png` and `SplashScreen@3x.png`. These are the files used by the storyboard. Replace their contents with the images you want.

4. To change the color used for the background, you can open the storyboard in the Xcode Interface Builder and change the color. Alternatively, you can open the storyboard file in an XML editor and change the `red`, `green`, and `blue` properties of the color with the `backgroundColor` key.

It's possible to use a storyboard file with any content you wish as your launch screen. To do this, you will need to use the Xcode Interface Builder. Prior to version **16.9**, Visual Studio included an iOS storyboard editor but this is no longer available. To edit a storyboard now, you need to open the project in Visual Studio for Mac, right-click on the file, and select **Open With | Xcode interface Builder**.

Updating the UWP app's splash screen

Similar to updating the app icon of your UWP app, use the `Package.appxmanifest` file and the **Visual Assets** tab. Select the **Splash Screen** tab and select the image you want to use for your splash screen. After this, uncheck **Apply recommended padding** and set **Splash screen background** to the background color you would like to use. In our case, this will be `#008CFF`. Now, click **Generate** to generate the splash screen images for the UWP app.

Updating the splash screen of the WASM app

To update the splash screen of your WASM head, add your new splash screen image inside the WASM project's **Assets** folder. After that, you only need to update the `AppManifest.js` file inside the `WasmScripts` folder to reference that image and update the splash screen color if necessary.

If you have followed the steps for our app successfully, you should be able to see the app in the app list on Android as seen on the left side of *Figure 5.5*. Once you start the app, your app should look as on the right side of *Figure 5.5* before showing the journey booking page. Note that the icon and splash screen provided are just examples here. In a real app, you would ensure that your app's icon looks good even this small:

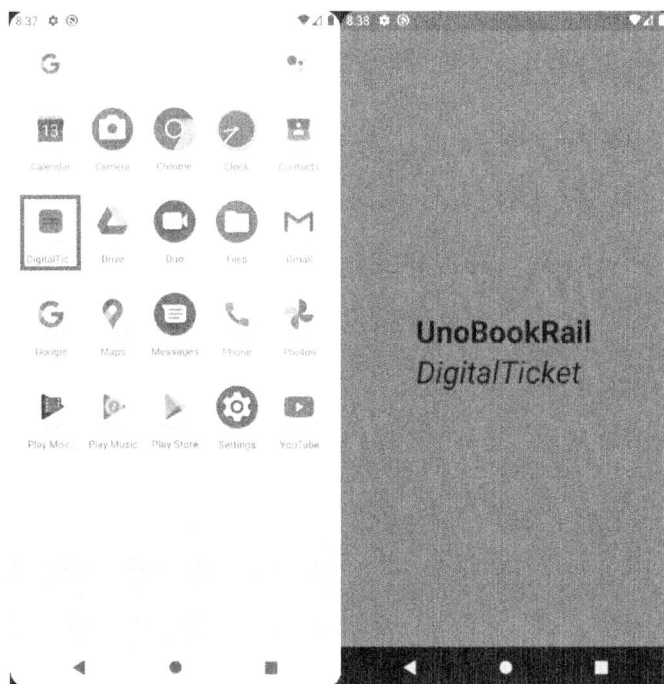

Figure 5.5 – Left: DigitalTicket in the list of apps; Right: Splash screen of DigitalTicket

Ensuring everyone can use your app

To make sure everyone can use your app, you need to make it accessible. Accessibility is key when developing apps. People with all levels of ability will use your app; your app not being accessible will make the life of your customers harder or might even make it impossible for them to use your app.

When thinking about accessibility, what comes to mind to most people is making your app accessible for blind people by adding labels and alt text for screen readers. However, accessibility is about so much more. For example, someone who has low vision but is not blind might not use a screen reader but instead might choose to use the high-contrast theme to make apps easier to use or might choose to increase the font size to make the text easier to read. Providing a dark theme is often seen as a purely aesthetic aspect; however, it is also important with regard to accessibility. Some people might be able to read text better while people with certain disabilities will have a harder time using your app.

If you are already familiar with the APIs available in UWP to make your app, there are a few things that are different when making your Uno Platform accessible. Since your app will run on different platforms and those platforms all have different APIs to provide accessible apps, Uno Platform only has a subset of properties available with regard to accessibility. At the time of writing, only the following properties are supported and work on every platform:

- `AutomationProperties.AutomationId`: You can set this property to allow easier navigation to controls with assistive technology.

- `AutomationProperties.Name`: Assistive technology will use this property to announce controls to users.

- `AutomationProperties.LabeledBy`: When setting this property, the control you are setting this on will be announced using the control specified by this property.

- `AutomationProperties.AccessibilityView`: Using this property, you can indicate that a control should not be read out to users by assistive technology or that you want to include controls that would commonly not be announced.

In addition to the properties listed previously, Uno Platform also supports the high-contrast theme on every platform. Since we are using the standard controls provided by Uno Platform, we won't need to watch out for this as Uno Platform already provides the right high-contrast look for our app. However, if you write your own controls, you should also check the high-contrast version of your app to ensure it is acceptable.

> **Important note**
> You should always localize the resources that will be used by assistive technology. Not doing this will potentially make your app inaccessible since users might encounter a language barrier, especially if assistive technology expects to read out words from a language and finds words from a different one.

To be able to ensure your app is accessible to people using assistive technology, you need to test your app using assistive technology. In the following section, you can find instructions to start a platform's default screen reader.

Starting the screen reader on different platforms

Since the steps to activate a system's assistive technology vary depending on the platform, we will go through them one by one, starting with Android.

TalkBack on Android

Launch the **Settings** app and open the **Accessibility** page. Press **TalkBack** and tap on the switch to enable TalkBack. Finally, press **OK** to close the dialog.

VoiceOver on iOS

Open the **Settings** app and open the **Accessibility** options under **General**. Then, tap on **VoiceOver** in the **Vision** category and tap on the switch to enable it.

VoiceOver on macOS

Launch **System Preferences** and click on **Accessibility**. Then, click on **VoiceOver** in the **Vision** category. Check **Enable VoiceOver** to use **VoiceOver**.

Narrator on Windows (for UWP and WASM)

To start the **Narrator** screen reader on Windows, you just need to press the Windows logo key, *Ctrl*, and *Enter* at the same time.

Updating our app to be accessible

In this chapter, we haven't ensured that our app is accessible. While a lot of controls are already accessible on their own, for example, the button control that will announce its content, there are still controls that we need to improve accessibility-wise. If a user were to use the app with assistive technology, not everything will be announced in a meaningful manner. Let's change this now by updating our app's UI to have all the necessary properties set. To do this, we will first update our journey booking page.

Both `ComboBox` control on our journey booking page currently will just be announced as `ComboBox` control, and as such, users with assistive technology have no idea what the `ComboBox` control is actually for. Since we have already added `TextBlock` element that describes their purpose, we will update them to use the `AutomationProperties.LabeledBy` property:

```
<TextBlock x:Name="StartPointLabel" x:Uid="StartPointLabel"
FontSize="20"/>
<ComboBox ItemsSource="{x:Bind journeyBookingVM.AllStations}"
x:Uid="StartPointComboBox"
    AutomationProperties.LabeledBy="{x:Bind
        StartPointLabel}"
SelectedItem="{x:Bind
        journeyBookingVM.SelectedStartpoint,Mode=TwoWay}"
    HorizontalAlignment="Stretch"
```

```
                DisplayMemberPath="Name"/>
<TextBlock x:Name="EndPointLabel" x:Uid="EndPointLabel"
FontSize="20"/>
<ComboBox ItemsSource="{x:Bind journeyBookingVM.
AvailableDestinations, Mode=OneWay}" x:Uid="EndPointComboBox"
    AutomationProperties.LabeledBy="{x:Bind EndPointLabel}"
    SelectedItem="{x:Bind
        journeyBookingVM.SelectedEndpoint,Mode=TwoWay}"
    HorizontalAlignment="Stretch"
    DisplayMemberPath="Name"/>
```

Now, when a user navigates to the ComboBox control using assistive technology, the ComboBox control will be announced using the text of the TextBlock element referenced by AutomationProperties.LabeledBy. Since the rest of the controls on that page are already taking care of accessibility for us, let's move on to the owned tickets page.

On the owned tickets page, there are two potential problems:

- The icons beside the station names will be announced as a blank icon.

- The QR code will only be announced as an image.

Since the icons are only for visual representation, we indicated to assistive technologies that the icons should not be announced using the AutomationProperties. AccessibilityView property and setting it to Raw. If you want to include a control for assistive technologies, you can set that property to Content.

To ensure that the QR code image will be announced in a meaningful way, we will add a descriptive name to it. For simplicity, we will just announce that it is the QR for the currently selected ticket. First, you need to update the image element as follows:

```
<Image x:Name="QRCodeDisplay" x:Uid="QRCodeDisplay"
    Source="{x:Bind ownedTicketsVM.CurrentQRCode,
            Mode=OneWay}"
    Grid.Row="4" MaxWidth="300" MaxHeight="300"
        Grid.ColumnSpan="2"/>
```

After this, add the following entries to the Resources.resw files:

English:

QRCodeDisplay.AutomationProperties.Name	QR Code of the currently selected ticket

German:

QRCodeDisplay.AutomationProperties.Name	QR Code des momentanen ausgewählten Tickets

By adding these entries, we have now provided a descriptive name for the QR code being displayed while also ensuring that this text will be localized.

Lastly, we also need to update the settings page. Since it only contains a single `ComboBox` control, which is missing a name, add the following entries to the `Resources.resw` files:

English:

LanguageOptionComboBox.AutomationProperties.Name	Select app language

German:

LanguageOptionComboBox.AutomationProperties.Name	Wähle Sprache der App

In this section, we briefly covered accessibility in Uno Platform; however, there are also certain limitations and things to watch out for that we did not mention. You can read more about these limitations in the official documentation: `https://platform.uno/docs/articles/features/working-with-accessibility.html`. If you wish to learn more about accessibility in general, you can take a look at the following resources:

- `https://docs.microsoft.com/en-us/learn/paths/accessibility-fundamentals/`
- `https://developer.mozilla.org/en-US/docs/Learn/Accessibility/What_is_accessibility`
- `https://developers.google.com/web/fundamentals/accessibility`

Summary

In this chapter, we built a customer-facing app that runs on iOS and Android. We covered how to store data using SQLite, how to make your app accessible, and making it ready for customers. As part of this, we covered how to localize your app, letting users choose the language of the app, and providing a custom splash screen for your app.

In the next chapter, we will write an information dashboard for UnoBookRail. The app will be targeted at employees of UnoBookRail and run on desktop and the web.

6
Displaying Data in Charts and with Custom 2D Graphics

This chapter will look at apps that need to show graphs, reports, and complex graphics. It's common for apps to include some sort of graph or chart. It's also becoming increasingly common to include elements in the UI that can't easily be made with standard controls.

As we progress through this chapter, we'll build a dashboard app for our fictional business that will display information appropriate to different parts of the business. Such apps are common as part of management reporting tools. You can imagine the different screens being displayed on monitors mounted on the walls in each department. This enables staff to instantly see what's going on in their part of the business.

In this chapter, we'll cover the following topics:

- Displaying graphs and charts
- Creating custom graphics with SkiaSharp
- Having the UI layout respond to changes in the screen size

By the end of this chapter, you'll have created a dashboard app that shows financial, operational, and network information that runs on UWP and the web. It will also adjust to different screen proportions, so the contents of each page account for different screen sizes and aspect ratios.

Technical requirements

This chapter assumes that you already have your development environment set up, including installing the project templates, as was covered in *Chapter 1, Introducing Uno Platform*. The source code for this chapter is at `https://github.com/PacktPublishing/Creating-Cross-Platform-C-Sharp-Applications-with-Uno-Platform/tree/main/Chapter06`.

The code in this chapter makes use of the library from `https://github.com/PacktPublishing/Creating-Cross-Platform-C-Sharp-Applications-with-Uno-Platform/tree/main/SharedLibrary`.

Check out the following video to see the code in action: `https://bit.ly/3iDchtK`

Introducing the app

The app we'll build in this chapter is called **Dashboard**. It's an application that displays the current activity within the business divided by department. This isn't something that would be available to all staff, but to allow us to focus on the features and areas of interest in this chapter, we'll not concern ourselves with how access is controlled. The real version of this app would have many features, but we're going to only implement three:

- Displaying current financial information
- Displaying live operational information
- Showing where the trains currently are in the network

As this application will be used by staff members in their offices, it will be available on desktop (via UWP) and in a web browser (with a WASM version).

Creating the app

We'll start by creating the solution for the app:

1. In Visual Studio, create a new project with the **Multi-Platform App (Uno Platform)** template.

2. Give the project the name `Dashboard`. You can use a different name, but you'll need to adjust all subsequent code snippets accordingly.

3. Remove all the platform head projects *except* for the **UWP** and **WASM** ones.

4. To avoid the need to write more code than necessary, we'll now add a reference to the shared library project. Right-click on the solution node in **Solution Explorer** and select **Add | Existing Project…**, navigate to the `UnoBookRail.Common.csproj` file, and click **Open**.

5. For each platform-specific project, we need to add a reference to the common library project. Right-click on the **UWP** project node in **Solution Explorer** and select **Add | Reference… | Projects**, then check the entry for `UnoBookRail.Common` and click **OK**. Now *repeat this process for the WASM project*.

With the basic solution structure now ready, we can add some functionality to the main page.

Creating the individual pages

We'll use a separate page for each area of functionality we're going to show:

1. Create a new folder in the **Shared** project called `Views`.

2. In the `Views` folder, add *three* new pages named `FinancePage.xaml`, `OperationsPage.xaml`, and `NetworkPage.xaml`.

We'll now update the main page to be able to navigate between these new pages.

Creating the main page

The app already contains the file `MainPage.xaml`, and we'll use it as the container for the ability to navigate between the other pages:

1. Replace the grid in `MainPage.xaml` with the following `NavigationView` control that contains options for each of the separate pages we'll implement:

```
<NavigationView
    PaneDisplayMode="Top"
    SelectionChanged="NavItemSelected"
    IsBackEnabled="{Binding Path=CanGoBack,
                    ElementName=InnerFrame}"
    BackRequested="NavBackRequested"
    IsSettingsVisible="False">
    <NavigationView.MenuItems>
```

```
        <NavigationViewItem Content="Finance" />
        <NavigationViewItem Content="Operations" />
        <NavigationViewItem Content="Network" />
    </NavigationView.MenuItems>
    <Frame x:Name="InnerFrame" />
</NavigationView>
```

2. We now need to add the handler for the `NavItemSelected` event mentioned previously to do the actual navigation between pages. Add the following to `MainPage.xaml.cs`:

```
using Dashboard.Views;

private void NavItemSelected(NavigationView sender,
NavigationViewSelectionChangedEventArgs args)
{
    var item = (args.SelectedItem as
               NavigationViewItem).Content.ToString();

    Type page = null;

    switch (item) {
      case "Finance":
        page = typeof(FinancePage);
        break;
      case "Operations":
        page = typeof(OperationsPage);
        break;
      case "Network":
        page = typeof(NetworkPage);
        break;
    }

    if (page != null && InnerFrame.CurrentSourcePageType
        != page) {
      InnerFrame.Navigate(page);
    }
}
```

3. We also need to implement the `NavBackRequested` method to handle the user pressing the back button to navigate back through the pages. Add the following to do this:

```
private void NavBackRequested(object sender,
NavigationViewBackRequestedEventArgs e)
{
    InnerFrame.GoBack();
}
```

> **Navigation**
>
> This app uses a custom-defined frame and a stack-based navigation style. This allows the user to press the built-in back button to return to a previous page. While this may not be considered the most appropriate for this app, it is one of the most popular ways that developers implement navigation within a UWP app. For this reason, we thought it appropriate to include this in this book and show it can be incorporated into an Uno Platform app.

4. The preceding will allow us to navigate between the pages when an item is selected from the menu, but we also want a page to be shown when the app is first opened. To do this, add the following call at the *end* of the `MainPage` constructor:

```
InnerFrame.Navigate(typeof(FinancePage));
```

> **Important note**
>
> The code in this section shows the simplest way to enable navigation between pages in a `NavigationView` control. This is certainly not the only way to do this or a recommendation that it should always be done this way.

With all the basics in place, we're now ready to add a graph to the finance page.

Displaying charts with controls from SyncFusion

SyncFusion is a company that makes UI components for web, desktop, and mobile development. Their Uno Platform controls are in the beta state at the time of writing and are free to use during this preview period via their community license (`https://www.syncfusion.com/products/communitylicense`). Many different chart types are available, but we'll use a line chart to create a page like the one shown in *Figure 6.1*. The chart is displayed along with some arrows that provide some general trend data so that the person viewing them has an at-a-glance summary of the data. Imagine them representing how the data compares to the same day in the previous week, month, and year:

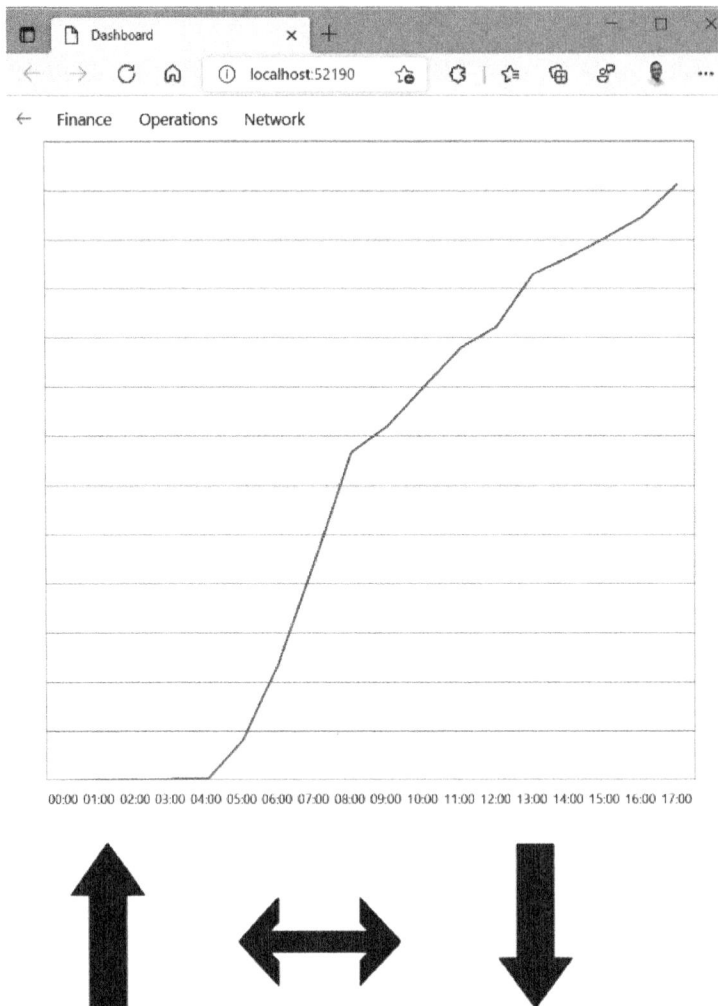

Figure 6.1 – Finance information including a graph from SyncFusion

Updating references to include the SyncFusion controls

The beta version of the SyncFusion Uno chart controls is available with the full source code on GitHub:

1. Download or clone the code from `https://github.com/syncfusion/Uno.SfChart`.

2. Add the **Syncfusion.SfChart.Uno.csproj** project to the solution by right-clicking on the solution and selecting **Add | Existing Project…**.

3. Update the **Syncfusion.SfChart.Uno** project to use the latest version of the **Uno.UI** package. This is to avoid any issues from trying to use different versions of the library in different projects within the solution.

4. Reference the **Syncfusion.SfChart.Uno** project from the *UWP* and *WASM* projects.

We're now ready to use the controls in the app.

> **Important note**
>
> As the SyncFusion controls are only available from the source, while not expected, they may have changed when you read this. Hopefully, compiled versions of the controls are available, but if you need to get to a state comparable to when this was written, use commit **43cd434**.

Drawing a line chart

We can draw a simple line chart by following these steps:

1. Start by adding this namespace to `FinancePage.xaml`:

    ```
    xmlns:sf="using:Syncfusion.UI.Xaml.Charts"
    ```

2. Now replace the grid with the following:

    ```
    <RelativePanel HorizontalAlignment="Center">
      <sf:SfChart
          x:Name="MainChart"
          MaxWidth="600"
          MaxHeight="600">
        <sf:SfChart.PrimaryAxis>
          <sf:CategoryAxis LabelPlacement="BetweenTicks"
              ShowGridLines="False" />
    ```

```
    </sf:SfChart.PrimaryAxis>
    <sf:SfChart.SecondaryAxis>
      <sf:NumericalAxis ShowGridLines="True"
          Visibility="Collapsed" />
    </sf:SfChart.SecondaryAxis>
    <sf:LineSeries
        ItemsSource="{x:Bind DailySales}"
        XBindingPath="Hour"
        YBindingPath="TotalSales" />
  </sf:SfChart>
  <TextBlock
      x:Name="SecondaryItem"
      FontSize="200"
      FontWeight="Black"
      RelativePanel.Below="MainChart"
      RelativePanel.AlignHorizontalCenterWithPanel=
          "True"
      Text="{x:Bind TrendArrows}" />
</RelativePanel>
```

This is the simplest `SfChart` class we can specify. We define a `PrimaryAxis` class (for the X-axis), which reflects the hours of the day, with a `SecondaryAxis` class (for the Y-axis) representing the numeric values and a set of data as a `LineSeries` class.

We also specify a `TextBlock` element to appear below the chart but be horizontally aligned. This will display arrows indicating trend information relating to the graph.

3. To provide the data, we need to add the following to the class in `FinancePage. xaml.cs`:

```
public List<HourlySales> DailySales
    => FinanceInfo.DailySales
        .Select(s => new HourlySales(s.Hour,
            s.Sales)).ToList();


public string TrendArrows => FinanceInfo.TrendArrows;
```

4. These properties require you to add this `using` declaration:

    ```
    using UnoBookRail.Common.DashboardData;
    ```

5. We must also create the following class that the `SfChart` object will use to find the named properties we referenced in the XAML:

    ```
    public class HourlySales
    {
        public HourlySales(string hour, double totalSales)
        {
            Hour = hour;
            TotalSales = totalSales;
        }
        public string Hour { get; set; }
        public double TotalSales { get; set; }
    }
    ```

We've obviously only created a simple chart here, but the critical point is to notice how easy it was. A real dashboard would likely show more than a single chart. You can see examples of the charts you could include in the sample app included in the repository at `https://github.com/syncfusion/Uno.SfChart`.

We've seen how easy it was to include a chart from one vendor to show financial information. Let's now add a chart from another to display some different information.

Displaying charts with controls from Infragistics

Infragistics is a company that provides UI and UX tools for a variety of platforms. They also have a selection of controls to use in Uno Platform apps that are free to use while in preview.

You can learn more about these controls at `https://www.infragistics.com/products/uno-platform` or follow along as we add a chart to the app to show information relating to the current operation of the UnoBookRail business and create a page that looks like the one in *Figure 6.2*:

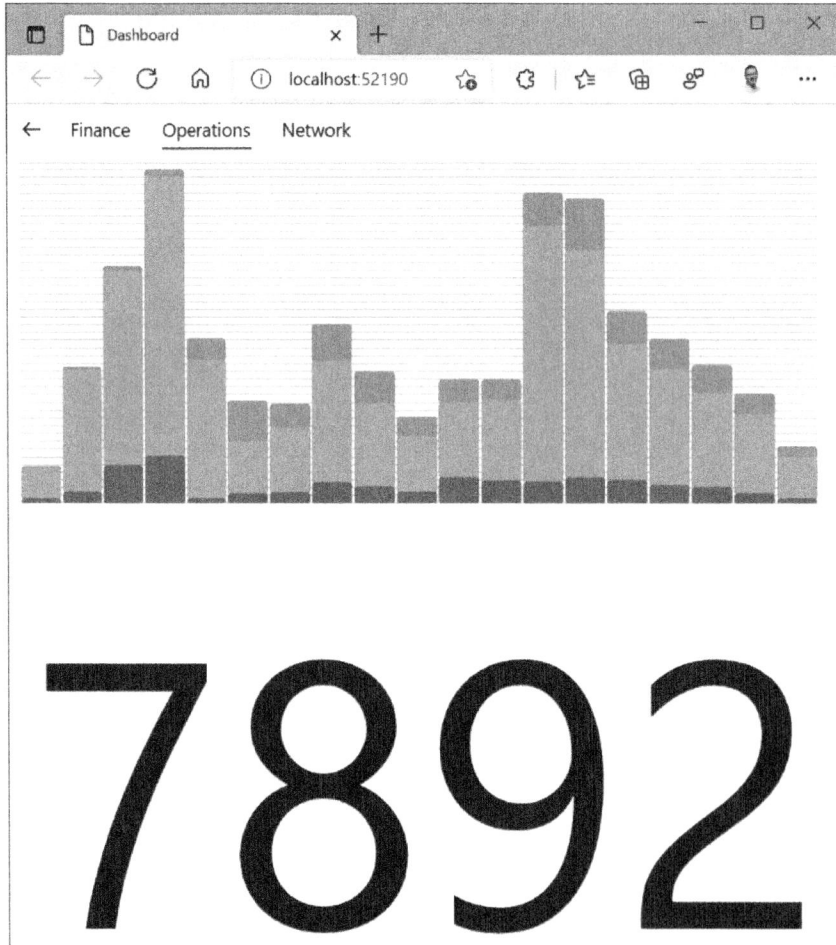

Figure 6.2 – Network operations details shown on a chart from Infragistics

Updating references

To be able to use the controls in our app, we must first make the following modifications:

1. Reference the `Infragistics.Uno.Charts` NuGet package in the **UWP** project:

    ```
    Install-Package Infragistics.Uno.Charts -Version 20.2.59-
    alpha
    ```

2. Reference the `Infragistics.Uno.Wasm.Charts` NuGet package in the **WASM** project:

```
Install-Package Infragistics.Uno.Wasm.Charts -Version
20.2.59-alpha
```

3. Reference the `Uno.SkiaSharp.Views` and `Uno.SkiaSharp.Wasm` NuGet packages in the **WASM** project. This is necessary because the Infragistics controls use SkiaSharp to draw the controls. This is different from the SyncFusion control we used previously, which uses XAML:

```
Install-Package Uno.SkiaSharp.Views -Version 2.80.0-
uno.493
```

```
Install-Package Uno.SkiaSharp.Wasm -Version 2.80.0-
uno.493
```

With those simple modifications, we can now add the chart to our app.

> **Important note**
>
> If you notice any strange compilation behaviors after making the preceding changes, try cleaning the solution, closing all open instances of Visual Studio, and then reopening the solution. This shouldn't be necessary, but we have found this to be required on a few occasions.
>
> You may also see entries in the error list from the SyncFusion project despite it successfully compiling. These errors can be safely ignored.

Drawing a column chart

We'll now add content to the **Operations** page of the app. For simplicity, we're going to only add two pieces of information. We'll add a chart to show how many of each ticket type has been used each hour today. Additionally, we'll display the number of people currently on trains or in stations, based on people presenting tickets to enter a station but not having subsequently exited:

1. Add the following namespace to the `Page` element of `OperationsPage.xaml`:

```
xmlns:ig="using:Infragistics.Controls.Charts"
```

2. Now add the following XAML as the contents of the page:

```
<Grid>
    <Grid.RowDefinitions>
```

```xml
    <RowDefinition Height="*" />
    <RowDefinition Height="*" />
</Grid.RowDefinitions>
<Grid.ColumnDefinitions>
  <ColumnDefinition Width="*" />
  <ColumnDefinition Width="*" />
</Grid.ColumnDefinitions>


<ig:XamDataChart Grid.Row="0" Grid.ColumnSpan="2"
    x:Name="PassengerChart">
  <ig:XamDataChart.Axes>
    <ig:CategoryXAxis x:Name="XAxis"
        ItemsSource="{x:Bind Passengers}" />
    <ig:NumericYAxis x:Name="YAxis" MinimumValue="0"
        Interval="500" Label="{}{}" />
  </ig:XamDataChart.Axes>
  <ig:XamDataChart.Series>
    <ig:StackedColumnSeries
            XAxis="{Binding ElementName=XAxis}"
            YAxis="{Binding ElementName=YAxis}"
            ItemsSource="{x:Bind Passengers}">
    <ig:StackedColumnSeries.Series>
        <ig:StackedFragmentSeries
            ValueMemberPath="Children" />
        <ig:StackedFragmentSeries
            ValueMemberPath="Adults" />
        <ig:StackedFragmentSeries
            ValueMemberPath="Seniors" />
    </ig:StackedColumnSeries.Series>
    </ig:StackedColumnSeries>
  </ig:XamDataChart.Series>
</ig:XamDataChart>


<TextBlock x:Name="CurrentCount"
            Grid.ColumnSpan="2" Grid.Row="1"
            Text="{x:Bind PsngrCount}"
```

```
        FontSize="300"
        HorizontalAlignment="Center"
        VerticalAlignment="Center" />
  </Grid>
```

There are three parts to the preceding code. We started by defining two rows and two columns. The content currently spans the columns, but the columns will be used in other ways later.

The chart is a XamDataChart class. Within this, we specify the *x* and *y* axes and the data to display as a StackedColumnSeries element. Within the series, we detail the paths to the data for each fragment of the stack.

Finally, we added the TextBlock element that displays the current passenger count.

3. Add the following using directive to OperationsPage.xaml.cs:

```
using UnoBookRail.Common.DashboardData;
```

These are needed for the properties we'll add to this file.

4. Add the following to the OperationsPage class providing the data shown in the chart:

```
public string PsngrCount => OperationsInfo.
CurrentPassengers;


private List<PersonCount> Passengers
    => OperationsInfo.Passengers.Select(p
        => new PersonCount(p.Hour, p.Children,
            p.Adults, p.Seniors)).ToList();
```

5. Now we need to add the PersonCount class we've just referenced:

```
public class PersonCount
{
    public PersonCount(string hour, double child,
        double adult, double senior)
    {
        Hour = hour;
        Children = child;
```

```
        Adults = adult;
        Seniors = senior;
    }
    public string Hour { get; set; }
    public double Children { get; set; }
    public double Adults { get; set; }
    public double Seniors { get; set; }
}
```

With that, we now have a simple page charting the number of passengers traveling each hour.

As with the SyncFusion charts, Infragistics has many more charts and other controls available. You can find examples of these at `https://github.com/Infragistics/uno-samples`.

Now that we've seen different ways of displaying more complex controls using libraries from third parties, let's look at drawing something more complicated ourselves.

Drawing custom graphics with SkiaSharp

UWP and Uno Platform include support for creating shapes and provide basic drawing capabilities. However, sometimes you need to display something in your app that can't easily be done with standard controls, you require fine-grained control, or you encounter performance issues when manipulating large numbers of XAML controls. In these situations, it can be necessary to draw directly onto the UI yourself. One of the ways to do this is with SkiaSharp. SkiaSharp is a cross-platform 2D graphics API based on Google's Skia graphics library that we can use in our Uno Platform apps. To show how simple it is to use, we'll create the final part of our application, which shows on a map where the trains in the network currently are. In just a few lines of code, we'll create something that looks as in the screenshot shown in *Figure 6.3*:

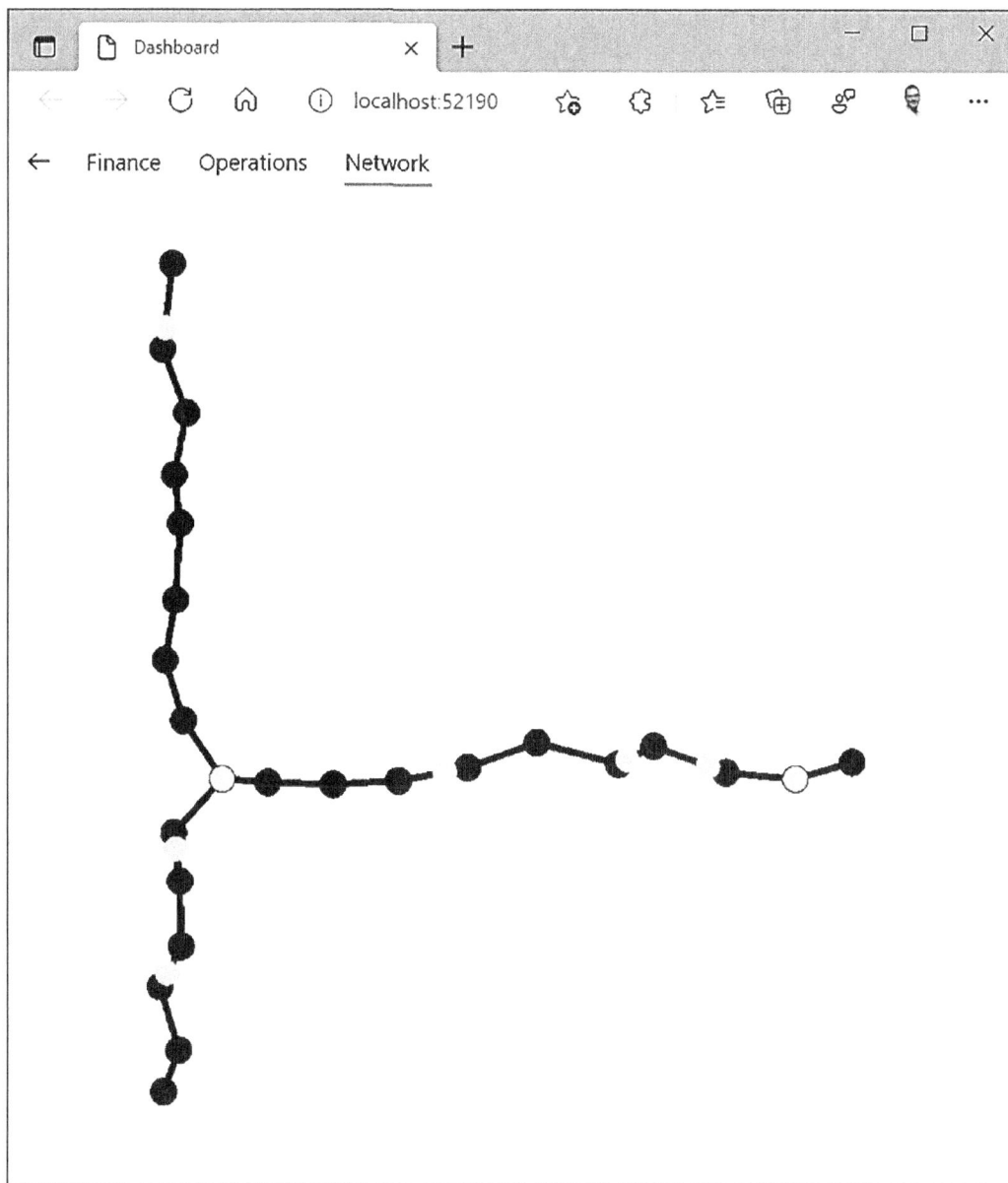

Figure 6.3 – The network map shown in the app when running in a browser

Now you've seen what we're going to create, let's get on and do it.

Updating project references

The references we need to use SkiaSharp in our app have already been added as part of the references we added to use the Infragistics controls. If you've made these changes, there's nothing to do here.

If you are following along and *haven't* added the Infragistics controls in the last section, you'll need to make the following change to your solution:

- Reference the `Uno.SkiaSharp.Views` and `Uno.SkiaSharp.Wasm` NuGet packages in the **WASM** project:

```
Install-Package Uno.SkiaSharp.Views -Version 2.80.0-
uno.493
```

```
Install-Package Uno.SkiaSharp.Wasm -Version 2.80.0-
uno.493
```

With the relevant references added, we're now ready to draw the network map.

Drawing the network map

To draw the network map in the app, we need to take the following steps:

1. In `NetworkPage.xaml`, add the following as the only content. This is the control that will show our drawing:

```
<skia:SKXamlCanvas xmlns:skia="using:SkiaSharp.Views.UWP"
PaintSurface="OnPaintSurface" />
```

2. To draw the map on the `SKXamlCanvas` control, we'll need to add the following using declarations to `NetworkPage.xaml.cs`:

```
using SkiaSharp;
using SkiaSharp.Views.UWP;
using UnoBookRail.Common.Mapping;
using UnoBookRail.Common.Network;
```

3. Next, we must add the `OnPaintSurface` method we referenced in the XAML. This method is called by the control whenever it needs to redraw the image. This will be when the control is first loaded and whenever the rendered size of the control changes:

```
private void OnPaintSurface(object sender,
SKPaintSurfaceEventArgs e)
{
```

```
    var canvas = SetUpCanvas(e);
    DrawLines(canvas);
    DrawStations(canvas);
    DrawTrains(canvas);
}
```

4. Add the SetUpCanvas method to initialize and position the image correctly:

```
private SKCanvas SetUpCanvas(SKPaintSurfaceEventArgs e)
{
    var canvas = e.Surface.Canvas;
    var relativeWidth = e.Info.Width / ImageMap.Width;
    var relativeHeight =
        e.Info.Height / ImageMap.Height;
    canvas.Scale(Math.Min(relativeWidth,
        relativeHeight));
    var x = 0f;
    var y = 0f;
    if (relativeWidth > relativeHeight)
    {
      x = (e.Info.Width - (ImageMap.Width *
          relativeHeight)) / 2f / relativeHeight;
    }
    else {
      y = (e.Info.Height - (ImageMap.Height *
          relativeWidth)) / 2f / relativeWidth;
    }
    canvas.Translate(x, y);
    canvas.Clear();
    return canvas;
}
```

The SetUpCanvas method sizes our drawing area to be as big as possible without
distorting or stretching it and ensures it is always centered horizontally and
vertically. Finally, it clears the canvas and returns it, ready for the other methods
to draw upon it.

5. Add the `DrawLines` method to draw the branch lines on the canvas:

```
void DrawLines(SKCanvas canvas)
{
    var paint = new SKPaint
    {
        Color = SKColors.Black,
        StrokeWidth = 1,
    };
    var northPnts =
        ImageMap.GetStations(Branch.NorthBranch);
    var mainPnts =
        ImageMap.GetStations(Branch.MainLine);
    var southPnts =
        ImageMap.GetStations(Branch.SouthBranch);

    SKPoint[] ToSKPointArray(List<(float X, float Y)>
        list)
        => list.Select(p => new SKPoint(p.X,
            p.Y)).ToArray();

    void DrawBranch(SKPoint[] stnPoints)
        => canvas.DrawPoints(SKPointMode.Polygon,
            stnPoints, paint);

    DrawBranch(ToSKPointArray(northPnts));
    DrawBranch(ToSKPointArray(mainPnts));
    DrawBranch(ToSKPointArray(southPnts));
}
```

In the preceding code, the station positions returned by the library are converted to a Skia-specific array used to draw a polygon connecting all the points.

6. Add the `DrawStations` method to draw the station positions on the branch lines:

```
void DrawStations(SKCanvas canvas)
{
    var paint = new SKPaint
```

```
    {
        Color = SKColors.Black,
        Style = SKPaintStyle.Fill,
    };

    foreach (var (X, Y) in ImageMap.Stations)
    {
        canvas.DrawCircle(new SKPoint(X, Y), 2,
            paint);
    }
}
```

The `DrawStations` method is simple as all it does is draw a circle for each station.

7. Add the `DrawTrains` method to show where the trains currently are on the map:

```
void DrawTrains(SKCanvas canvas)
{
    var trainPaint = new SKPaint
    {
        Color = SKColors.Cyan,
        Style = SKPaintStyle.Fill,
    };
    foreach (var train in ImageMap.GetTrainsInNetwork())
    {
        canvas.DrawCircle(new SKPoint(
            train.MapPosition.X, train.MapPosition.Y),
                1.8f, trainPaint);
    }
}
```

The `DrawTrains` method is again simple as it loops through the provided data and draws a cyan circle at each position. Because this is drawn after the station circles, it will appear above them when a train is at a station.

> **Important note**
> In this chapter, we've only used a few circles and lines to create our map. However, SkiaSharp is capable of much more than we have space to cover here. You might want to explore the other functionality available by extending the map we've just created to include the names of stations or add other details that show the direction a train is heading or if it is at a station.

We now have all the pages of our app implemented, but we can further improve things by having the content adjust depending on the size of the screen or window.

Responding to changes in the UI

Your apps will need to run on different sized screens and windows. Some of these differences will be due to the different devices the app will run on, but you may also need to account for windows that can be resized by the user.

It's possible to design multiple versions of a page and load the appropriate one at runtime. However, it's usually much easier to create a single page that adjusts to the available dimensions. We'll look at how to do that with the features available.

Changing the page layout

Uno Platform allows you to create a responsive UI by switching between `VisualStates`.

It's possible to create **StateTriggers** elements (to trigger changes between states) for many scenarios, but the most common is to use an `AdaptiveTrigger` element that fires based on the size of the control to which it is attached. We'll now use adaptive triggers to adjust the **Finance** and **Operations** pages to better lay out their contents based on the available width:

1. Add the following as the first child of `RelativePanel` in `FinancePage.xaml`:

```
<VisualStateManager.VisualStateGroups>
  <VisualStateGroup>
    <VisualState>
      <VisualState.StateTriggers>
        <AdaptiveTrigger MinWindowWidth="1200" />
      </VisualState.StateTriggers>
      <VisualState.Setters>
        <Setter Target="SecondaryItem.
```

```
                         (RelativePanel.AlignTopWithPanel)"
                      Value="True"/>
               <Setter Target="SecondaryItem.
                  (RelativePanel.AlignVerticalCenterWithPanel)"
                      Value="False"/>
               <Setter Target="SecondaryItem.
                  (RelativePanel.RightOf)"
                      Value="MainChart"/>
               <Setter Target="SecondaryItem.
                  (RelativePanel.Below)"
                      Value="{x:Null}"/>
               <Setter Target="SecondaryItem.Margin"
                  Value="0,200,0,0"/>
            </VisualState.Setters>
          </VisualState>
        </VisualStateGroup>
     </VisualStateManager.VisualStateGroups>
```

This defines an `AdaptiveTrigger` element that's applied when the panel is at least 1,200 relative pixels wide. When this visual state is triggered, the `TextBlock` element is set to the right of the chart and has its alignment adjusted accordingly. The left-hand side of *Figure 6.4* shows how this looks.

2. We can now do a similar thing with the grid in the `OperationsPage.xaml` page. Add the following immediately below the row and column definitions:

```
<VisualStateManager.VisualStateGroups>
   <VisualStateGroup>
     <VisualState>
       <VisualState.StateTriggers>
         <AdaptiveTrigger MinWindowWidth="1200" />
       </VisualState.StateTriggers>
       <VisualState.Setters>
         <Setter Target="PassengerChart.
             (Grid.ColumnSpan)" Value="1"/>
         <Setter Target="PassengerChart.(Grid.RowSpan)"
             Value="2"/>
         <Setter Target="CurrentCount.(Grid.Row)"
             Value="0"/>
```

```
        <Setter Target="CurrentCount.(Grid.Column)"
            Value="1"/>
        <Setter Target="CurrentCount.
            (Grid.ColumnSpan)" Value="1"/>
        <Setter Target="CurrentCount.
            (Grid.RowSpan)" Value="2"/>
    </VisualState.Setters>
  </VisualState>
 </VisualStateGroup>
</VisualStateManager.VisualStateGroups>
```

With these setters, we're making use of the row and column definitions we created earlier. While the initial code put the controls in separate rows, here we're changing the controls so they are in different columns and span the rows when the window is wider. As you can see in *Figure 6.4*, this means that the number of people currently on trains is displayed beside the chart, rather than below it:

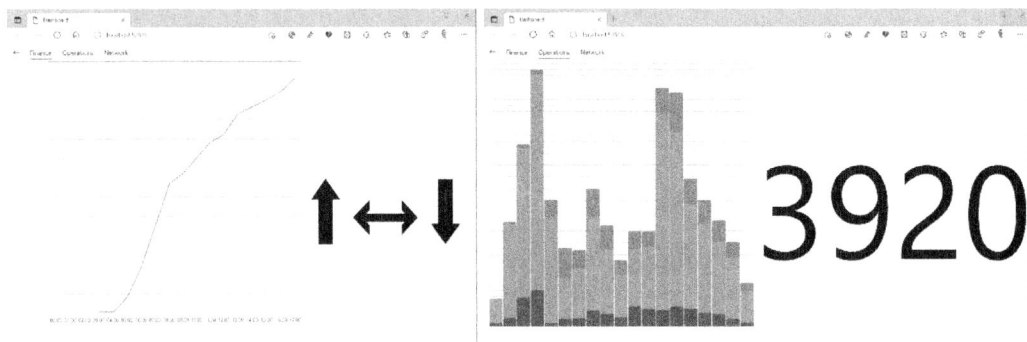

Figure 6.4 – The Finance and Operations pages shown in a landscape layout

With these two examples, we've seen different ways of changing how the elements on a page can be repositioned to change the layout. There is no one right way to adjust all pages for different amounts of available space. State triggers can be used to change any property on an element, and it's also possible to have multiple triggers so you could, for example, have different layouts for small, medium, and large screens.

Changing the layout of the elements on the screen isn't the only way to adjust what's shown. It's also possible to have the controls themselves adjust, resize, and redraw themselves to fit the space.

Stretching and scaling content to fit the available space

One of the strengths of XAML is its ability to dynamically lay out controls and not rely on providing specific sizes for each element. It's possible to resize individual XAML controls by setting the `HorizontalAlignment` and `VerticalAlignment` properties to control how they make use of the available space. Setting the values of these properties to `Stretch` will allow them to take up all the available space in their parent element. For more complex scenarios, you can also use a `ViewBox` element to transform controls by stretching them in different ways and directions.

If you wish to know more about creating layouts with XAML elements, you'll find some useful links at `https://platform.uno/docs/articles/winui-doc-links-development.html#layouting`.

Many controls also automatically adjust to use all or as much of the available space as appropriate. We did this with the map we drew with SkiaSharp. The map was drawn as large as possible without distorting it. It was aligned in the center of the available space regardless of whether the window was of a portrait or landscape aspect ratio.

Now that all the pages adjust to the available space, our app and this chapter are complete.

Summary

In this chapter, we built an app that works on UWP and in a web browser. The app used graphing controls from SyncFusion and Infragistics. We also created a custom map with SkiaSharp. Finally, we looked at how to adjust the UI layout in response to different and changing screen sizes.

This chapter is the last in this part of the book. In the next part, we'll move on from building apps to look at how to test and deploy them. In the next chapter, we'll look at how to use the `Uno.UITest` library as part of your broader testing strategy. When building applications that run on multiple platforms, automating the testing across those platforms can save lots of time and boost your productivity.

Section 3: Test, Deploy, and Contribute

This final part of the book focuses on app development after the code has been written. Specifically, it focuses on how you can test the UI of the apps you create and then deploy them to the cloud (in the case of WebAssembly) or an app store. Finally, it shows you where to go for more resources, help, or information, before ending by looking at how you can contribute to the wider project.

In this section, we include the following chapters:

- *Chapter 7, Testing Your Apps*
- *Chapter 8, Deploying Your Apps and Going Further*

7
Testing Your Apps

In the previous chapters, we covered developing multiple different types of apps using Uno Platform. Uno Platform not only allows apps to be written, however; it also allows automated UI tests to be written that will run on Android, iOS, and WebAssembly using the Uno.UITest framework. During this chapter, we will write our first test using Uno.UITest and run it on different platforms, including using emulators. After this, you will also learn how to write tests for Windows using WinAppDriver.

In this chapter, we'll cover the following topics:

- Setting up the `Uno.UITest` project for your app
- Authoring `Uno.UITest` tests for your Uno Platform app
- Running your tests against the WASM, Android, and iOS versions of your app
- Writing unit tests for your Uno Platform app
- Using WinAppDriver to author automated tests for the UWP head of your app
- Why manual testing is still important

By the end of this chapter, you'll have learned how to write tests using `Uno.UITest` and WinAppDriver for your app, how to run those tests on different platforms, and why manually testing your app is still important.

Technical requirements

This chapter assumes that you already have your development environment set up, including installing the project templates, as was covered in *Chapter 1, Introducing Uno Platform*. The source code for this chapter is available at `https://github.com/PacktPublishing/Creating-Cross-Platform-C-Sharp-Applications-with-Uno-Platform/tree/main/Chapter07`.

The code in this chapter makes use of the library from `https://github.com/PacktPublishing/Creating-Cross-Platform-C-Sharp-Applications-with-Uno-Platform/tree/main/SharedLibrary`.

Check out the following video to see the code in action: `https://bit.ly/3iBFZ2e`

Getting started with Uno.UITest

Before we get started with Uno.UITest, let's cover what Uno.UITest is and what its aim is. Uno.UITest is a library developed and maintained by the Uno Platform team to allow developers to write unified UI tests for their Uno Platform apps. These UI tests allow you to simulate users interacting with your app and verify the UI of your app to ensure that user interactions work correctly and that your app behaves as designed. With Uno.UITest, you can write **UI tests** (also sometimes referred to as interaction tests), which you can run against the **Android**, **iOS**, and **WASM** heads of your app.

Under the hood, Uno.UITest uses **Xamarin.UITest** to run tests against the Android and iOS head of the app. For the WASM version of the app, Uno.UITest uses **Selenium** and **Google Chrome**. Using these libraries, Uno.UITest allows you to write tests that mimic user interactions with the UI of your app, including mimicking mouse input such as clicking, and keyboard input such as entering text.

But when should you use UI tests? When writing complex apps, ensuring that changes to your code did not break existing features can often be difficult to test, especially as some changes only become noticeable when using the app, not when testing components or classes alone. UI tests are ideal for this kind of scenario as you can write tests simulating a normal user using your app without having to manually go through dozens or hundreds of steps. A common scenario for writing UI tests is to check whether users can successfully achieve certain tasks within your app, for example, sign in to your app or search for a specific thing. While UI tests are good for testing these kinds of scenarios, UI tests are no silver bullet and also have their drawbacks. Since UI tests simulate user input, they are slower to run compared to normal unit tests, which are only testing single objects or classes. In addition to this, since the UI testing framework or library needs to find a way to interact with your app, UI tests can sometimes break when updating the UI of your app or changing texts or names within your app.

Nonetheless, when developing an app, writing UI tests is very important when you try to ensure that no bugs have snuck into the app. This is especially useful when writing apps that will run on a variety of different devices having different screen sizes, capabilities, and OS versions as this makes it easier to test your app on a lot of different configurations as manual testing is slow and error-prone.

Before we use Uno.UITest, we first need an app that we can use to write tests for. For this, let's start by creating a new solution for our app that we will use to write tests for:

1. Create a new project with the **Multi-Platform App (Uno Platform)** template.

2. Name the project UnoAutomatedTestsApp. Of course, you can use a different name; however, in this chapter, we will assume that the project is named UnoAutomatedTestsApp.

3. Remove all the platform head projects *except* for Android, iOS, UWP, and WASM.

4. Now we need to add a reference to our shared library. To do this, right-click on the solution file, select **Add > Existing Project…**, navigate to the UnoBookRail. Common.csproj file, and then click **Open**.

5. Reference the shared library project in every head project. For this, right-click on the head project, select **Add > Reference… > Projects**, check **UnoBookRail. Common**, and click **OK**. Since we need a reference to the library in every head, repeat this process for every head, in other words, Android, iOS, UWP, and WASM.

Now that we have created the project, let's add some content to our app that we can test:

1. Add xmlns:toolkit="using:Uno.UI.Toolkit" to the **Page** element at the root of MainPage.xaml.

2. Replace the Grid control inside your MainPage.xaml file with the following:

```
<StackPanel Spacing="10" Padding="10"
    toolkit:VisibleBoundsPadding.PaddingMask="All"
    Background="{ThemeResource
        ApplicationPageBackgroundThemeBrush}">
    <StackPanel x:Name="SignInForm" Spacing="10">
        <TextBox x:Name="UsernameInput"
            AutomationProperties.AutomationId=
                "UsernameInput"
            TextChanged="Username_TextChanged"
                Header="Username"/>
        <PasswordBox x:Name="PasswordInput"
```

```
            AutomationProperties.AutomationId=
                "PasswordInput"
            PasswordChanged="Password_PasswordChanged"
                Header="Password"/>
        <TextBlock x:Name=
            "SignInErrorMessageTextBlock"
                AutomationProperties.AutomationId="
                    SignInErrorMessageTextBlock"
            Foreground="{ThemeResource
                SystemErrorTextColor}"
                    Visibility="Collapsed"/>
        <Button x:Name="SignInButton"
            AutomationProperties.AutomationId=
                "SignInButton"
            Click="SignInButton_Click"
                Content="Sign in" IsEnabled="False"
            HorizontalAlignment="Center"
                BorderThickness="1"/>
    </StackPanel>
    <TextBlock x:Name="SignedInLabel"
        AutomationProperties.AutomationId=
            "SignedInLabel"
        Text="Successfully signed in!"
            Visibility="Collapsed"/>
</StackPanel>
```

3. This is a simple sign-in interface that we will write tests for later in this chapter. It includes sign-in controls, a sign-in button, and a label that will be shown when signed in.

4. Now, add the following two methods to the `MainPage` class:

```
using UnoBookRail.Common.Auth;

...

private void Username_TextChanged(object sender,
TextChangedEventArgs e)
{
    SignInButton.IsEnabled = UsernameInput.Text.Length
        > 0 && PasswordInput.Password.Length > 0;
}
```

```csharp
private void Password_PasswordChanged(object sender,
RoutedEventArgs e)
{
    SignInButton.IsEnabled = UsernameInput.Text.Length
        > 0 && PasswordInput.Password.Length > 0;
}
private void SignInButton_Click(object sender,
RoutedEventArgs args)
{
    var signInResult = Authentication.SignIn(
        UsernameInput.Text, PasswordInput.Password);
    if(!signInResult.IsSuccessful &&
        signInResult.Messages.Count > 0)
    {
        SignInErrorMessageTextBlock.Text =
            signInResult.Messages[0];
        SignInErrorMessageTextBlock.Visibility =
            Visibility.Visible;
    }
    else
    {
        SignInErrorMessageTextBlock.Visibility =
            Visibility.Collapsed;
        SignInForm.Visibility = Visibility.Collapsed;
        SignedInLabel.Visibility = Visibility.Visible;
    }
}
```

This code adds handlers that allow us to enable the sign-in button as soon as the user has entered a username and password. Otherwise, the sign-in button will be disabled. In addition to this, we also handle the sign-in button click and update the UI accordingly, including showing the error message if the sign-in failed.

Now, if you start the UWP head of your app, you will see something like *Figure 7.1*:

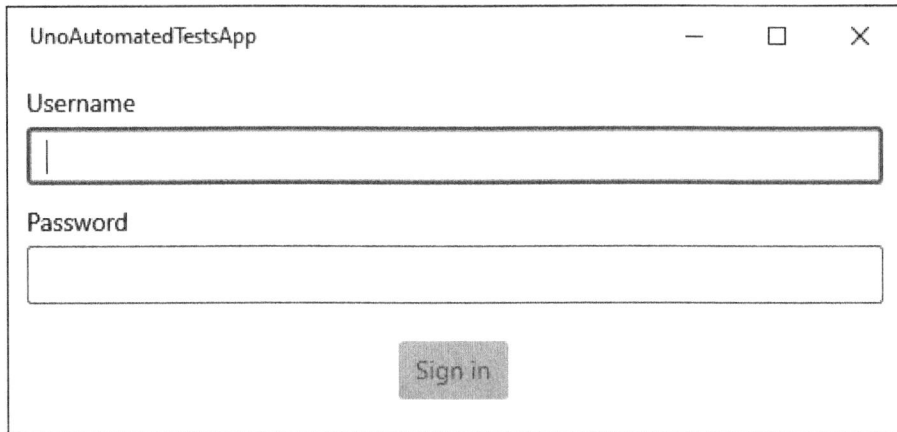

Figure 7.1 – Screenshot of the running app with the sign-in form

Now that we have added a simple test app that we can test again, we can now add our **Uno.UITest** tests project:

1. If you want to run tests for the WASM head of your app, make sure you have Google Chrome installed.

2. First, you will need to update the project files for the Android, iOS, and WASM heads. For that, add the following entries before the last closing project tag of the `.csproj` files for those projects:

```
<PropertyGroup Condition="'$(Configuration)'=='Debug' or
'$(IsUiAutomationMappingEnabled)'=='True'">
    <IsUiAutomationMappingEnabled>
        True</IsUiAutomationMappingEnabled>
    <DefineConstants>$(DefineConstants);
        USE_UITESTS</DefineConstants>
</PropertyGroup>
```

3. For the iOS project, add a reference to the `Xamarin.TestCloud.Agent` NuGet package. Since, as of the time of writing, the latest stable version was **0.22.2**, we will use that.

    Inside the `OnLaunched` method of your `App.xaml.cs` file, add the following at the beginning of the method:

```
#if __IOS__ && USE_UITESTS
        // Launches Xamarin Test Cloud Agent
```

```
        Xamarin.Calabash.Start();
    #endif
```

Since the Uno.UITest library uses Xamarin.UITest under the hood, for the iOS app, we need to add the preceding code. Otherwise Xamarin.UITest can't interact with the running iOS app and the tests won't work.

4. Since the Uno.UITest project type is not included in the Uno Platform Visual Studio templates extension, make sure you have the Uno Platform `dotnet new` templates installed. You can find the instructions for this in *Chapter 1, Introducing Uno Platform*.

5. Inside the `UnoAutomatedTestsApp` folder, create a folder named `UnoAutomatedTestsApp.UITests`.

6. Inside the newly created folder, run the following command:

```
dotnet new unoapp-uitest
```

This will create a new Uno.UITest project inside the folder and also add the project to the solution file.

7. Update the Android and iOS apps package names. For Android, replace the **package** entry inside the `Properties/AndroidManifest.xml` file of the Android project with `package="UnoBook.UnoAutomatedTestsApp"`. To replace the iOS package name, open the `Info.plist` file inside the iOS project and replace `Bundle Identifier` with `UnoBook.UnoAutomatedTestsApp`.

8. Now we need to update the `Constants.cs` file inside the Uno.UITests app project to point to the correct app. For this, replace lines 13, 14, and 15 with the following:

```
public readonly static string iOSAppName = "UnoBook.
UnoAutomatedTestsApp";
public readonly static string AndroidAppName = "UnoBook.
UnoAutomatedTestsApp";
public readonly static string WebAssemblyDefaultUri =
"http://localhost:[PORT]/";
```

Since the port of the WASM app is generated randomly, replace `[PORT]` from the preceding code with the following information

> **Note**
>
> We need to update the `Constants.cs` file since Uno.UITest needs to be able to find the app through the app name or app URI in the case of WASM. To find out which URI your WASM head is running on, open `Properties/launchSettings.json` inside the WASM head. Inside there, depending on whether you will be using the **IIS Express** or the `[ProjectName].Wasm` target, either use `applicationUrl` from the **iisSettings** option or `applicationUrl` from the `[Project name].Wasm` profile to ascertain the port. In this chapter, we will be using **IIS Target**. The iOS app name is defined by the Bundle identifier inside the `Info.plist` file located inside the iOS project. For the Android app name, refer to the package property inside the `Properties/AndroidManifest.xml` file of the Android project.

Inside the **UnoAutomatedTestsApp.UITests** project, you will find three files:

- `Constants.cs`: This contains the configuration to find the running app using the app package name or URL of the app, as explained earlier.

- `Given_MainPage.cs`: This is a sample test file with a small test showing how to write a test.

- `TestBase.cs`: This file contains all the bootstrap code that takes care of starting and tearing down the app and also exposes an `IApp` instance (more on this in the next section). This file also exports a `TakeScreenshot` function that you can use to take screenshots of the running app being tested.

Now that we have covered how to set up the Uno.UITest project and its structure, let's continue by writing our first Uno.UITest and learn how to run those tests.

Writing and running your first test

Before we start writing our first test, we will cover how you can use Uno.UITest to interact with your apps. For this, we will first start by covering the basics of the addressing elements using Uno.UITests query feature objects.

How Uno.UITest works

Since UI tests need to address UI elements of your app, every UI testing library needs to have a way to allow developers to address those elements. `Uno.UITest` does this using the `IAppQuery` interface to define queries and the `IApp` interface to run those queries and inject input.

The `IApp` interface provides you with the necessary APIs to interact with your app, including clicking elements, simulating scrolling, and injecting text input. As part of the creation of the `Uno.UITest` project, the `TestBase` class will provide you with an `IApp` instance. Since the `IApp` interface allows you to simulate input to your app and most interactions require a specific control to be the target of your interaction, most methods on the `IApp` interface require you to specify the `AutomationID` property of the control or by using the `IAppQuery` interface.

In the following example, we will use `AutomationID` to click the button, as defined by the following XAML:

```
<!-- Setting AutomationId to reference button from UI test -->
<Button AutomationProperties.AutomationId="SignInButton
Content="Sign in"/>
```

When writing a Uno.UITest test, we can then press the button using the following code:

```
App.Tap("SignInButton");
```

In contrast to using `x:Name/AutomationID` of a control to specify the element, by using the `IAppQuery` interface, you can address controls based on other properties, for example, their type, or based on specific properties being set on a control. When working with `IAppQuery`, you will notice that the `IApp` interface does not expect to get an element of the `IAppQuery` type, but rather an element of the `Func<IAppQuery, IAppQuery>` type. Since the `IApp` interface relies heavily on this, you will often see the following `using-alias` statement:

```
using Query=System.Func<Uno.UITest.IAppQuery,Uno.UITest.
IAppQuery>;
```

This allows developers to write queries more easily since you can simply use the `Query` type alias instead of having to write it out every time. For simplicity, in this chapter, we will also use this `using` statement and use the `Query` type.

If we take the XAML from before, pressing the button with the `IAppQuery` interface can be done as follows:

```
Query signInButton = q => q.Marked("SignInButton");
App.Tap(signInButton);
```

When we created the Uno.UITest project, you may have also noticed that a reference to the NUnit NuGet package was added. By default, Uno.UITest uses NUnit for assertions and their tests. Of course, this does not mean that you have to use NUnit for your tests. However, if you wish to use a different testing framework, you will need to update the `TestBase.cs` file since it uses NUnit attributes to hook into the setup and teardown of the tests.

Now that we covered the basics of how `Uno.UITest` works, we will now continue by writing tests for our sign-in interface.

Authoring your first test

We will start by writing our first tests for the sign-in interface we added at the start of this chapter. For simplicity, we will use NUnit since `Uno.UITest` uses this by default when creating a new `Uno.UITest` project, meaning that we don't have to update the `TestBase` class. We begin by creating a new file for our tests:

1. First, remove the existing `Given_MainPage.cs` file.
2. Create a new folder called `Tests`.
3. Create a new class called `SignInTests.cs` inside the `Tests` folder.
4. Update `SignInTests.cs` with the following code:

   ```
   using NUnit.Framework;
   using Query = System.Func<Uno.UITest.IAppQuery, Uno.UITest.IAppQuery>;
   namespace UnoAutomatedTestsApp.UITests.Tests
   {
       public class SignInTests : TestBase
       {
       }
   }
   ```

   We are inheriting from `TestBase` to access the `IApp` instance of the current test run and to be able to send input to our app. In addition to that, we are also adding a using statement for the `NUnit` library as we will use it later and add the named using statement we covered in the section *How Uno.UITest works*.

Now, let's add our first test. Let's start by simply checking whether the email and password input fields and the sign-in button exist. For the rest of this section, we will only be working inside the `SignInTests.cs` file since we are writing tests for the sign-in user interface:

1. Start by adding a new public function, which will be our test case. We will name the function `VerifySignInRenders`.

2. Add the **Test** attribute. This lets `NUnit` know that the function is a test.

3. Now, add the following code inside the function:

```
App.WaitForElement("UsernameInput");
App.WaitForElement("PasswordInput");
App.WaitForElement("SignInButton");
```

Your `SignInTests` class should now look something like this:

```
public class SignInTests : TestBase
{
    [Test]
    public void VerifySignInRenders()
    {
        App.WaitForElement("UsernameInput", "Username input
            wasn't found.");
        App.WaitForElement("PasswordInput", "Password input
            wasn't found.");
        App.WaitForElement("SignInButton", "Sign in button
            wasn't found.");
    }
}
```

Now what our test does is try to find the elements with the automation ID `UserNameInput`, `PasswordInput`, and `SignInButton`, and fail the test if it can't find any of those elements.

Now that we have written our first test, let's try it out! To do this, we'll first cover how to run those tests.

Running your tests on Android, iOS, and WASM

Running your `Uno.UITest` tests against the Android, iOS, and WASM head of your app is fairly simple, although the process is always slightly different depending on what platform you are trying to start.

Running tests against the WASM head

Let's start by running our test against the WASM head of our app:

1. First, you will need to deploy the WASM head of the app. For this, select the **UnoAutomatedTestsApp.Wasm** start up project and select the **IIS Express** target, as shown in *Figure 7.2*. Then, press *Ctrl + F5*, which will deploy the project.

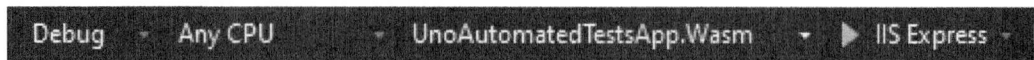

| Debug ▾ | Any CPU ▾ | UnoAutomatedTestsApp.Wasm ▾ | ▶ IIS Express ▾ |

Figure 7.2 – WASM project with IIS Express selected

2. Update `Constants.cs` and change `Constants.CurrentPlatform` to `Platform.Browser`. If you haven't updated the `Constants.WebAssemblyDefaultUri` property, do that as in the *Getting started with Uno. UITest* section.

3. Open **Test Explorer** by clicking **View** in the menu bar and clicking on **Test Explorer**. Now, expand the tree and right-click the **VerifySignInRenders** test. Click the **Run** option from the popup. Now, the test will run against the app running in Chrome.

> **Important note**
>
> At the time of writing, due to a known bug with Uno.UITest, running the tests against the WASM head might not work as Chrome might fail to start. Unfortunately, no workaround is known yet. To learn more about the current state of this bug, refer to the following GitHub issue: `https://github.com/unoplatform/Uno.UITest/issues/60`.

Once the tests have started, Chrome will be started in headless mode and once the tests have finished, the test will be marked as passed in the Visual Studio Test Explorer.

Running tests against the Android version of your app

In addition to running your tests against the WASM head, you can also run the tests against the Android version of your app running on an emulator or running on an Android device. To do this, follow these steps:

1. Ensure that **Android Emulator** is running and that the app has been deployed. To deploy the Android version of your app, select the Android project as the start up project and press *Ctrl + F5*. If you want to run the tests against the app running on your Android device, make sure the app is deployed on the device and that your device is connected to your computer.

2. Update `Constants.cs` and change `Constants.CurrentPlatform` to `Platform.Android`. In case you haven't updated the `Constants.AndroidAppName` property, do that as in the *Getting started with Uno. UITest* section.

3. As was the case with WASM, now right-click the test in **Test Explorer** and click on **Run**. The app will start inside the emulator or on your Android device and the tests will be running against the running Android app.

Running tests against the iOS version of your app

You can also run your UI tests against the iOS version of your app running on an emulator or on an iOS device. Note that macOS is required for this. To run the tests against the iOS head, follow these steps:

1. Ensure that the iOS simulator is running and that the app has been deployed. To deploy the iOS version of your app, select the iOS project as the start up project and run the app. If you want to run the tests against the app running on your iOS device, make sure the app is deployed on the device and that it is connected to your computer.

2. Update `Constants.cs` and change `Constants.CurrentPlatform` to `Platform.iOS`. Set `iOSDeviceNameOrId` to the name of the emulator or tethered device you wish to use.

    If using a tethered device, you may also need to change `iOSAppName` and the **Bundle Identifier** in `info.plist` so that it is compatible with your developer certificate.

3. Now, right-click the test project in the **Tests** window and click on **Run Test**. The app will start and the tests will be run.

> **Additional information**
>
> Running the UI tests on a mac requires having compatible versions of the test libraries, tools, and OS versions. If you encounter errors when running the tests, ensure you have the latest versions of OS X, Xcode, Visual Studio for Mac, and the NuGet packages you are using in the test project. You may also need to ensure that the device or simulator you are running against is the latest iOS version (including any updates).
>
> Running the UI tests on a simulator can be resource-intensive. You may find it necessary to run the tests on a connected device if they don't start on the simulator.
>
> If testing on a physical device, UI automation must be enabled. Enable this at **Settings** > **Developer** > **UI Automation**.
>
> Hopefully, more documentation will be added that will make testing and debugging tests on a Mac easier. For progress on this, see `https://github.com/unoplatform/Uno.UITest/issues/66`.

Now that we have covered how to run your tests against the Android, iOS, and WASM versions of the app, we will dive deeper into writing tests by writing more UI tests for our sign-in interface.

Writing more complex tests

So far, we have only tested the very basic example of our sign-in interface rendering. However, we also want to make sure that our sign-in interface actually works and allows users to sign in. For this, we will write a new test that ensures that when a username and password are being provided, the sign-in button is clickable:

1. Create a new function, `VerifyButtonIsEnabledWithUsernameAndPassword`, inside the `SignInTests.cs` file and add the **Test** attribute to it.

2. Since we will use those queries more often, add the following `Query` objects to the `SignInTests` class:

```
Query usernameInput = q => q.Marked("UsernameInput");
Query passwordInput = q => q.Marked("PasswordInput");
Query signInButton = q => q.Marked("SignInButton");
```

3. Now, let's simulate entering text in the username and
    password fields by inserting the following code into the
    `VerifyButtonIsEnabledWithUsernameAndPassword` test:

```
App.ClearText(usernameInput);
App.EnterText(usernameInput, "test"); App.
ClearText(passwordInput);
App.EnterText(passwordInput, "test");
```

> **Important note**
>
> Due to a bug with Xamarin.UITest, the testing library Uno.UITest uses
> for Android and iOS, clearing and entering tests does not work on every
> Android device or emulator. You can find more information on this
> bug here: `https://github.com/microsoft/appcenter/`
> `issues/1451`. As a workaround, you can use an Android emulator with
> API version 28 or lower as those Android versions are not affected by this bug.

This will simulate a user entering the text `test` into the username input field
and the same text into the password input field. Note that in this and the following
tests, we will always clear the text beforehand to ensure that the correct text has
been entered.

> **Note**
>
> When running multiple tests as a group, for example, by selecting multiple
> tests or their root node in the Test Explorer, Uno.UITest will not reset the app
> between the individual tests. That means that you will need an initialization
> code for your tests if those rely on a specific initial app state.

4. Now, let's verify that the sign-in button is enabled by using the following code:

```
var signInButtonResult = App.WaitForElement(signInButton);
Assert.IsTrue(signInButtonResult[0].Enabled, "Sign in
button was not enabled.");
```

For this, we ensure that the button exists and grab the `IAppResult[]` object for
that query. We then check that the button is enabled through the `IAppResult.`
`Enabled` property. Note that we added a message to the assert that will be
displayed when the assert fails by providing a second parameter.

Now, if you run the test for Android, the app will start on your Android device or the
emulator. `Uno.UITest` will then enter text inside the **Username** and **Password** input
fields and you should see the sign-in button become clickable.

Let's now test whether invalid sign-in credentials provide a meaningful error message. For this, we will write a new test:

1. Create a new function, `VerifyInvalidCredentialsHaveErrorMessage`, inside the `SignInTests.cs` file and add the **Test** attribute to it.

2. Now, add a new query to the `SignInTests` class that we will use to access the error message label:

```
Query errorMessageLabel = q =>
q.Marked("SignInErrorMessageTextBlock");
```

3. Now, let's enter credentials that are definitely invalid and press the **Sign in** button using the following code:

```
App.ClearText(usernameInput);
App.EnterText(usernameInput, "invalid");
App.ClearText(passwordInput);
App.EnterText(passwordInput, "invalid");
App.Tap(signInButton);
```

4. Since we will be using `Uno.UITest` extensions methods and `Linq` inside our test, add the following `using` statements:

```
using System.Linq;
using Uno.UITest.Helpers.Queries;
```

5. Lastly, we need to verify the error message using the following code. By that, we check that the error label is displaying the appropriate error message:

```
var errorMessage = App.Query(q => errorMessageLabel (q).
GetDependencyPropertyValue("Text").Value<string>()).
First();

Assert.AreEqual(errorMessage, "Username or password
invalid or user does not exist.", "Error message not
correct.");
```

6. If you run this test now, you will see how the username **"invalid"** and the password **"invalid"** will be entered. After that, the test clicks on the sign-in button and you will see the error message **Username or password invalid or user does not exist.**.

Lastly, we want to verify the fact that with valid credentials, users can sign in. For this, we will use the username `demo` and the password `1234`, as these are known to the authentication code as a demo user:

1. As with the previous tests, create a new function with the name `VerifySigningInWorks` inside the `SignInTests.cs` file and add the `Test` attribute to it.

2. Since we will use the `SignedInLabel` to detect whether we are signed in, add the following query as we will use it later to detect whether the label is visible.

3. Add the following code to enter the demo user credentials and sign in:

```
App.ClearText(usernameInput);
App.EnterText(usernameInput, "demo");
App.ClearText(passwordInput);
App.EnterText(passwordInput, "1234");
App.Tap(signInButton);
```

4. Lastly, check whether we are signed in by verifying that the signed-in label is visible and displaying the correct text using the following code:

```
var signedInMessage = App.Query(q => signedInLabel(q).
GetDependencyPropertyValue("Text").Value<string>()).
First();
Assert.AreEqual(signedInMessage, "Successfully signed
in!", "Success message not correct.");
```

5. If you run this test, you will see how the username `demo` and the password `1234` have been entered. After the sign-in button gets clicked by the test, the sign-in form will disappear and you will see the text **Successfully signed in**.

While we covered writing tests using Uno.UITest, of course, we didn't cover all the available APIs. *Figure 7.3* shows a list of different APIs available as part of Uno.UITest and how you can use them:

Uno.UITest IApp interface API	Use cases
DoubleTap	You can use this API to simulate double-tapping something.
DragAndDrop	This API can be used to simulate drag and drop behavior, for example, dragging tabs around in a TabView control.
PinchToZoomIn and PinchToZoomOut	With these two APIs, you can simulate users zooming in or out, for example, when displaying an image.
PressVolumeUp and PressVolumeDown	As the title suggests, these APIs simulate a user pressing volume up or volume down on the device.
ScrollDown, ScrollDownTo, ScrollUp, and ScrollUpTo	These APIs allow you to simulate the scrolling of controls, for example, to scroll a list of messages.
SetOrientationLandscape and SetOrientationPortrait	Using these APIs, you simulate users changing the orientation of the device to test how your app handles those scenarios.
SwipeLeftToRight and SwipeRightToLeft	You can use these APIs to simulate users swiping from one side to the other, for example, to swipe in a menu from the side.

Figure 7.3 – List of additional APIs available as part of Uno.UITest

Now that we have covered writing tests using Uno.UITest, let's look at tools you can use to write automated tests for your app, including using WinAppDriver to write UI tests for the UWP head of your app.

Test tools beside Uno.UITest

`Uno.UITest` is not the only tool you can use to write automated tests for your Uno Platform app. In this section, we will cover writing UI tests for the UWP head of your project using WinAppDriver and Selenium and writing unit tests for the UWP head of the project.

Testing the UWP head of your app with WinAppDriver

At the time of writing, Uno.UITest does not support running the tests against the UWP head of your app. However, you might also want to run UI tests against the UWP version of your app. Luckily, **WinAppDriver** and **Appium** allow us to achieve this. WinAppDriver is a tool developed by Microsoft that allows developers to simulate input to Windows apps, including UWP apps. While WinAppDriver allows you to interact with Windows apps, it does so by starting a web server locally and allows interaction with apps by communicating with WinAppDriver through a web-based protocol. To make the development process easier for us, we will use **Appium.WebDriver** as our library to write the UI tests. We will start by creating our test project and adding the necessary tests. Note that we will be creating a new project since we don't want Appium.WebDriver to interfere with Uno.UITest and we can't use Appium and WinAppDriver from inside a UWP project, meaning we can't reuse our UWP Unit test project:

1. First, you will need to install WinAppDriver. For this, go to the releases page of WinAppDriver (`https://github.com/Microsoft/WinAppDriver/releases`) and download the latest MSI installer. At the time of writing, the latest stable release was version **1.2.1**, and we will be using this version for this chapter. After downloading the MSI installer, run it to install WinAppDriver. Note that you will later need to start the `WinAppDriver.exe` file and if you install WinAppDriver in a different folder, you should make a note of the installation folder.

2. Open the **UnoAutomatedTestsApp** solution and create a new Unit Test project. To do this, right-click on the solution node and click **Add** > **New Project**.

3. In the dialog, search for `Unit Test App` and select the option highlighted in *Figure 7.4*:

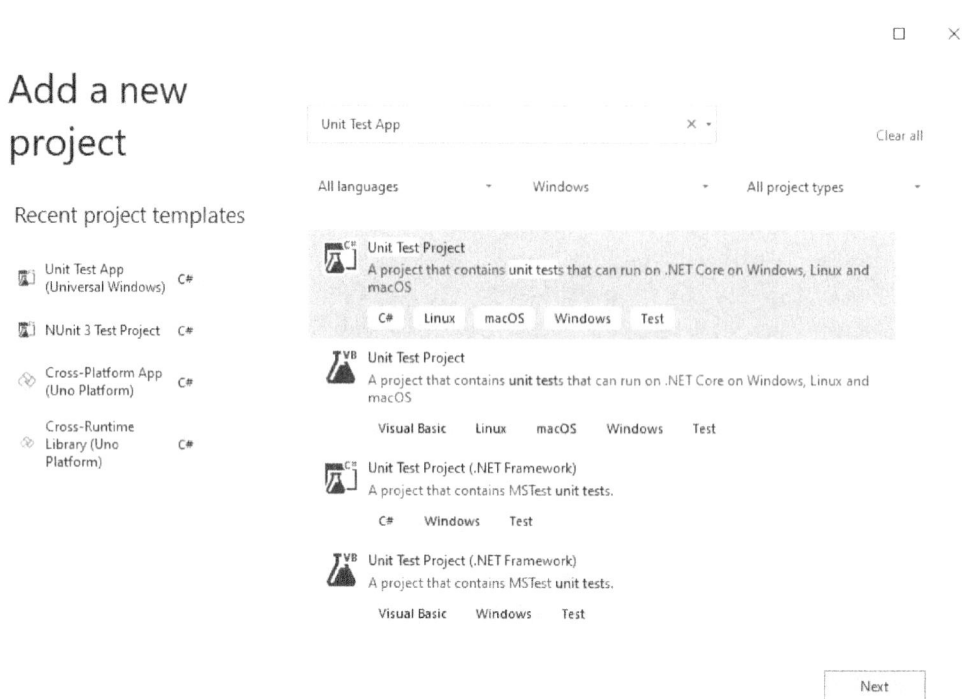

Figure 7.4 – Unit Test Project template in the new project dialog

4. Press **Next** and enter the project name. We will name the project `UnoAutomatedTestsApp.UWPUITests`. Of course, you can name the project differently; however, we will assume that the project is named `UnoAutomatedTestsApp.UWPUITests` in this chapter. Then, press **Next**.

5. Now, select the target framework; we will be using **.NET 5.0**. Now, click **Create** to create the project.

6. Once the project is created, right-click the project in the solution view and click on **Manage NuGet Packages…**. Now, install the **Appium.WebDriver** package by searching for `Appium.WebDriver` in the **Browse** section and installing the package.

Now that we have created the unit test project, we can write our first UI test using `Appium.Webdriver`. We will only cover how to write your first test using Appium and WinAppDriver. You can find more information about WinAppDriver and writing tests in their official documentation:

1. Before we write our first test, first rename the `UnitTest1.cs` file to `SignInTests.cs`. and also rename the `UnitTest1` class to `SignInTests`.

2. Open the `Package.appxmanifest` file located inside the UWP head of the app and change the **package name** located under **Packaging** to `UnoAutomatedTestsApp`. Now, deploy the UWP head of your app by selecting the UWP head and pressing *Ctrl + F5*. Since we have changed the package name, we want the test to start the app using the updated package name.

3. Add the following `using` statements to the `SignInTests` class:

```
using OpenQA.Selenium.Appium;
using OpenQA.Selenium.Appium.Windows;
```

4. Now, add the following code to the `SignInTests` class.

```
private static WindowsDriver<WindowsElement> session;
[AssemblyInitialize]
public static void InitializeTests(TestContext _)
{
    AppiumOptions appiumOptions = new AppiumOptions();
    appiumOptions.AddAdditionalCapability("app",
        "UnoAutomatedTestsApp_cdfyh0xbha7kw!App");
    appiumOptions.AddAdditionalCapability(
        "deviceName", "WindowsPC");
    session = new WindowsDriver<WindowsElement>(new
        Uri("http://127.0.0.1:4723"), appiumOptions);
}
```

This will start the app using the app's package identity and connect to the running WinAppDriver. Since we will use the created `WindowsDriver` object to interact with the app, we store a reference to it. Note that the highlighted section will be different for your app. To get the correct value, open the `Package.appxmanifest` file and open the **Packaging** tab. Then, replace the highlighted part with the **Package family name** value.

5. Now, remove the existing `TestMethod1` test and add the following test:

```
[TestMethod]
public void
VerifyButtonIsEnabledWithUsernameAndPasswordUWP()
{
    var usernameInput =
        session.FindElementByAccessibilityId(
            "usernameInput");
    usernameInput.SendKeys("test");
    var passwordInput =
        session.FindElementByAccessibilityId(
            "passwordInput");
    passwordInput.SendKeys("test");
    var signInButton =
        session.FindElementByAccessibilityId(
            "signInButton");
    Assert.IsTrue(signInButton.Enabled, "Sign in
        button should be enabled.");
}
```

Like the `VerifyButtonIsEnabledWithUsernameAndPassword` test we wrote in the Uno.UITest section, this test verifies that when a username and password have been entered, the sign-in button is enabled.

Now that we have written our first test, let's run it! To do this, you will first need to start WinAppDriver. If you have installed WinAppDriver in the default folder, you will find the `WinAppDriver.exe` file in the `C:\Program Files (x86)\Windows Application Driver` folder. If you have chosen a different installation folder earlier, open that folder and start the `WinAppDriver.exe` file inside there. Upon starting, you should see something as shown in *Figure 7.5*:

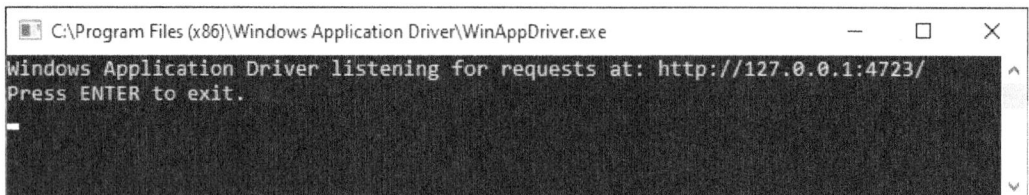

Figure 7.5 – Window running WinAppDriver

Now, you can start the test by right-clicking the
VerifyButtonIsEnabledWithUsernameAndPasswordUWP test inside the test explorer
and clicking on **Run**. The test will start the app, enter the text, and then check whether the
sign-in button is enabled.

Automated accessibility testing with Axe.Windows

In addition to writing normal UI tests, you can also add **Axe.Windows** to your testing
suite to automatically check your app for accessibility issues as part of the UI testing
strategy. Axe.Windows is a library developed and maintained by Microsoft that aims
to detect accessibility issues in apps. Adding Axe.Windows to your UI tests is simple:

1. Add a reference to the Axe.Windows package in the **UnoAutomatedTestsApp.
    UWPUITests** project. To do this, right-click the project and click on **Manage
    NuGet Packages…**. Search for Axe.Windows and install the package.

2. Now, add the following two using statements to the SignInTests.cs file:

    ```
    using Axe.Windows.Automation;
    using System.Diagnostics;
    ```

3. Lastly, add the following test to the SignInTests class:

    ```
    [TestMethod]
    public void VerifySignInInterfaceIsAccessible()
    {
        var processes = Process.GetProcessesByName(
            "UnoAutomatedTestsApp");
        Assert.IsTrue(processes.Length > 0);
        var config = Config.Builder.ForProcessId(
            processes[0].Id).Build();
        var scanner = ScannerFactory.CreateScanner(
            config);
        Assert.IsTrue(scanner.Scan().ErrorCount == 0,
            "Accessibility issues found.");
    }
    ```

Since `Axe.Windows` needs to know the process ID, we first get the process ID of the running app using the **System.Diagnostics.Process** API. We then create a new `Axe.Windows` configuration using the process ID, which we then use to create a new **Axe. Windows scanner**. The `Axe.Windows` scanner allows us to scan our app for accessibility issues using the **Scan** function. Since `Scan()` returns a scan result object telling us that all accessibility issues have been found, we assert that we have found zero accessibility errors. When writing UI tests for more complex apps, you would scan the app more often to ensure that every scenario and view inside your app will be covered by this accessibility scan. For example, you could scan the app for accessibility issues every time you navigate to a different view. If you now run the test, the test app will start and after a few seconds, the test will be marked as **Passed** since our sign-in interface has no accessibility issues that can be found by `Axe.Windows`.

In this section, we have only scratched the surface in terms of testing with WinAppDriver and Axe.Windows and there is a lot more we could cover. If you would like to learn more about authoring tests with WinAppDriver, you can find more information in their authoring test scripts documentation (`https://github.com/microsoft/ WinAppDriver/blob/master/Docs/AuthoringTestScripts.md`) or take a look at their sample code: `https://github.com/microsoft/WinAppDriver/ tree/master/Samples/C%23`. If you wish to learn more about Axe.Windows, you can visit their GitHub repository: `https://github.com/microsoft/ axe-windows`.

In the next section, we will cover how to write unit tests for your Uno Platform app, including the different approaches to it.

Writing unit tests for your Uno Platform app

As app complexity increases, ensuring that your app's logic is working becomes increasingly difficult to validate without tests. While you can use UI tests to validate the logic, you can only verify logic that gets exposed as part of the UI. Things such as network access or error handling, however, become very difficult to validate using UI tests as those things are generally exposed through the UI. In addition to that, UI tests are slower since they are mimicking user interaction and rely on the rendered UI to update.

This is where **unit tests** come in. Unit tests are small tests that verify single units of your code. Most commonly, classes or functions are treated as individual units and tests are grouped based on the class or function they are testing; in other words, for every class you want to test, there is a set of tests only targeting that class and not any other class. As the complexity of your app increases, unit tests allow you to verify that single classes are still working as expected.

> **Important note**
>
> Unit tests are no silver bullet! While unit tests allow you to verify the behavior of single pieces of functionality, larger and more complex apps also require more tests besides unit tests, in other words, UI tests to ensure that the app as a whole works as expected. Only because single classes work correctly in isolation, this does not mean that the whole construct works together as expected and is bug-free!

Since, at the time of writing, only creating unit tests against the UWP head is well supported, we will focus on this. We will now cover the different ways to create the unit test project.

Different approaches to adding a unit test project

Since most, if not all, of your app's logic sits inside a shared project, writing unit tests is a bit more complex. Since the shared project does not actually produce an assembly that you can reference, there are different ways to test your app's logic, which both come with their own benefits and drawbacks.

The first option is to create a project containing the unit tests for the platform you want to run the tests on and reference the shared project in that project. This is the easiest way to get started since you just need to create a new project and reference the shared project. One of the downsides is that since shared projects don't allow references such as NuGet packages to be added to them, any libraries you are using inside your shared project also need to be referenced by your test project. In addition to this, since the shared project does not create a binary but is compiled into the projects that are referencing it, changes made to the shared project will always result in the tests project recompiling.

The next option is to leave your code inside the shared project and reference the platforms head project inside the unit test projects; for example, create a UWP Unit test project and reference the UWP head of your app inside it. This option is better than the first option since you don't encounter the issues of library references needing to be added to the test project since the platform head references the libraries for us. We will use this approach in this chapter.

The last option is to move the code inside the shared project into a **Cross Platform Library (Uno Platform)** project and reference the library in the platform heads and unit test projects. This approach has the benefit that you can add library references to the library project on its own and don't have to manually add the reference to the individual projects. One of the downsides is that you have to switch to a cross-platform library project type instead of being able to use the existing shared project. This approach also has the downside that the cross-platform library will always be compiled for all platforms, thereby increasing the build time when only requiring specific platforms.

Let's now add a unit test to our app by using the second option previously discussed, that is, adding a reference to the platforms head project.

Adding your first unit test project

Since we will reference the UWP platform head, we need a UWP unit test app. For this, we first need to add a new project:

1. Right-click the solution and click **Add** > **New Project**.

2. In the dialog, search for the **Unit Test App (Universal Windows)** text and select the **Unit Test App (Universal Windows)** project type, as shown in *Figure 7.6*:

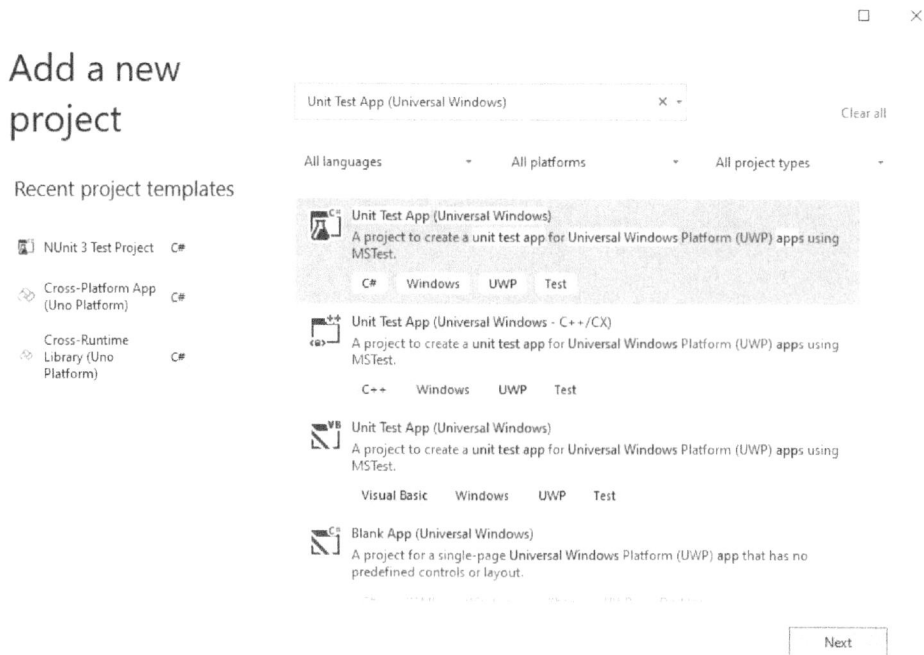

Figure 7.6 – Unit Test App (Universal Windows) project type in a new project dialog

3. Click **Next** and name the project `UnoAutomatedTestsApp.UWPUnitTests`. You can name the project differently, of course; however, in this and the following sections, we will assume that the project is named as mentioned previously.

4. Select the minimum and target version. We will use **18362** for both since the UWP head of the app also uses those. Not using the same minimum and target version of the UWP head might result in build errors, so you should always aim to match the UWP head.

5. Now, add a reference for the UWP head to the Unit Test App project. For this, right-click the **UnoAutomatedTestsApp.UWPUnitTests** project in the solution view, click **Add > Reference… > Projects**, check **UnoAutomatedTestsApp.UWP**, and then click **OK**.

6. Since the reference to the UWP head will also copy the `Properties/Default.rd.xml` file into the build output folder, this will result in a build issue as there are two `Default.rd.xml` files that the compiler wants to copy into the same folder. Because of that, rename the `Default.rd.xml` file of the unit test app to `TestsDefault.rd.xml`. Then, also update the `UnoAutomatedTestsApp.UWPUnitTests.csproj` file to point to that file. If you are renaming the file from the **Solution** view, you just need to select the project and press *Ctrl + S*.

7. In addition to that, we also need to rename the image assets of the unit test project. For this, prepend all images inside the `Assets` folder with `UWPUnitTestApp-`.

We are now able to write and run unit tests for everything included inside the UWP head, including classes included inside the shared project. For larger apps that also have platform conditional code, you will only be able to reference classes and code inside the UWP unit test project that are getting compiled for the UWP head. Now that we have created the project, let's write a small unit test. In contrast to the Uno.UITest tests project, the Unit Test App (Universal Windows) project type uses **MSTest** as the testing framework. Of course, you can change this, but for simplicity, we will stick with MSTest. Note that you can't use NUnit for UWP unit tests as it does not support UWP:

1. Since we don't have many classes we can test now, let's add a new class to the shared project. To do this, create a new class named `DemoUtils`.

2. Replace the code of the file with the following:

```
namespace UnoAutomatedTestsApp
{
    public class DemoUtils
    {
        public static bool IsEven(int number)
```

```
        {
            return number % 2 == 0;
        }
    }
}
```

We will just use this code so that we have something easy to write unit tests for.

3. Now, rename the `UnitTest.cs` file inside the **UnoAutomatedTestsApp. UWPUnitTests** project to `DemoUtilsTests.cs`.

4. Now, replace the content of the `DemoUtilsTests.cs` file with the following:

```
using UnoAutomatedTestsApp;
using Microsoft.VisualStudio.TestTools.UnitTesting;
namespace UnoAutomatedTests.UWPUnitTests
{
    [TestClass]
    public class DemoUtilsTests
    {
        [TestMethod]
        public void VerifyEvenNumberIsEven()
        {
            Assert.IsTrue(DemoUtils.IsEven(2),
                "Number 2 should be even");
        }
    }
}
```

This is a small unit test to verify that our `DemoUtils.IsEven` function successfully determines that the number **2** is even.

We have now added our first unit test. As is the case with the UI test, you can run the test by opening the test explorer, expanding the tree, right-clicking the **VerifyEvenNumberIsEven** test, and clicking on **Run**. The test will then compile, deploy the unit test app, and start it. Your tests will be run and the unit test app will then close.

In the last section of this chapter, we will cover manual testing, why it is important, and how to approach testing accessibility manually using **Accessibility Insights**.

Performing manual testing and why it is important

While automated tests help to find bugs and issues, there are certain things they cannot cover that still require manual testing. When developing apps that make use of features such as a camera, Bluetooth, or other device capabilities, writing automated tests is hard and sometimes even impossible. In these scenarios, manual testing is necessary. This is especially important with connectivity features to see how your app handles unstable connections and whether your app still provides a good user experience, especially with varying connection quality. More importantly, testing using emulators makes it hard to verify how the app will feel on actual devices, especially when thinking about the user experience, such as elements being the right size and easily tappable on screens.

In addition to testing specific features that are hard to simulate as part of an automated test such as GPS or roaming data access, manual testing is also critical to ensure that your app is great usability-wise. While during development, running the app inside your emulator is fine, manual testing becomes more and more important as development progresses.

Besides manually testing your app by using the app on a device or emulator, another important aspect is manually testing your app for accessibility. Ensuring that your app is accessible by users is crucial when developing apps, and while automated tests, such as `Axe.Windows` tests, can help find issues, they are not perfect. Since people with all levels of ability might use your app, making your app not accessible makes your app harder or even impossible to use for those customers. Since everyone should be able to use your app regardless of their level of ability, there are different tools when testing your app for accessibility. In this section, however, we will focus on using assistive technology and using the **Accessibility Insights** scanning tool.

Accessibility insights is a tool that allows you to scan your app for accessibility issues manually, similar to what `Axe.Windows` does. In fact, **Accessibility insights for Windows** uses `Axe.Windows` under the hood. In contrast to `Axe.Windows`, Accessibility Insights also allows the testing of your web app and Android app for accessibility issues. In this chapter, you will learn how you can use Accessibility Insights for Windows. If you wish to learn more about Accessibility Insights, including using Accessibility Insights for Web and Accessibility Insights for Android, you can check out the official website: `https://accessibilityinsights.io/`.

Now, let's get started by using Accessibility Insights for Windows by using it on the UWP head of the UnoAutomatedTestsApp:

1. To do this, first, you need to download Accessibility Insights for Windows from `https://accessibilityinsights.io/docs/en/windows/overview/` by clicking on **Download for Windows**. If you have already installed Accessibility Insights for Windows, you can proceed with *step 4*.

2. Once the download has finished, run the MSI Installer to install Accessibility Insights.

3. Once the installation process has finished, **Accessibility Insights for Windows** should start and you will see something similar to that shown in *Figure 7.7* after dismissing the telemetry dialog:

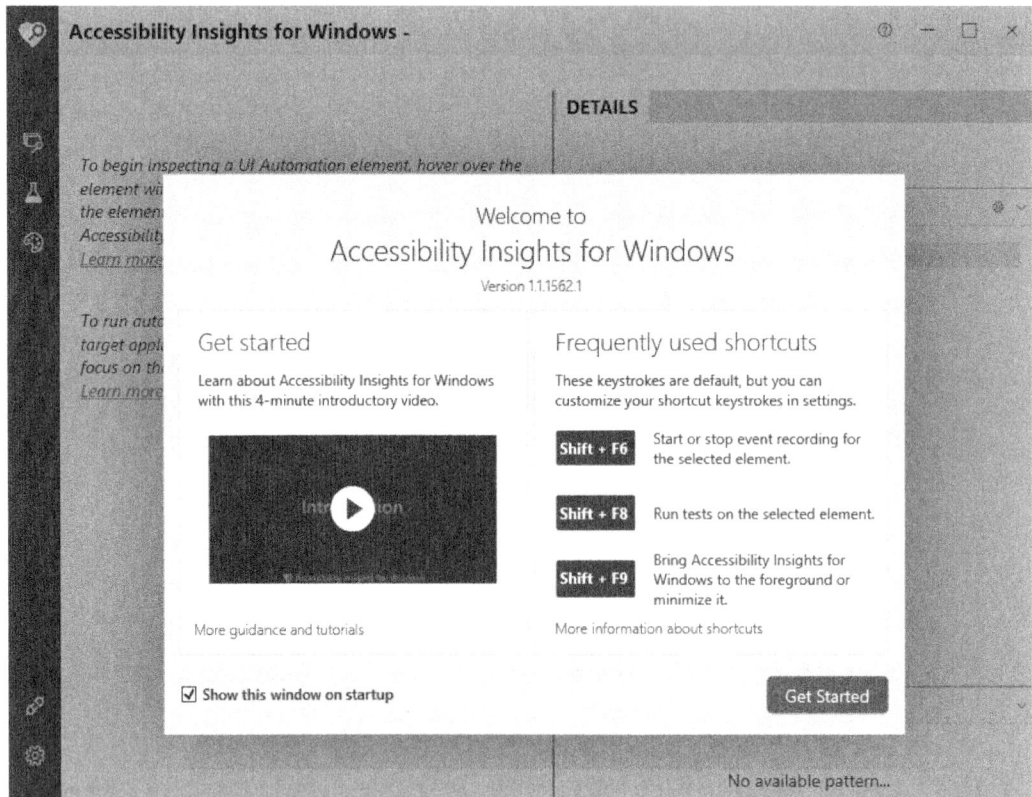

Figure 7.7 – Screenshot of Accessibility Insights

4. Once you have closed the popups, start the UWP head of
    `UnoAutomatedTestsApp`.

    Now, if you hover over the app, you will notice that the area you are hovering over
    and the controls in that area will be surrounded by a dark blue area. In Accessibility
    Insights, you can see the different UI automation properties of the control, for
    example, the control's `control type` or whether they are keyboard-focusable.
    To scan a control, you can either select the control from **Live Inspect tree** or click
    on the scan button in the top-right corner of the blue rectangle, as shown in
    Figure 7.8:

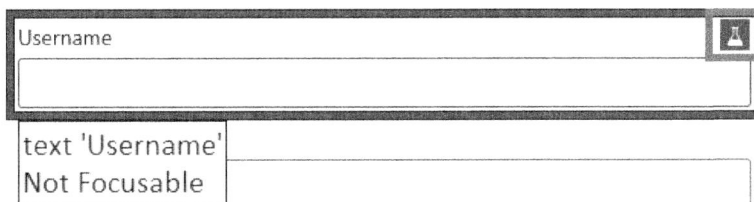

Figure 7.8 – Highlighted scan icon on control

While Accessibility Insights is a useful tool for finding accessibility issues, testing your app
by using it with assistive technology is crucial to ensure that your app can be used by users
with all levels of ability. For this, we will manually test the UWP head using Narrator.
However, similar testing can be done on Android, iOS, and macOS. To learn how to start
the assistive technology on different platforms, please refer to the *Starting the screen reader
on different platforms* section in *Chapter 5, Making Your App Ready for the Real World*.

Let's walk through our app now using Narrator. To do this, start Narrator by pressing
Windows logo key, *Ctrl*, and *Enter* at the same time and open **UnoAutomatedTestsApp**.
Narrator should then announce **UnoAutomatedTestsApp, Window**. Using the *Caps Lock*
key and the *arrow* keys, you can navigate through the app. As you navigate through the
app, Narrator will then announce the header of the username input, the password input,
and then the sign-in button. This also allows us to find potential accessibility issues that
`Axe.Windows` and Accessibility Insights for Windows did not catch. For this, enter a
username by navigating to the username input field, entering the text `invalid`, and
repeating the process for the password field. Upon navigating to the sign-in button and
hitting the space bar, you will notice that you are
not being notified of any error messages. This is an accessibility issue as users relying
on assistive technology will not be notified of the error message and will not know
what happened.

For larger apps, navigating through the app will be more complicated. While our test app is small and all controls are accessible, for larger apps using this testing, you can find crucial accessibility issues, for example, controls that have an unhelpful or even misleading representation for assistive technology. Finding these issues early in the development process makes them easier to fix and prevents them from impairing users.

In this section, we scratched the surface of manual testing and why it is necessary. We also covered how to approach accessibility testing using Accessibility Insights and assistive technology.

Summary

In this chapter, we have learned how to write automated UI tests for your app using `Uno.UITest` and Selenium. We also then learned how to run those tests on different platforms, including running them on your app running on an emulator. After that, we covered how to write UI tests for the UWP head of the app using WinAppDriver and also write unit tests for the UWP head. Lastly, we covered manual testing and how to test for accessibility issues.

In the next chapter, we'll talk about deploying your app and how you can bring your `Xamarin.Forms` app to the web using Uno Platform. We will also cover how to build for other platforms and cover how you can join and even contribute to the Uno community.

8
Deploying Your Apps and Going Further

This chapter concludes our introduction to Uno Platform, but there's still a lot more to cover before we finish. You already know that Uno Platform allows for the creation of apps that run in multiple environments. This does not apply just to new apps. A large part of the appeal of Uno Platform is that it enables developers to also take existing apps and run them in new environments. Because it is built on UWP and WinUI, Uno Platform provides an excellent way for you to take existing apps and run them in new environments.

In this chapter, we'll cover the following topics:

- Bringing `Xamarin.Forms` apps to WebAssembly
- Deploying a Wasm Uno Platform app to the web
- Deploying your app to a store
- Engaging with Uno Platform community

By the end of this chapter, you'll know how to deploy your applications, and you'll be confident about the subsequent steps to take in your journey with Uno Platform.

Technical requirements

This chapter assumes that you already have your development environment set up, including installing the project templates. This was covered in *Chapter 1, Introducing Uno Platform.*

This chapter will also use source code that was created in *Chapter 6, Displaying Data in Charts and with Custom 2D Graphics.* This is available at the following URL: `https://github.com/PacktPublishing/Creating-Cross-Platform-C-Sharp-Applications-with-Uno-Platform/tree/main/Chapter06`.

Check out the following video to see the code in action: `https://bit.ly/3xDJDwT`

Bringing Xamarin.Forms apps to WebAssembly

If you use .NET for your development and have previously created a mobile (iOS and/or Android) app, you may have used `Xamarin.Forms`. If you have mobile apps built with `Xamarin.Forms` that you now want to run on WebAssembly, you may be worried that a rewrite of code is in order, but it's not.

`Xamarin.Forms` can create UWP apps. Uno Platform allows UWP apps to run on other platforms. Therefore, it's possible to use the UWP app produced by `Xamarin.Forms` and pass that as input for Uno Platform to use to create a Wasm app. Fortunately, and for simplicity, all the connecting of project inputs and outputs is taken care of by a provided template.

> **Tip**
> It's also possible to use Uno Platform controls within a Xamarin app. Doing so is simple, and there's a guide showing how at the following URL: `https://platform.uno/docs/articles/howto-use-uno-in-xamarin-forms.html`.

To show how a UWP app created by `Xamarin.Forms` can be used by Uno Platform to create a Wasm app, let's create a new `Xamarin.Forms` app and add a Wasm head using Uno. You can, of course, do the same thing with an existing `Xamarin.Forms` app, but *only if it has a UWP head*. If you have an existing `Xamarin.Forms` app without a UWP head, you'll need to add one before you can create a Wasm head:

1. Inside **Visual Studio**, create a new project with the **Mobile App (Xamarin.Forms)** project template.

2. Give the project (and solution) the name **UnoXfDemo**. You can, of course, use a different name, but you will need to need to adjust all subsequent references accordingly.

3. Check the **place solution and project in the same directory** box.

4. Select the **Blank** template option and be sure to check the option to say you plan to develop for **Windows (UWP)**.

    We'll use a blank application template for simplicity. Most `Xamarin.Forms`-specific content should work fine. However, you are advised to test this early in your process to identify any possible issues you may encounter with custom UI or third-party controls.

5. Right-click on **Solution node** in **Solution Explorer** and select **Open in Terminal**.

6. The **Developer PowerShell** windows will open in the directory of the solution. In it, type the following:

    ```
    dotnet new -i Uno.ProjectTemplates.Dotnet::*
    ```

    This will ensure that you have the latest versions of the templates installed.

7. Now type the following:

    ```
    dotnet new wasmxfhead
    ```

    This will add the new project to the solution.

8. Select **Reload**, when prompted, to reload the solution and you'll see **UnoXfDemo. Wasm** as a new project inside the solution.

9. Downgrade all the references of **Xamarin.Forms** to be version **5.0.0.1931**, as this is the latest version supported by Uno Project.

10. Add a reference to the `Xamarin.Forms` package in the Wasm project, as follows:

    ```
    Install-Package Xamarin.Forms -Version 5.0.0.1931
    ```

    Note that all versions of `Xamarin.Forms` referenced from the projects in the solution should be the same, and they must also match the version supported by the `Uno.Xamarin.Forms.Platform` package. If they don't, you'll get an error explaining the different versions referenced and how to address them.

11. Update the version of **Uno.Xamarin.Forms.Platform** used by the Wasm project to **5.0.0-uno.1799**. This is to ensure compatibility with version **5.0** of `Xamarin. Forms` that, at the time of writing, is referenced in the latest version of the templates.

12. Set the **UnoXfDemo.Wasm** project as the start up project, and then start debugging. You'll see something that looks similar to *Figure 8.1*:

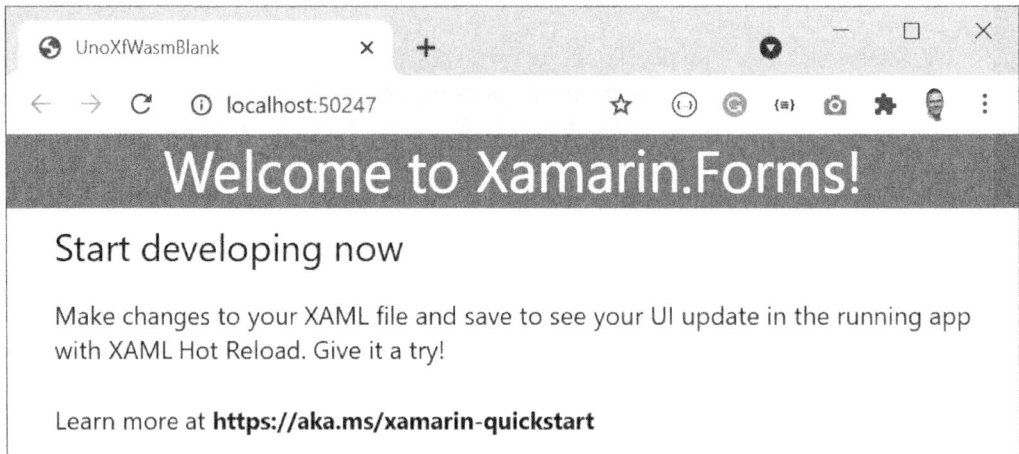

Figure 8.1 – A default (blank) Xamarin.Forms app running through WebAssembly

Of course, you can continue developing the app, adding or changing features or functionality, and then deploy the latest version to WebAssembly like any other project in the solution.

Now, we've seen how simple it is to use Uno Platform to have a Xamarin.Forms app run as a Wasm app.

> **Important note**
> In addition to being able to take an existing Xamarin.Forms app and have it work with Uno Platform, it's also possible to take an existing UWP app and convert that to use Uno Platform to target other operating systems too. The Uno Platform team has published an official guide on how to do this at the following URL: https://platform.uno/docs/articles/howto-migrate-existing-code.html.

After you've created the Wasm version of your app (whether it started out as a Xamarin.Forms app or not), you'll want to make it available on the web so that other people can use it. We'll look at that now.

Deploying a Wasm Uno Platform app to the web

Building a Wasm app and having it running locally on your machine is an exciting step that shows the power and potential of Uno Platform. However, running locally on your machine makes it hard for other people to use it. What you need to do is host the app somewhere that everyone can access it.

Probably the most popular choice for hosting a .NET-based web application is on Azure. You can host your app anywhere, and the process is very similar for all services as there is no server-side processing needed. On the assumption that Azure is where you're likely to want to host your app, let's now see how this is done. If you've never deployed a web app or used Azure before, it can seem daunting, but you'll see how easy it is and that there's nothing to fear.

> **Try Azure for free**
>
> If you don't already have an Azure account, you can sign up for a free trial by visiting the following URL: `https://azure.microsoft.com/free/`.

Rather than create a new app purely to show it being deployed, let's use the app we created in *Chapter 6, Displaying Data in Charts and with Custom 2D Graphics*:

1. Open the **Dashboard** app you created previously (or download the version from `https://github.com/PacktPublishing/Creating-Cross-Platform-C-Sharp-Applications-with-Uno-Platform/tree/main/Chapter06`).

2. Right-click on the **WASM** project and select **Publish…**.

3. You'll see that there are many places you can publish your app to, but as we want to publish the app to Azure, select the **Azure** option and click **Next**.

4. For the specific target, we'll select the **Azure App Service (Windows)** option, although you could use any of the other options.

> **Important note**
>
> Static Web Apps is another suitable way of hosting a Wasm app. See `https://azure.microsoft.com/services/app-service/static/` for more details.

5. If you haven't already done so, sign in to your Azure linked account.

6. We'll create a new app service to host the app, so click on the **plus sign** for **Create an Azure App Service**.

7. A default name for your app will be automatically assigned. As this will be used as the subdomain where the app will be made available, this must be unique. The default name will have a number appended to the project name based on the current date and time. You can change this if you wish, but if the value you specify isn't unique, you'll see a warning that the name is not available, and you must choose another.

8. If you have multiple subscriptions linked to your account, select the one you want to use for this app.

9. Select or create new resource groups and hosting plans. For demonstration purposes, you can use a **Free** hosting plan for now. If the needs of your app mean this is insufficient, you can change this in the future.

> **Important note**
>
> When you move on from the free trial and have an app in production, it's vital that you fully understand the options and billing-related choices you have configured for your web app. This will avoid any unexpected charges to your credit card, or a critical app being disabled when you run out of credit. The appropriate settings for you and your app will depend on your app and individual requirements. Details of the billing options can be found at the following URL: `https://azure.microsoft.com/pricing/details/app-service/windows/`.

10. Click the **Create** button and the service will be created for you. This may take a few seconds, and a message will be shown in the corner of the screen while this takes place.

11. You'll now see something like *Figure 8.2*. This shows I've used the name
    UnoBookRailDashboard, so the app will be available at the following URL:
    `https://unobookraildashboard.azurewebsites.net/`. Now click
    Finish, and the app will be built ready for deployment:

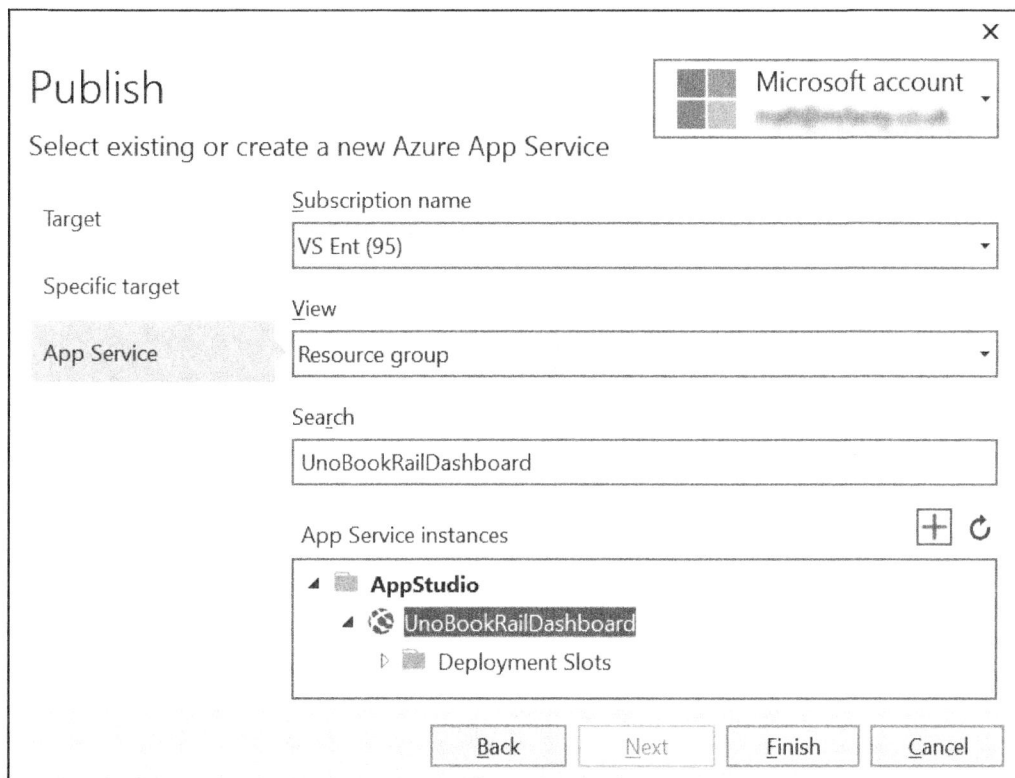

Figure 8.2 – The Azure Publish dialog ready to publish the app

12. Now that you've set up your web app, you're ready to publish the app. Click the
    Publish button at the top right of the window.

It might take a minute or two, but eventually, the browser will open a new tab with your app running from Azure. This should look similar to *Figure 8.3*:

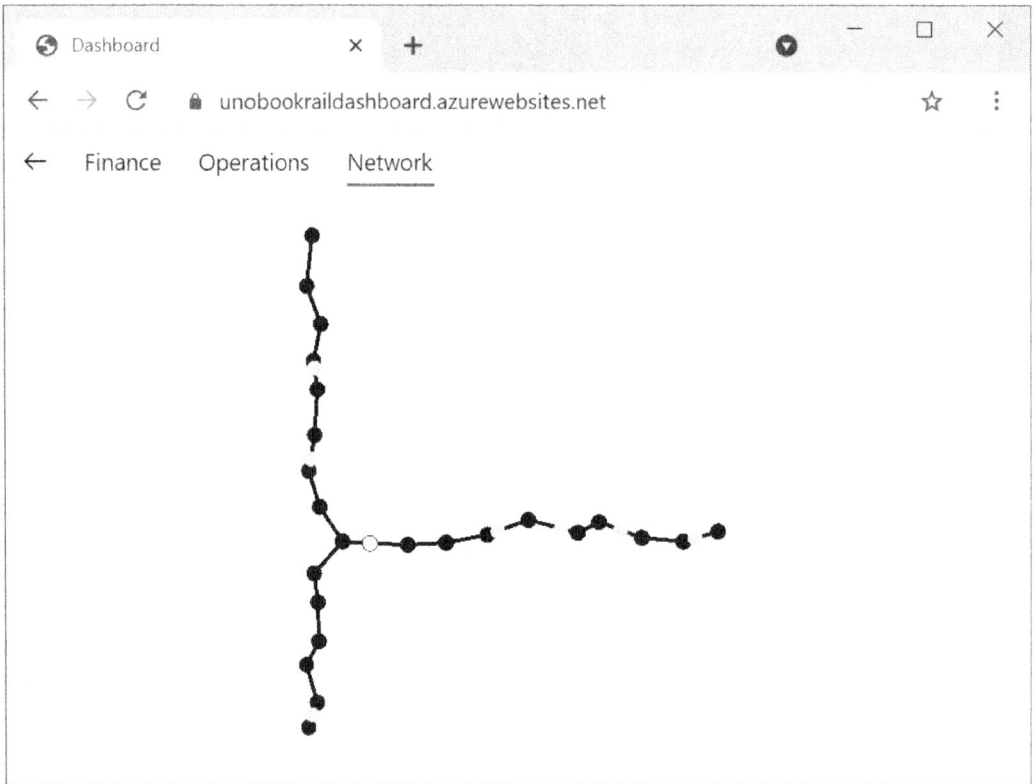

Figure 8.3 – Dashboard app running on Azure

If you're not hosting your app on Azure, you may find helpful guidance by searching how to deploy a **Blazor** app, as the process is likely to be similar. Ultimately, an Uno Platform-based WebAssembly app is all static files and can be deployed to any server capable of hosting static content.

Publishing from Visual Studio is convenient. However, it is not desirable in terms of creating a tracked, repeatable process. Ideally, you should set up an automated process to deploy your app. Having **continuous integration and deployment** (**CI/CD**) processes is what we'll look at next.

Automating build, tests, and distribution

Ideally, you'll be using an automated process to build, test, and deploy your application, and not rely on doing it all manually, as manual processes are more error-prone.

This is where a CI/CD process is essential. As we've just manually deployed a Wasm app to Azure, let's start by looking at automating that process. Fortunately, the Visual Studio tooling makes it simple.

If you go through the **Publish** wizard for a project that is in a source control repository, after creating the web app, you'll be presented with an extra step (as seen in *Figure 8.4*). This can be used to create a YAML file with the workflow configured for you:

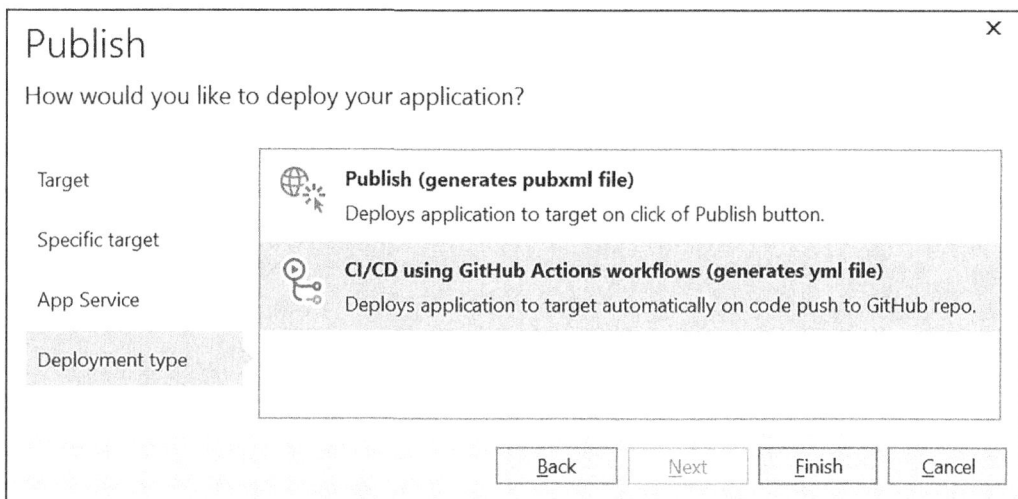

Figure 8.4 – Creating a GitHub action to publish your Wasm app via the Publish wizard

The generated file will only need a single modification to account for the solution structure used by the Uno Platform templates. The working directory will need to be changed to Dashboard\Dashboard.Wasm.

Once you've made any changes and pushed them to GitHub, the code will be built and deployed automatically.

You can see an example of a GitHub Actions workflow file that deploys an Uno Platform-based Wasm app at the following URL: https://github.com/mrlacey/UnoWasmGithubActions/blob/main/.github/workflows/UnoWasmGithubActions.yml.

GitHub isn't the only place where you may store your code, and GitHub Actions isn't the only CI/CD pipeline option. For developers working with .NET, Azure DevOps (previously Visual Studio Online) is a popular solution.

Nick Randolph has created a comprehensive guide to creating an Azure DevOps-based build pipeline for Uno Platform apps at the following URL: `https://nicksnettravels.builttoroam.com/uno-complete-pipeline/`.

Lance McCarthy has also created an example repository that shows multiple Azure DevOps build pipelines being used with a repository hosted on GitHub. This can serve as a helpful reference if you need to do something similar, and can be found at the following URL: `https://github.com/LanceMcCarthy/UnoPlatformDevOps`.

Due to the number of platforms that Uno Platform allows you to create, and the variety of ways you can build and deploy those apps, it is impractical to provide walk-throughs of all scenarios. Fortunately, because Uno Platform is built on top of other well-known technologies, the build processes for those other technologies are also the same ones you'll use to build your Uno Platform-based apps. For example, because the Android, iOS, and macOS apps are built on top of Xamarin, the build and deployment processes are likely to be the same as if building with Xamarin directly.

We started this section on CI/CD by looking at deploying the Wasm-based version of an app built with Uno. This isn't the only place you may need to deploy your app. App stores are where you're likely to need to deploy at least some of the apps you build, so we'll look at them next.

Deploying your app to a store

Suppose you're building an app for public use. In that case, you'll likely need to deploy it via the appropriate app store for that operating system. The rules, policies, and restrictions that a store applies for an app built with Uno Platform are the same as for an app built with any other toolset.

The policies for each store can change frequently (typically, at least a couple of times each year) and are also quite long. For this reason, we saw no value in reproducing them here. Instead, you should look to the official documentation in the following list:

- **Windows Store** (for UWP): `https://docs.microsoft.com/windows/uwp/publish/`
- **Google Play Store** (for Android): `https://support.google.com/googleplay/android-developer#topic=3450769`
- **iOS App Store**: `https://developer.apple.com/ios/submit/`
- **macOS App Store**: `https://developer.apple.com/macos/submit/`

The process for distributing your Uno-based app is the same as for any other app. You'll need to create a developer account for each of the stores you wish to deploy through, and then upload the relevant files, packages, and bundles to the store as required.

As the Android, iOS, and Mac apps are all built on top of platform-specific Xamarin technologies, you may also find their publishing-related documentation useful:

- **Google Play Store**: `https://docs.microsoft.com/xamarin/android/deploy-test/publishing/publishing-to-google-play/`

- **iOS App Store**: `https://docs.microsoft.com/xamarin/ios/deploy-test/app-distribution/app-store-distribution/publishing-to-the-app-store`

- **macOS App Store**: `https://docs.microsoft.com/xamarin/mac/deploy-test/publishing-to-the-app-store/`

The preceding links point to general information for each of the stores. If you do encounter any specific Uno-related issues, there is a large community ready to help you.

Engaging with the Uno Platform community

That Uno Platform is an open source project is part of its appeal for many people. Like many open source projects, a core team helps lead a community of contributors. It's this broad community that you can look to for information, help, and become a part of.

Sources of information

Beyond this book (obviously!), the central place to go for information is the official website at the following URL: `https://platform.uno/`. On the website, you'll find documentation, guides, samples, and a blog. Subscribing to the blog is an excellent way of keeping up with all future announcements, as is following the official Twitter account at the following URL: `https://twitter.com/unoplatform`.

The official website also includes information on topics beyond the scope of this book, such as using Uno Platform to target Windows 7 or on Linux (see `https://platform.uno/uno-platform-for-linux/`).

The official website is chock full of information, but with so many features and things you might want to do in your apps, you'll reach a point where you have questions that need answering.

Sources of help

There are four places you can go to for help relating to working with Uno Platform:

- Stack Overflow

- Discord

- GitHub

- Professional support

Stack Overflow is the internet's repository of software development-related questions and answers. It's your first port of call for questions about how to use Uno Platform. You'll find many of the core team and regular contributors answering questions there. Make sure your questions are tagged with **uno-platform**, and ask at the following URL: `https://stackoverflow.com/questions/tagged/uno-platform`.

How to ask for help

As with most things, you get more out when you put in more effort. This applies to asking for help too. If you're not familiar with it, Stack Overflow has a guide to asking questions at the following URL: `https://stackoverflow.com/help/how-to-ask`.

There are two general principles behind asking for help well. Firstly, remember that you're asking for help, not for someone else to do the work for you. Secondly, making it easier for someone to help you increases the likelihood that they can and will do so.

A good request for help includes all and only the necessary specific information needed to provide an answer. A vague description of a problem or your code is a lot less helpful than providing details of what you've tried or a simple, minimal way of reproducing the problem.

If your questions relate to the internals of Uno Platform, or you're working with the latest preview versions, you're better off asking your questions on **Discord**. The **UWP community** server has an **uno-platform** channel that includes lots of enthusiastic community members and members of the core team. You can join this by going to the following URL: `https://discord.com/invite/eBHZSKG`.

Using Uno Platform, as with any open source project, comes with a level of responsibility. Open source software is a collective process where everyone is working to enable everyone to have better software. This means there is an expectation that you will report a bug, even if you can't fix it yourself. If you think you have found a bug in the platform, a sample, or the documentation, you should file an issue on GitHub at the following URL: `https://github.com/unoplatform/uno/issues/new/choose`. As with a request for help, you should provide as much appropriate information as possible, including a minimal way of reproducing the issue, to make it easy for the issue you have found to be reproduced and fixed. Be sure to provide all the requested information, as this helps issues be addressed quickly and without wasted effort, or the need for people to ask for more information.

Finally, if you need an issue addressed promptly, or you have deeper support requirements than can be handled on Stack Overflow or Discord, **professional paid support** is also available from the company behind Uno Platform. Go to `https://platform.uno/contact` to discuss your requirements.

Contributing

There's a common misconception that contributing to an open source project means adding code, but as with any software project, there is a lot more involved in having something successful and valuable than just the code. Of course, if you want to help contribute code, you'll be warmly welcomed. Start by looking at issues labeled **good first issue**, and check out the contribution guide at the following URL: `https://platform.uno/docs/articles/uno-development/contributing-intro.html`. But remember, there are lots of other things you could do instead.

It's a cliché, but it's true that everything helps, no matter the size. Sharing your experiences is one of the easiest but also most valuable things you can do. This could be providing a formal how-to guide or code sample. Alternatively, it might be as simple as answering the question of someone who wants to know how to do something you've already done.

Whether large or small, we look forward to seeing how you contribute.

Summary

In this chapter, we've looked at various areas to round out your introduction to Uno Platform. You've seen how Uno Platform can extend an existing `Xamarin.Forms` app so that it can run via WebAssembly. You saw how to deploy the Wasm version of your app to Azure. We looked at continuous integration and deployment. You saw where to go to further your learning, and we looked at how you can engage with the Uno Platform developer community.

With that, we have come to the end of this book. If you've worked your way through each chapter, you will now have the knowledge and confidence to use Uno Platform to build apps that run on multiple operating systems. We look forward to seeing what you create.

Thanks for reading!

Packt>

Other Books You May Enjoy

If you enjoyed this book, you may be interested in these other books by Packt:

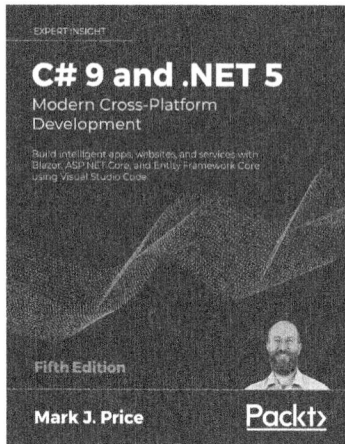

C# 9 and .NET 5 – Modern Cross-Platform Development - Fifth Edition

Mark J. Price

ISBN: 978-1-80056-810-5

- Build your own types with object-oriented programming
- Query and manipulate data using LINQ
- Build websites and services using ASP.NET Core 5
- Create intelligent apps using machine learning
- Use Entity Framework Core and work with relational databases
- Discover Windows app development using the Universal Windows Platform and XAML
- Build rich web experiences using the Blazor framework
- Build mobile applications for iOS and Android using Xamarin.Forms

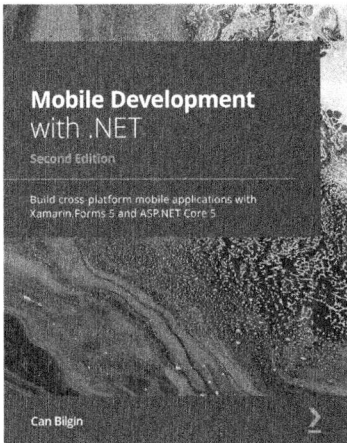

Mobile Development with .NET - Second Edition

Can Bilgin

ISBN: 978-1-80020-469-0

- Discover the latest features of .NET 5 that can be used in mobile application development

- Explore Xamarin.Forms Shell for building cross-platform mobile UIs

- Understand the technical design requirements of a consumer mobile app

- Get to grips with advanced mobile development concepts such as app data management, push notifications, and graph APIs

- Manage app data with Entity Framework Core

- Use Microsoft's Project Rome for creating cross-device experiences with Xamarin

- Become well-versed with implementing machine learning in your mobile apps

Packt is searching for authors like you

If you're interested in becoming an author for Packt, please visit `authors.packtpub.com` and apply today. We have worked with thousands of developers and tech professionals, just like you, to help them share their insight with the global tech community. You can make a general application, apply for a specific hot topic that we are recruiting an author for, or submit your own idea.

Hi!

We're Matt Lacey and Marcel Alexander Wagner, authors of *Creating Cross-Platform C# Applications with Uno Platform*. We really hope you enjoyed reading this book and found it useful for increasing your productivity and efficiency in developing cross platform Applications.

It would really help us (and other potential readers!) if you could leave a review on Amazon sharing your thoughts on *Creating Cross-Platform C# Applications with Uno Platform*.

Go to the link below or scan the QR code to leave your review:

`https://packt.link/r/1801078491`

Your review will help us to understand what's worked well in this book, and what could be improved upon for future editions, so it really is appreciated.

Best wishes,

Index

Printed in Great Britain
by Amazon